otra vez
para la familia
Eva y Rey

and for the people
and places
of my home state:
"When I dream about the moonlight
on the Wabash . . ."

TO THE TEACHER

THIS BOOK is designed to give beginning film students guidance in viewing, describing, and analyzing films. In the following pages, readers will be encouraged to formulate their own descriptions and analyses after attentive viewings and practice in formulating and revising their responses.

By using this book, students or general readers will be able to develop and explain their responses. They will also gain awareness of their own and others' critical assumptions plus greater understanding of the film medium. And, I hope, they will be motivated and prepared to move on to more advanced studies in filmmaking, film history, and film theory or aesthetics.

Compared to other books on the same subject, this book has four distinctive features:

- It emphasizes practical criticism rather than theory and history. For most beginning students, who mainly just enjoy going to the movies, the combination of criticism, theory, and history is overwhelming.
- The book is geared toward beginners, who may lack skills in viewing, analyzing, and explaining.
- The book combines information and exercises to help viewers develop critical skills.
- The emphasis is on film viewing and viewer responses, rather than on filmmaking/filmmakers and viewer responses.

The book is divided into five parts. Part One, Subject and Methods, introduces the subject of the book and illustrates how a film might be examined and discussed. Part Two, Films and Examining Films, contains chapters on the distinctive qualities of fictional films, characterization and plot; on cinematic images and sound; and on different kinds of viewer responses. Part Two concludes with two lists that may be used in the study of any film: Questions for Thought/Discussion/Writing and Exercises for Examining Films. Part Three, Writing Analyses, is made up of three chapters intended to help students convey their responses with clarity and precision. Part Four, Issues in Analysis, discusses some issues in film presentation and study. Part Five, Sources for Eight Films, provides background information, combined outline and frame enlargements, questions and observations, and annotated bibliography for eight representative films often studied in beginning film classes. The information shows students some of the kinds of resources available or that can be devised. It also saves time and makes possible greater accuracy and detail in analyses of those frequently studied films.

The book concludes with a glossary including numerous cross-references, an annotated bibliography, and an index.

Throughout the book I have focused on fictional films, especially feature-length commercial films, mainly because I believe that most beginning film students will more likely be drawn into the study of films if they begin with something familiar and enjoyable. I have also restricted the scope of the book because a single book covering fictional, documentary, and experimental film with any pretense at accuracy and balance will have many shortcomings. Nevertheless, although the focus is on fictional films, many sections of this book may also be used to study documentary and experimental films.

In the hope of stimulating student interest and insight, I have included numerous study questions; eight outlines of films; exercises in viewing, listening, writing, reading, and discussing; a chapter on writing about films; ten sample student analyses; a chapter on film and video; numerous drawings, photographs, tables, and publicity stills on the making or marketing of films; over eighty frame enlargements, all in the original aspect ratio; and quotations from critics.

In the Instructor's Manual I have supplied a sample course syllabus, numerous suggested classroom strategies, tips on helping students write more effectively, a sample essay assignment and final examination, and a bibliography for teachers, including a section on Securing Films, Videotapes, and Videodiscs and Showing Them.

I hope the book will provide some answers to deans and faculty who occasionally peek into our classrooms, shake their heads, and wonder what it is we do in the dark. My main aim, however, has been to encourage students in the serious study of film. I hope to help students discover for themselves some of the wonders of films and their reactions to them, yet guide them so that their accounts of their responses are thoughtful and meaningful to others. My goal has been to help beginning film students discover that films can be enjoyed *and* studied, so that they will look and see.

ACKNOWLEDGMENTS

THE following libraries and archives have aided me in my research: Library, California State College, Stanislaus; Pacific Film Archives; Theater Arts Library, UCLA; Cinema Library, USC; Margaret Herrick Library, Academy of Motion Picture Arts and Sciences; Library, American Film Institute, Los Angeles; Library and Film Center, Museum of Modern Art, New York; Billy Rose Theatre Collection in the Lincoln Center Branch and the Film Department of the Donnell Branch, New York Public Library; Elmer Holmes Bobst Library, New York University; Library, French Institute (Alliance Française), New York; Motion Pictures, Broadcasting and Recorded Sound Division, U.S. Library of Congress; Resource Center, American Film Institute, formerly in Washington, D.C.; National Film Archive and Information Division (Library Services and Education), British Film Institute; Filmoteca nacional de España in Madrid; Biblioteca, Filmoteca nacional, Barcelona; Biblioteca, Collecció cinematográfica catalana in Barcelona; Biblioteca del Cinema Delmiro de Caralt, Barcelona; and Museo del Teatro, sección de cinematografía, Barcelona.

As I did my research, the following people were especially helpful: Paula J. Crawford, Robert Leroy Santos, Jane Johnson, Britten Dean, and Samuel Oppenheim, all of California State College, Stanislaus; Anne G. Schlosser, Library Director, American Film Institute in Los Angeles; Michael R. Miller and William K. Everson, both of New York City; Barbara Humphrys, Library of Congress; Susan Julian Huxley, British Film Institute; María Dolores Devesa, Alicia Potes, Carlos Serrano de Osma, José Fernández Guarpón, and Florentino Soria Heredia (Director), Filmoteca nacional de España; and Ramón Sala, Filmoteca nacional in Barcelona.

A number of people have read parts of the manuscript and made helpful suggestions and corrections: colleagues William H. Hayes, Owen Porter, George Settera, and Hope Werness at California State College, Stanislaus; Richard Ekker at Modesto Junior College; David Shepard, Directors Guild of America; Robert Carringer and Steven P. Hill, both of the University of Illinois; Peter Bondanella and James Naremore of Indiana University; Jack Shadoian, University of Massachusetts; Vance Kepley, University of Wisconsin; Jameson Goldner, San Francisco State University; Al LaValley, USC; Roger Manvell,

Boston University; Pamela Baker, Northeast Louisiana University; and Charles H. Harpole, University of Texas at Dallas.

Processing of the frame enlargements is by Image Photographic Laboratory in Washington, D.C.; Ursula Shelehov of the Burbank Studios Photo Lab; Quang Bui of Modesto, California; Noble Dinse, a talented colleague; and Gig Goodman in New York, who skillfully made up most of the prints. Vicki Eden—graphic artist at California State College, Stanislaus—did most of the drawings.

A sabbatical leave award from California State College, Stanislaus, helped fund much of the travel and research. Dr. Reuben Torch, Vice President for Academic Affairs, made a word processor accessible to the faculty and thus speeded my work and increased its accuracy. Colleague George Settera with his usual good spirits helped me learn how to use the thing, and Marion McCardia typed in many of the chapters at a time when I needed all the time I could get. Over the years Dr. Paul Harder, as dean and then assistant vice president at Cal State, has consistently supported film studies and my work. He merits special thanks.

At Holt, Rinehart and Winston, Anne Boynton-Trigg saw the distinctiveness and merit of my approach and helped me discover a more effective way to organize the material, and Carla Kay, Project Editor, was both helpful and pleasant to work with.

My wife, Eva Santos Phillips, did more than I can remember or adequately thank her for. She helped with translations from Spanish and French, and with proofreading, questions, suggestions. And she heard me out. Many times. *Gracias. Merci.* Thank you.

C·O·N·T·E·N·T·S

Analyzing Films
A Practical Guide

P·A·R·T

ONE

SUBJECT
AND
METHODS

THE first section of the book explains what the book is about: experiences of films and thoughtful explanations of those experiences. Part One also illustrates some of the kinds of things we viewers can discover about a film if we examine it closely. The first part concludes by illustrating how several viewers explained in writing their responses to a film.

· 1 ·

To the Student

SUBJECT OF THIS ,BOOK
Films
Descriptions
Analysis
BOOK'S STRUCTURE AND GOALS

You must look at a thing until sight becomes insight.
                                        Attributed to Robert Frost
Failure, according to popular definition, consists of an attempt to do something which does not succeed immediately.
To that, I say "HUMBUG!"
That isn't failure, that's *education*.   Gene Olson, *Sweet Agony*

It's magic. We go into a darkened world, cut off from outside distractions. With eyes wide open we are hypnotized by larger-than-life images. Often our fantasies are played out; our dreams and nightmares, too. We see details unavailable to us in life. We see colors and shapes that *look* like life but are not. The characters on the screen are more attractive or uglier than their human counterparts. We see objects appear, disappear, blend into each other. We travel in space and time. We hear music. We are moved.

Later, we may talk briefly about the experience; then, in all probability, we largely forget about it and move on to the next film. We take so much for granted. But what happens if we see a film, then examine it and formulate our responses and (sometimes) see it more than once, reexamine it, and reformulate our responses? This book will help you discover answers to that question, answers revealing details about individual films and insight into the achievements and potential of the film medium itself.

3

You will be encouraged

- To learn something about the film to be seen and analyzed
- To see the film
- To examine it through discussion and exercises and to begin thinking out and expressing your responses
- Sometimes, to see the film a second time (often taking notes)
- To reassess your responses to a film seen a second time and explain your responses in greater detail.

The book is built upon the assumption that close analysis of films increases understanding and enjoyment of those films and of the film medium itself. Practice in analysis also increases analytic and communicative skills, two major goals of the liberal arts education.[1]

By using the methods of this book, you will be able to view any film more alertly, to describe it more accurately, and to explain your responses to it more persuasively. You will be more alert in the dark and more convincing in the light.

Subject of this Book

Films

Films may be divided into three major groups: fictional, documentary, and experimental (see Figure 1.1). Whenever one considers a large and varied group of objects—whether books, statues, or films—and tries to divide and classify them, not all of the objects fit neatly into a category. So it is with films. For instance, the classic German film *The Cabinet of Dr. Caligari* is sometimes classified as an experimental film that presents fascinating shapes and textures and only secondarily tells a story. *(Battleship) Potemkin,* an early Soviet film, is sometimes defined as a documentary that seems to re-create past events. Some fiction films blend with the experimental or documentary category or (rarely) both.

Although this book concentrates on fictional films originally shown in theaters, many of its observations and techniques can also be used in examining and discussing documentary and experimental films. Throughout the book I have attempted to use the term "films" to mean fictional, documentary, and experimental films and "fictional films" to mean films with characters (as distinguished from people)

---

[1] Unlike specialized practical programs designed to prepare people for specific jobs, the liberal arts education attempts to prepare students to gather and organize information and ideas and to reason and express themselves; such education also acquaints them with a variety of knowledge in the arts, social sciences, and physical and natural sciences deemed significant by the faculty of the college.

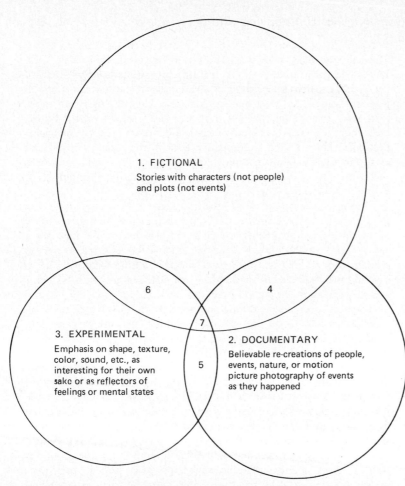

1. FICTIONAL
Stories with characters (not people)
and plots (not events)

6

4

7

3. EXPERIMENTAL
Emphasis on shape, texture,
color, sound, etc., as
interesting for their own
sake or as reflectors of
feelings or mental states

5

2. DOCUMENTARY
Believable re-creations of people,
events, nature, or motion
picture photography of events
as they happened

4. Films that blend documentary and fiction, e. g., Italian neorealists
5. Films that combine documentary and experimental (rare)
6. Films that blend fictional and experimental, e.g., those directed by Cocteau
7. Films that combine all three kinds of films (extremely rare)

1.1 Types of films

and plots. (For more explanation of the characteristics of fictional films, see Chapter 4.)

Descriptions

In discussing and writing about a film, we viewers always use some description, or words that suggest pictures and sounds. To illustrate what is meant by description, let's consider the last 50 seconds of *The*

Godfather, Part II, beginning with the ending of a long scene. Picture this:

The action evidently takes place at the Corleone residence in New York. We have learned earlier in this scene that it's Pearl Harbor Day, December 7, 1941. Michael Corleone, as a young man who has just quit college and joined the Marines, sits alone at a large dining room table. (The rest of the family has left the room and is nearby in the house, welcoming the godfather Vito to a surprise birthday party.) Michael is dressed in light-colored clothing; the light in the scene is bright and even. He is sitting and smoking a cigarette. The only sound we hear is that of the rest of the family, off-frame, greeting Vito and singing "For He's a Jolly Good Fellow."

During a slow lap dissolve to the next scene (one image fades out as the next fades in), the singing of "Jolly Good Fellow" continues to be heard. Stringed instruments and flute are also heard. We now see a slowly moving train in Sicily sometime in the 1920s (from elsewhere in the film, we can infer this with confidence). In a train window, Vito as a young man has one arm around his son Michael and with his other arm helps the boy wave good-bye.[2]

The next scene begins during another slow lap dissolve, as the song "For He's a Jolly Good Fellow" and the music from the previous shot continue to be heard. We now see the adult Michael sitting outdoors, presumably at his Lake Tahoe compound in 1959. He is on the right side of the frame, seen from the waist up. He's wearing dark clothing. He has a cigarette in his right hand. He puts his left loose fist up to his mouth and keeps it there for the rest of the scene. Leaves are on the ground. In the far background we get a glimpse of four people walking away and to the right. As the camera begins to move forward, the music from the Sicily scene dies out. Also as the camera dollies in, the background goes out of focus, and only Michael on the right foreground is in focus. As the camera dollies in, it also tilts down: the horizon in the background goes out of the top of the frame, and we view Michael from a slightly high angle. As the camera approaches Michael, the right side of his face falls into darkness; the left side remains in harsh light. The camera stops with Michael in medium close-up and even more out of the frame on the right. After a brief pause, the theme music begins (strings, harp, woodwinds) as Michael continues to look straight ahead and contemplate we know not what. As the image fades to blackness, the theme music continues into the end credits.

This is a rather detailed description of the concluding 50 or so seconds of the film. In words it attempts to re-create the original sights and sounds. We often use descriptions to stress particular de-

[2] This shot is the same as the last part of a shot used to show the end of Vito's trip to Sicily, where he took revenge on an old family enemy. The music is identical, too. But in the earlier shot, Robert De Niro, as the young Vito, is heard saying, "Michael, say good-bye," and the sounds of the moving train are heard.

tails, to aid the reader or listener in noticing or remembering some aspect of a film. When the reader or listener has not seen the film, the description conveys a sense of what the film is like. Description is of most use when it is accurate, vivid, and complete (or at least chooses representative details). It is most effective when it is full of specifics yet free of unnecessary words. It is especially useful in outlines, plot summaries, and transcriptions (as in cutting continuity scripts that describe the finished film). Description is also invaluable when used to support explanations of our responses to a film.

Analysis

As I see it, the critic's job is to understand, to explain, to interpret and above all to appreciate the work of art, to try to share his or her enthusiasms with others.   Richard Roud, *Cinema: A Critical Dictionary*

In discussing and writing about a film, we inevitably use description. In analysis, however, we explain convincingly what in the film made us think and feel the way we do. Notice how in the following analysis I use description to clarify and support some of my responses to the final 50 seconds of *The Godfather, Part II*.

I notice that the images center on Michael and show him at three stages of his life: as a young, idealistic man; as his father's boy in his father's hands, which shortly before had killed an old man; and finally as a mature man. As a child, he is guided by his affectionate father; as an adult he is alone. In the concluding scene we don't know what he is feeling, but his expression suggests he is not happy. It's cold; the leaves on the ground suggest it is the dead time of year. The same mood is symbolized by his dark clothes, and part of his face is lit in hard, uncomplimentary light (toward the end of the shot, half of his face is in the dark). He shows no sign of relaxation or enjoyment, even though he is in a beautiful, though cold, setting. Toward the end of the shot, only Michael is in focus: he is seen cut off from everything else. Michael seems to be reflecting on things past. Like his father, he has gained power and settled old scores, but he lacks his father's warmth and skill with people. His father, as the sound track reminds us, was seen by his family as a jolly good fellow, but by this point, Michael is alienated from his family.

If we have seen the earlier film, *The Godfather*, which presents events earlier in Michael's life, the closing scenes of *The Godfather, Part II* have further importance. We recall from the earlier film the high hopes Michael's father had for him and how Michael initially resisted the criminal life of his family, then became involved because of his love for his father. To me, the concluding images of *Part II* (intensified by the accompanying music) evoke the loss of innocence and unrealized dreams, and are quite moving. The 50 seconds are rich in meaning, feeling, and importance for all of *Part II*, indeed for the complete godfather story.

Implied in my discussion above is, I think, a strong admiration for this filmmaking. It is complex, yet subtle. Its techniques—lighting, camera work, acting, sound, and so on—are appropriate and effective, yet they do not call attention to themselves and so they avoid detracting from the film's impact. The concluding seconds of the film create a unified and appropriate final reaction to the film as a whole. Many viewers, however, miss the significance of the brief shot of Michael as a child with his father on the train. The dialogue accompanying the earlier use of this footage has been dropped; the scene is so short and the film so long and complex that many forget its earlier appearance.

Whenever we view a film, think about what we have experienced, then explain our responses and what it is in the film that elicited those responses, we are giving a film review or film analysis. The terms "review" and "analysis" are similar yet not identical. They are similar in that both refer to explanations of our responses to a film showing. The explanations may be in speech, or, more often, writing. As shown in Table 1.1, however, reviews and analyses differ in their goals, in the thoroughness of the examination used to reach them, and in the thoroughness of their explanations. Reviews and analyses differ in degree, not kind, and some explanations of responses are difficult to classify as either a review or an analysis. Many of Pauline Kael's essays in the *New Yorker,* for example, are detailed analyses, although they usually appear biweekly and are often thought of as reviews. Most responses to films, however, are clearly reviews *or* analyses. Reviews appear in newspapers and in weekly and monthly magazines after a film opens and on television programs such as "At the Movies" and "Sneak Previews." (For an example of a film review, see the essay reprinted from *Time* in Chapter 3.) Analyses appear in film journals and film books. (For examples of analyses, see Chapters 3, 8, and 9.)

To read or write an analysis about any kind of film is to take part in a dialogue about it. The best analyses, like the best conversations, show enthusiasm for the subject (and often for the language used to describe it). They also convey a sense of sharing, understanding, and reasoned and reasonable evaluations. Film analysis is a way of explaining what the viewer sees and hears in a film, and how and why the viewer reacts. Given the immense variety of viewers and the complexities of a film, no two analyses will be exactly alike, and no single analysis will be the complete and final word about the film. Not that all analyses are equally valuable. Careless analyses are of little help or interest. The challenge in doing film analysis is to share enthusiasm, insight, and reasonable evaluations about the film(s). When supported with accurate examples from the film, analysis can persuade other viewers or listeners to reconsider the film or some aspect of it. Sometimes an analysis can confirm viewers' original responses and help

Table 1.1
Reviews and Analyses

	Review	Analysis
Goal	To provide basic factual information and to help reader/listener decide whether to see a particular film	To communicate individual responses to a film in detail and to persuade reader/listener that the responses are reasonable
Examination	Often one viewing of the film and some thinking about the experience	Often two or more viewings, examination of particular parts of the film, readings, discussion with others
Formulation of responses	Usually shorter and less detailed than in an analysis; often done under pressure of a deadline	Usually longer and having more details on each aspect covered; author usually has more time to formulate and revise than is the case for reviewer

them understand those responses more completely. Well-done analyses can make viewers want to see the film again with renewed enjoyment and perception.

Potentially, nearly all viewers have interesting and worthwhile observations to make about films. Each person has a unique combination of experience and outlook that can be applied to film analysis. For example, one person is a shrewd judge of character; another knows history well and sees how it is reflected in films. Most people, too, enjoy seeing at least certain kinds of films and discussing them. The trouble is that most people lack the training and experience to sort out their impressions, note significant detail, discover principles, and express their responses specifically and persuasively (see Figure 1.2). Proficiency in viewing and analysis is also scarce because both ever-present commercial television and many of the most popular movies make few demands on audience attentiveness, intelligence, and sensitivity. Yet, like every worthwhile skill—such as playing a musical instrument or learning a foreign language—skill in film analysis can be developed through guidance, encouragement, practice, and persistence.

This book tries to help viewers become more aware of their responses to films and to help them answer such questions as the following:

- What do we know about films? How do we know it?
- How certain are we about what we think we know and why do we say so?

BLOOM COUNTY   by Berke Breathed

1.2 Critic at work. © 1982, The Washington Post Company, reprinted with permission.

- To what extent are our responses shaped by our individual backgrounds, preoccupations, values? To what degree are they determined by our culture: the place and time and people of our lives?
- How and why do other viewers react as they do?
- Which responses and analyses are truest to the films?

To find answers to these and other questions, viewers are encouraged to examine individual films carefully, and sometimes repeatedly, and to make their descriptions of their responses as clear, accurate, thorough, and persuasive as they can. In practicing doing so, viewers improve critical and communicative skills. The film experience includes the interaction of many factors, and in examining it closely viewers may also gain understanding of their own tastes and standards, other viewers, and occasionally of cultural influences. They also build a foundation for understanding both film history and the nature and potential of film—what is usually called "film theory."

Many people tend to do film analysis from a particular perspective. Thus, some people "see" films from the point of view of Marxist economic and political theory. Others are feminist critics, who are especially sensitive to the implications of the depictions of the sexes on film. Some are semiologists, who use the technical language of linguistics to study what the components of film mean or signify. Still others believe that the best way to understand films is to study the films of a dominant filmmaker, usually the director (*auteur* theory). Some viewers prefer to compare and contrast a film with many other similar films, such as other westerns or other musicals (genre criticism). These and other approaches are widely used in film journals and advanced film courses, and they are often interesting and useful. These advanced critical approaches, however, can bewilder beginning film students, who first need guidance in finding their own voice and practice in speaking clearly with it.[3]

Book's Structure and Goals

In order to help viewers understand responses to films and to communicate that understanding effectively, the book is organized into five parts. Part One, Subject and Methods, includes this introductory chapter plus a sample examination of a film and a chapter of sample written reviews and analyses. Part Two, Films and Examining Films, contains three chapters that explain the basics of fictional stories, the sights and sounds of cinema, and viewer responses. Part Two concludes with two lists, Questions for Thought/Discussion/Writing and Exercises for Examining Films. Part Three, Writing Analyses, has a chapter on writing and revising essays plus two chapters of sample student essays. Part Four, Issues in Analysis, discusses some major issues in presenting and studying films, including consideration of the uses and limitations of video, the consequences of different film versions, and other possible problems or misconceptions. Part Five, Sources for Eight Films, presents background information, outlines with accompanying frame enlargements, questions, observations, and bibliographies for eight films useful to beginning film classes. The book concludes with a glossary; selected, annotated bibliography; and an index.

The book is designed to help readers—in the classroom and out—see and hear any film attentively and to describe their responses thoughtfully and persuasively. Exercises in discussing, observing, listening, reading, and writing are used as ways to strengthen critical skills, and viewers are guided through the steps of reaching their own clear and accurate descriptions and their own informed and defensible analyses. The approach advocated in this book helps maximize insight into the film while minimizing the chances of distorting an account of the film, as often happens, for example, in the typical situation where the viewer just sees the film once and discusses it briefly.

[3] An anthology that explains and illustrates some different critical perspectives is Bill Nichols, ed., *Movies and Methods* (Berkeley: University of California Press, 1976).

· 2 ·

Sample Examination of a Film

As was mentioned in the previous chapter, the five-step approach to analyzing a film (learning background information, seeing the film, examining it, viewing the film a second time, and reassessing earlier responses) is ideal, though not always possible. In this chapter, let's examine *The Third Man* (the title is no longer protected by U.S. copyright laws, and good 16 mm prints and videotape copies are readily available). If we apply the five-step approach, what might we learn about the film? What we learn about *The Third Man* will illustrate some of what we may learn about any film examined closely.

If you will not be seeing *The Third Man* before you read this chapter, read the following plot summary at least twice, then read the rest of the chapter as an illustration of the kinds of things that can be learned about a film by using various techniques and strategies.

Plot Summary

In *The Third Man*, Holly Martins, an American writer of western fiction, arrives in Vienna to do "publicity work for some kind of charity" that his friend Harry Lime is running. Shortly after Martins arrives, he learns that Lime had recently been hit by a car and killed. Soon Martins is suspicious about the circumstances of Lime's death, and he stays on in Vienna to try to solve the mystery. In three eventful days, Martins meets Lime's girlfriend, Anna, and Lime's associates: Kurtz, Dr. Winkel, and Popescu. He also keeps meeting up with Major Calloway, who is presumably in charge of the police in the British section of occupied Vienna, because Calloway is trying to get evidence about the men involved in Lime's criminal activities. Unexpectedly, Martins meets up with the third man who, it was reported, helped carry Lime's body from the street after the accident. The consequences of that chance encounter have serious repercussions for all the film's major characters.

Now for a more detailed plot summary.

I. Prologue

During various shots of Vienna, Austria, actor Joseph Cotten reads the following lines:[1]

> I never knew the old Vienna before the war, with its Strauss music, its glamour, and its easy charm. I really got to know it in the classic period of the black market. [See Figures 2.1 and 2.2.] They could get anything if people wanted it enough and had the money to pay. Of course, a

2.1 Shot early in Prologue: statue of Beethoven. © 1949 London Film Productions.

---

[1] In a British version of the film, director Carol Reed delivers slightly different lines. The two versions, American and British, are quite similar in all other respects. When the film was first shown, it was shown in a 93-minute version, and occasionally that version is still shown instead of the 104-minute version described in the following paragraphs.

2.2 Next shot after the one represented in Figure 2.1: two black-marketeers. © 1949 London Film Productions.

situation like that does tempt amateurs, but you know of course they don't last long, not really, not like professionals. Now the city is divided into four zones, you know—American, British, Russian, and the French—but the center of the city, that's international, policed by an International Patrol, one member of each of the four powers. Wonderful! You can imagine what a chance they had, all of them strangers to the place and no two of them speaking the same language. Oh, they were good fellows on the whole and did their best. [*Pause*] Vienna doesn't look any worse than a lot of other European cities, bombed a little, of course. [See Figure 2.3.] Anyway, I was dead broke when I

2.3 Last shot of Prologue, before Martins's train arrives at station. © 1949 London Film Productions.

got to Vienna. A close pal of mine had wired me offering me a job doing publicity work for some kind of charity he was running. I'm a writer. Name's Martins. Holly Martins. Anyway down I came all the way to old Vienna, happy as a lark and without a dime.

II. First Day

Holly Martins arrives at the Vienna train station. He shows his passport to a military policeman and explains that he has come to Vienna to visit a friend, Harry Lime. Next, he arrives at Lime's apartment building (see Figure 2.4). In the hallway, a porter tells Martins that Lime has been hit by a car and killed. Martins arrives at the cemetery before the end of Lime's funeral and afterward accepts a ride back to town with Major Calloway, a British officer who is evidently in charge of the military police in the British section of Vienna. In a bar, Martins is intoxicated and becomes upset when Calloway calls Lime a racketeer. In a military hotel reception area, Sergeant Paine, Calloway's assistant, tells a Mr. Crabbin that Martins is a famous writer, and Crabbin invites Martins to speak to the "Cultural Re-education Section" and stay on in Vienna as their guest. At about the same time, Martins also receives a telephone call from Kurtz, a friend of Lime. At an outdoor café, Kurtz and Martins talk about Harry. Outside Lime's flat, Kurtz describes Lime's accident to Martins, and Martins questions the porter. Back at the hotel reception desk, Martins rejects an airplane ticket Calloway has sent, and goes out.

2.4 Martins's arrival at Lime's building: he walks under a ladder. © 1949 London Film Productions.

III. First Night

In a theater dressing room, Martins learns from Anna, Harry Lime's lover, more about the circumstances of Harry's death. At Harry's apartment, Anna helps Martins question the porter, who becomes angry when Martins presses him, and orders Martins to leave. At Anna's building, Martins and Anna learn that the International Police are searching Anna's rooms. The police, under Calloway's charge, take possession of Lime's letters to Anna and her passport, then take Anna away for questioning. In Calloway's office, Anna sees a Soviet officer examining her passport. Martins arrives at the residence of Dr. Winkel (Harry's physician) and questions him, but learns nothing new. In Calloway's office, the Soviet officer is eager to take Anna into custody and repatriate her. Martins and Anna arrive at the Casanova Club, where. Kurtz works. Martins chats with Crabbin, then Kurtz, who introduces Martins to Popescu, another associate of Lime's who happened to be present at Harry's accident. Popescu makes a veiled threat to Martins.

IV. Second Day

On a bridge, Popescu, Kurtz, and Dr. Winkel meet with an unidentified fourth man. Outside Harry's flat, the porter sets up a meeting with Martins for that night; then the porter turns and presumably sees someone behind him (see Figure 2.5). At about 6:00 P.M., Martins arrives at Anna's room. They talk about Harry, then leave to go see the porter.

2.5 Reaction shot of porter. © 1949 London Film Productions.

V. Second Night

On Harry's street, Martins and Anna see a crowd outside Harry's building. The porter has been murdered. A boy who had witnessed the porter's anger with Martins cheerfully points out Martins as the murderer. Anna and Martins run off, pursued by the crowd. Martins and Anna elude the pursuers by going into a cinema. As Martins arrives back at the hotel reception desk, he finds a driver waiting for him. Under ominous circumstances, Martins is sped off for an unknown meeting—at the Cultural Re-education Section (see Figure 2.6). During a question and evasive answer session after Martins's talk, Popescu and two other men arrive, and Popescu makes thinly veiled threats to Martins. Soon Popescu's two assistants are chasing Martins, who slips outside and manages to elude his pursuers. In Calloway's office, Calloway, with Paine's assistance, presents Martins with evidence of Lime's criminal activities, and the Soviet officer gets Anna's passport. At a cabaret bar, Martins is drinking and is evidently depressed. He avoids the bar girls, buys flowers, and leaves. At Anna's apartment, he says he has come to say good-bye, but Anna guesses that Calloway told him the truth about Lime. After Anna and Martins talk further about Harry, Martins reveals his feelings for her. Outside on the street, Martins gets a glimpse of Lime standing in a doorway (see Figure 2.7). Martins pursues him but loses his trail in a square. Later, Martins brings Calloway and Paine to the square. Calloway guesses that Lime may have gone into a kiosk and descended into the sewer. The three of them look around in the sewer. At the cemetery, Lime's coffin is dug up. It contains the body of Joseph Hobbin, an

2.6 Subjective camera and dutch-angle shot: what Martins sees upon his arrival at Cultural Re-education Section. © 1949 London Film Productions.

2.7 First view of Lime. © 1949 London Film Productions.

orderly who used to steal penicillin from military hospitals and sell it to Lime. Under Soviet orders, the International Police arrive at Anna's apartment and take her away. At International Police headquarters, Calloway intercepts Anna and questions her about Lime once again.

VI. *Third Day*

On the street outside Kurtz's house, Martins tells Kurtz and Winkel that he wants to meet with Lime. Later, at the base of a Ferris wheel, Lime arrives. The two of them get in a Ferris wheel compartment and have a tense meeting. Later, at Calloway's office, Martins agrees to help Calloway capture Lime.

VII. *Third Night*

At the Vienna train station, Paine helps Anna onto a train. Before the train leaves, however, she spots Martins lingering nearby. In a snack bar, she guesses that Martins has made a deal with Calloway and that her freedom from the Soviets is part of the deal. She angrily leaves. At the International Police headquarters, Martins tells Calloway that he won't be a decoy after all. Calloway tricks Martins into a visit to a children's hospital, where Martins sees the results of Lime's diluted penicillin (see Figure 2.8). Soon afterward, Martins again agrees to help capture Lime. Later that night, Martins waits in a café for a meeting with Lime; outside are Calloway, Paine, assorted police, and an ominous shadow (see Figure 2.9). Anna makes a surprise appear-

2.8 In children's ward of hospital, Martins sees the results of Lime's drugs. © 1949 London Film Productions.

2.9 Shadow of balloon man. © 1949 London Film Productions.

ance in the café, says that "they [presumably Kurtz, Winkel, and Popescu] have just been arrested," and berates Martins; then Harry arrives, quickly realizes the situation, and draws a gun on Martins, but runs off as Paine shows up. In a nearby sewer to which he is chased, Lime shoots Paine. Calloway shoots Lime but does not kill him. While Calloway is distracted by Paine's injury, Martins takes Paine's pistol and walks away. The injured Lime tries to lift a grate and escape into the night (see Figure 2.10). Martins finds the cornered Lime. They exchange glances (see Figure 2.11). Offscreen, Martins (presumably) finishes off Lime with a shot.

VIII. Fourth Day

At the cemetery the next afternoon, Lime is buried. Afterward, as Calloway and Martins drive away, they pass Anna. Martins asks Calloway to stop, and Martins gets out. Calloway drives on. On the cem-

2.10 Harry trying to lift grate. ©1949 London Film Productions.

2.11 Last view of Lime. © 1949 London Film Productions.

etery road, Martins waits for Anna as she approaches him. Martins waits—and she walks past him (see Figure 2.12).

A reminder: If you will not be seeing the film, it's a good idea to read the plot summary again before reading the rest of this chapter.

2.12 Last shot of film. Note falling leaf above Anna's head. © 1949 London Film Productions.

Background Information

Most people who saw *E.T.* in 1982 understood the culture depicted in the film. If they did not have direct knowledge of a wealthy sub-urban California life-style, at least they had a cinematic or television acquaintance with it. However, a U.S. audience in the 1980s viewing *The Third Man*, which was first shown in 1949, is in a different position.

The film shows some events in Vienna shortly after the conclusion of World War II. Although the major language spoken is English, to modern American audiences the film is truly foreign, and some background information is helpful.

I'll take space here to stress only some of the most useful information. World War II had ended in 1945, with the United States, Soviet Union, Britain, and France as victorious allies. Soon afterward, tensions between the Soviets and the other allies mounted, and the "cold war" began. Europe in 1948 was torn by political uncertainty. In the spring of that year, Communists gained control of the government of Czechoslovakia, Austria's neighbor. Later in the year the Soviets blockaded Western access to Berlin; the United States began flying in supplies, and the feeling was widespread that war between the U.S. and the U.S.S.R. was imminent.

Like Berlin, Vienna of the late 1940s was also divided into occupied zones (British, American, French, Soviet). The city had many refugees, a thriving black market, and numerous spies. According to a British newspaper, at the time of the film's release in Vienna, it was reported that more than twenty intelligence and secret service organizations were operating there, so many that when a new political group formed in Vienna, "agents of all kinds formed a good part of the audience. Most of them recognised one another."[2]

The Third Man was conceived when British producer Alexander Korda approached Graham Greene, an English novelist and occasional scriptwriter, to write a script about the four-power occupation of Vienna. After Greene visited the city for a few weeks, he wrote a story that underwent extensive revisions before the film reached theaters. Evidently, most of the changes came about because of the close work of Greene and the film's director, Carol Reed (1906–1976).

The music for the film was arranged and played on the zither by Anton Karas. For some months after the film's release, the "Third Man Theme" was high on the popular music charts. The zither, an ancient stringed instrument, is held in the lap or set on a table and strummed or plucked with a pick or fingers. Usually it has five melody strings; it can have up to forty harmony strings (see Figure 2.13). It

2.13 Anton Karas playing the zither. Larry Edmunds Bookshop.

[2] *Manchester Guardian,* 11 March 1950.

is widely played in the Tyrols (Western Austria) and in Bavaria. In the 1940s, few feature films used a solo instrument as the only source of music.

The accompanying production stills—of filming on location in a sewer, recording the music, and mixing the sound (by blending various sources to make up the composite sound track)—convey some sense of the efforts in making the film (see Figures 2.14–2.16).

2.14 Filming on location in a sewer. Larry Edmunds Bookshop.

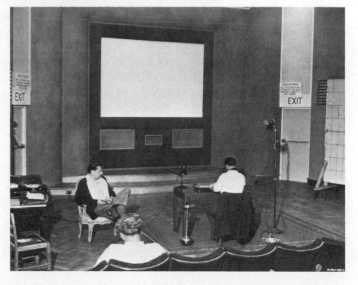

2.15 Director Carol Reed (left) and Anton Karas during a recording session. Larry Edmunds Bookshop.

2.16 Mixing sound for *The Third Man* on a mixing board. Larry Edmunds Bookshop.

The film features two American actors, Joseph Cotten as Martins and Orson Welles as Harry Lime. Both came from a background in theater and radio drama; both also worked in the classic film *Citizen Kane* (see Chapter 15). Welles's performance in *The Third Man* attests to his commanding voice and extraordinary presence. Many viewers remember him vividly from this film, indeed remember the film as an Orson Welles film, even though he appears late in the film and only briefly.

The other characters and performers:

Major Calloway: Trevor Howard (1916–   )
Anna Schmidt: Alida Valli (1921–   ), an Italian actress of
   Austrian background

Sergeant Paine: Bernard Lee (1908–1981)
'Baron' Kurtz: Ernst Deutsch
Popescu (puh PESS ko): Siegfried Breuer
Dr. Winkel: Erich Ponto
Porter: Paul Hoerbiger
Crabbin: Wilfrid Hyde-White

First Viewing

During the first showing, nearly all viewers will be caught up in the mystery and will be asking such questions of themselves as Who is the third man? Who killed Lime? Will Martins be killed? Will Martins and Anna become lovers? Viewers will naturally try to understand and evaluate the characters, especially the most important ones: Lime, Martins, Anna, and Major Calloway. Of course, viewers will also have their individual interests. Some will notice certain details; others will notice other aspects. Some will make certain judgments; other viewers will disagree. For instance, some will be so disgusted by Harry Lime's actions that they will feel no pity at his death. Other viewers will feel some compassion for him.

Questions and Exercises

Some Discussion Questions

After seeing a film, most people like to talk about the experience, and that is often an excellent way to begin to formulate an analysis. For *The Third Man,* the following eleven sets of questions encourage people who have seen the film to consider various aspects; the questions also give focus to any discussion, though some of them cannot be answered after only one viewing. *If you have not seen* The Third Man, *don't try to answer these questions; merely look at them as kinds of questions that may be asked of a film.*

1. What do we learn about Lime in his conversation with Martins on the Ferris wheel? In the Ferris wheel compartment Lime draws a heart and writes Anna's name in it. What does that action tell you about Lime? What is Lime's relationship to the Soviet authorities in Vienna? How do you feel about Harry Lime? What is it about the film that makes you react that way toward him? Do we understand *why* he has done what he has done? What significance, if any, can you ascribe to the fact that in Anna's photograph of Harry he moved his head and evidently blurred the picture?

2. Is Martins right to try to help capture Lime? Why or why not? Is he right to shoot Lime? Why or why not?

3. How successful a detective is Martins? What is his responsibility for the deaths of the porter, Paine, and Lime?

4. What different reasons can you give to explain why Anna does not toss dirt into the grave during the first funeral but does toss dirt during the final funeral service? For what possible reasons does Anna walk past Martins at the end of the story?

5. After Lime and Martins talk on the Ferris wheel, Lime says to Martins: "Don't be so gloomy. After all, it's not that awful. Remember what the fellow said: in Italy for thirty years under the Borgias they had warfare, terror, murder, and bloodshed, but they produced Michelangelo, Leonardo da Vinci, and the Renaissance. In Switzerland they had brotherly love—and they had five hundred years of democracy and peace, and what did that produce? The cuckoo clock." What is Lime's point? How persuasive is his implied analogy? Why do you say so? What does Lime's implied argument reveal about him?

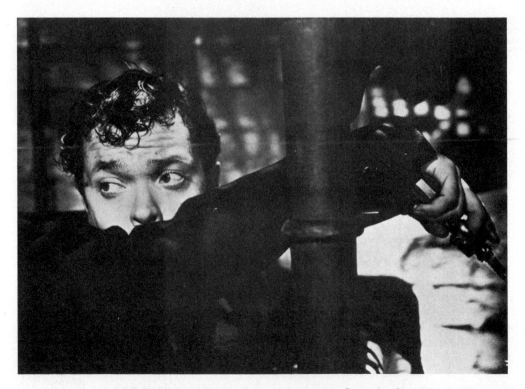

2.17 Publicity still, not frame enlargement from the film. The Academy of Motion Picture Arts and Sciences.

6. Study the publicity still (Figure 2.17), which was made by posing the actor Orson Welles before a still camera, and the comparable frame enlargement from the film (Figure 2.18). What mood and meaning does each image create? Why do you say so?

7. Discuss in detail the setting, composition, and mood of the film's last shot, one frame of which is reprinted in Figure 2.12.

8. In numerous shots in *The Third Man* the subject photographed appears to be on a tilted surface, not a horizontal one (Figures 2.6 and 2.8). Where else in the film are these dutch angles used? Where are high angles used? (See Figure 5.21.) Low angles? (See Figure 5.23.) What effects does each of the three kinds of angles create?

9. In many shots of this film much of the frame is covered in black, and the subject is illuminated by a single source of light (see Figures 2.7, 2.9, and 2.11). Where else in the film is this kind of lighting (called low-key lighting) used? What does it contribute to the scenes where it is employed?

10. The porter's death is not shown. It is implied by a shot of him presumably looking at his would-be murderer (Figure 2.5). Near the end of the film in the scene where Martins visits the hospital treating the victims of Lime's business, we are not shown the children, only Martins's reaction to them, and the reaction shots of Martins are medium shots, not close-ups (Figure 2.8). Where else in the film is less shown than might be shown? What is the consequence of showing less, rather than more?

2.18 Frame enlargement—an enlarged photograph of an individual frame from the film. © 1949 London Film Productions.

11. The film might be interpreted as a story about a well-meaning but largely naive and inept U.S. citizen looking at the same events as do the Europeans but seeing them differently and eventually learning about disillusionment and corruption in post–World War II Europe. *In detail,* defend or criticize such an interpretation.

Viewing Exercises

If viewers can see certain parts of a film again, they will be surprised by their discoveries. Later in the book, twelve viewing exercises for doing so are described. One of the most useful is simply to view a scene again without the sound turned up.

Looking at the prologue of *The Third Man,* for example, without listening to the sound track allows the viewer to concentrate on the visual information: we can *see* more clearly that Vienna is a city of culture yet criminal activity, war damage, and foreign military occupation (Figures 2.1–2.3).

Looking again at the scene of Lime's first funeral, we can see it takes place in autumn, the dying time of year, and we can see how sparsely attended it is, by two business associates/friends (we learn later), his lover (we learn later), a pallbearer, a priest, and his assistant. Calloway is far back from this group, viewing events. Martins approaches the grave site and looks at it and at Anna, while Kurtz and Winkel eye Martins. Anna does not respond to the priest's brief comfort, and she declines to toss a spoon of dirt into the grave, turns, scarcely notices Martins, and leaves. He steps forward, accepts the spoon, and tosses some dirt into the grave. Winkel is so caught up in looking at Martins that he forgets to leave the wreath for Lime's grave and has to be reminded by Kurtz to do so.

As in many film scenes, what is said is rather unimportant. But what is shown tells us much important information about the characters. Calloway is unmoved and observing from afar. Only a few characters attend Lime's funeral. Kurtz and Winkel show intense interest in the stranger: after Martins's arrival, they pay no more attention to the funeral service. Lime's two friends are not preoccupied with the service to begin with, as Anna is, and are easily distracted. Lime's friends seem suspicious of others. They are also mysterious: why, after all, would they take so much interest in a stranger? The scene is the first of many in the film showing characters looking at and trying to figure out other characters. We see Martins entering into a situation evidently without seeing all of what is going on: he does not seem to notice Kurtz and Winkel, though characteristically he does take an interest in the beautiful woman. And we see Anna caught up in her feelings and taking little notice of anyone. All this and much more is communicated visually in about 80 seconds.

Writing Exercises

Yes, writing is hard. But it's an excellent way to discover what we know and what we don't. It's also an excellent way to discover. Numerous writing exercises are described later in the book. Here I'll describe and illustrate only one of them.

I often ask students to write about the images in a film. What sticks in the mind after the showing? Why are those images so prominent? In doing this exercise for *The Third Man,* you may find yourself including references to the darkness, deep shadows, cold and damp (we often see breath in the air), falling leaves, bombed-out buildings, unpopulated streets, the cemetery at the beginning, middle, and conclusion of the film, dank and dark sewers, suspicious looks, the accompanying lies, the general unhappiness. In *The Third Man,* Anna isn't the only one who rarely gives an unforced smile.

Second Viewing

After seeing *The Third Man,* discussing it, and possibly doing at least one exercise, the viewer surely realizes that the film is more than an entertaining mystery story. The viewer also tends to have many questions that a second showing may help answer, perhaps including the following: Does Anna sense that Lime is not dead before she learns that he is not? How is the viewer to feel about Calloway? What makes Harry act as he does? These and similar questions are often not entirely answerable after one viewing. During the second showing, viewers are also apt to notice additional, significant details. For example, the unlucky Martins walks under a ladder just before he goes into Lime's building at the beginning of the film (Figure 2.4). At the first funeral Anna declines to toss some ashes or dirt into Harry's grave; at the second funeral, she does so. We see someone (presumably Dr. Winkel) carving a roasted bird, then see Winkel lurking in the shadows before we first see him in the light, and it's not very bright light at that. We may notice that the dog at Winkel's is Kurtz's and infer that Kurtz is visiting there. We may notice that in the taxi on the way to his lecture, Martins is seen from an angle showing him behind bars; indeed, he is a prisoner. During a second viewing, many viewers may notice the glances between Martins and the wounded, trapped Lime, whose eyes and slight nod imply that he is asking for release from his suffering (see Figure 2.11). Almost certainly the viewer will notice how very often dutch-angle shots are used (see Figures 2.6 and 2.8) and how many scenes take place in deep darkness. These and many other details are often missed in the first viewing.

Reconsideration

Now is the time to reconsider your earlier responses, perhaps by reconsidering the study questions or discussing your responses with others, or by doing various readings, or by writing an analysis.

One of the most useful readings is an analysis. How does another, experienced viewer respond to the film? Nearly always, it's interesting to find out. (Sometimes the analysis is more interesting and entertaining than the film!) For a review and two analyses of *The Third Man,* see the next chapter.

Another excellent way to reassess your responses to a film is to write your own analysis of it, or at least of one major aspect (see Part Three of this book). In writing your analysis, you're bound to gain greater understanding of the film.

By now, I hope it is clear that a fictional film is enormously and deceptively complex. So are our reactions to it. And so are the possible ways to examine those reactions. In this chapter I have illustrated only a few of the techniques and sources that can be used to reveal some of the complexity of a film. A full examination of *The Third Man* or any feature film requires at least a book to explain it.

Now that this chapter has illustrated some of what can be learned about a film by using various strategies, the next chapter will illustrate how three viewers reacted after close examination of a film.

· 3 ·

Sample Review and Analyses

Time **Magazine:** *Review of* The Third Man
David Denby: *Night World*
Lynette Carpenter: *"I Never Knew the Old Vienna": Cold War Politics and* The Third Man

THE previous chapter illustrates some of what could be discovered about a film if it is examined closely. This chapter illustrates what three writers discovered about *The Third Man*. Close reading of the following essays reveals that the writers examined the film closely; at the very least, they saw the film repeatedly. It is certain, too, that these writers wrote and rewrote their explanations of their responses; otherwise, their essays would not be so clear, detailed, insightful, and interesting.

I include these essays not as models for beginning film students, but rather as illustrations of how different writers react to the same film in different yet defensible ways.

Review of *The Third Man*
Time *Magazine*

*T*HE *Third Man* (Sir Alexander Korda; David O. Selznick) is already a smash hit in Britain, where most critics hailed it as the best movie of 1949. U.S. moviegoers are likely to find it one of the best of 1950. Like *The Fallen Idol,* by the same brilliant British team—Director Carol Reed and Scripter Graham Greene—it adds an extra depth of character insight and a new texture of pictorial eloquence to the kind of spellbinding thriller that made Alfred Hitchcock famous.

Set and filmed in a forlorn, postwar Vienna, *The Third Man* is crammed with cinematic plums that would do the early Hitchcock proud—ingenious twists and turns of plot, subtle detail, full-bodied bit characters, atmospheric backgrounds that become an intrinsic part of the story, a deft commingling of the sinister with the ludicrous, the casual with the bizarre. But the central characters are not mere pawns in a melodrama; they are motivated people who speak grown-up dialogue and feel contagious emotions. The film's most original touch: a unique musical sound track using only a hauntingly twanging zither* which speaks more tellingly than a full symphony orchestra.

The story employs the classic melodramatic gambit of the innocent who walks straight into somebody else's intrigue and can't get out. With an old friend's promise of a vague job, Joseph Cotten, an American hack writer of Western novelettes, arrives in Vienna just in time to rush to his benefactor's funeral. He learns that 1) his friend was mixed up in some sort of racket; and 2) his death may not have been as accidental as the dead man's Vienna associates—a seedy baron, a teak-faced doctor and a Rumanian fashionplate—so glibly assure him.

A well-meaning bungler in the tradition of Graham Greene heroes, Cotten decides to clear up his friend's death and reputation, goes about it with an ingenuous bravado that soon turns him from hunter into hunted. Along the way he becomes involved with a sardonic major of the British military police (Trevor Howard) who had hunted his friend, a melancholy actress (Valli) who had loved him, and finally, the villain (Orson Welles), a glad-handing, cynical American.

In Director Reed's hands, a shot of a body floating in the Danube tells a story of its own, a shot of a cat licking a man's shoe becomes a chilling premonition of shock. Reed gets a grotesquely comic sequence out of an eerie

*Played by Viennese Anton Karas, a Carol Reed protégé, whose recordings from the score quickly became bestsellers in British music shops (*Time,* Nov. 28).

four-year-old boy leading a street crowd in pursuit of Cotten while the accompanying zither jangles like a nickelodeon piano. At every turn, he exploits the hulking shadows and wet, back-lighted cobblestones of Vienna at night. Cameraman Robert *(Odd Man Out)* Krasker gives beautiful expression to Reed's photogenic tricks, e.g., as a train chugs out of the station, nothing is seen but the light patterns of its windows projected across a cloud of steam.

Even *The Third Man*'s flaws are largely the product of its brilliance. To build atmosphere, Reed has filmed much of the picture with the camera slightly askew; after a while, the angle calls too much attention to itself. He has a way of emptying the streets at his convenience and peopling them suddenly when it suits him. And toward the end, he stages a chase through the city's sewers which, for all its self-sustaining excitement, comes after the story's major suspense has been resolved. But these are minor faults in the work of a craftsman so skilled that he has earned the right to be judged as an artist.

Director Reed handles his actors as expertly as his story. Valli's playing of a girl numbed with loyal, grieving love is just right. Cotten and Howard fill out every corner of their characterizations; and a supporting cast of excellent European actors with new faces keeps the stars on their toes. The ultimate proof of Reed's powers as a director: he has managed to get a temperate, first-rate performance out of Orson Welles.

Night World

David Denby

. . . A favorite work of art, then, is one that we can relax with, one that we can repeatedly experience without risk of total involvement. We feel safe with it. It engages us without overwhelming us. Among the greatest movies, there are harrowing experiences of personal and social disintegration—*Greed, M, Umberto D, L'Avventura, Shame*—but I wouldn't include any of these, as much as I love and admire them, among my favorite movies. My favorites— the ones I watch most frequently—include the screwball comedies of the thir- ties, the Marx Brothers pictures, musicals like *Singin' in the Rain* and *The Band Wagon,* and, especially, fast-moving American melodramas like *Scarface, The Front Page, The Maltese Falcon, The Letter, Casablanca, The Big Sleep, All About Eve,* and *The Sweet Smell of Success. The Front Page* is shown rarely these days and *The Sweet Smell of Success* was a commercial failure when it came out, but this is still an extremely conventional list of films. It hardly seems a critic's list—it could be *anybody's* list. I don't particularly mind admitting that the popularity of these films enters into my experience of enjoying them the most personally. They are all good movies, and don't need critical defense, but it seems obvious that a good movie is defined as a favorite movie only when I can enjoy it repeatedly with friends—either old friends who come over to watch the movie on television or those spontaneous friends—the entire the- ater—that one discovers during a good night at a revival house. In such a case, the accumulated social experience of seeing the movie, with its associa- tions of companions, lovers, wisecracks, arguments, etc. becomes as important as the movie itself. I can't imagine wanting to see *Casablanca* by myself, nor can I dissociate *Casablanca* from the various people I've enjoyed it with. But I don't feel this way about many movies that are much better than *Casablanca.* I can remember my extreme annoyance after a showing of *Umberto D* when an acquaintance wanted to begin an immediate discussion and I only wanted to be alone. When we see a great movie, the experience is always silent, soli- tary and intensely personal; if we are deeply moved, even a stray, silly remark heard on the way out of the theater can be heartrending.

What are the qualities which turn a good movie into a favorite? With few exceptions my friends and I first saw the melodramas listed above on televi- sion in the middle fifties, when we were twelve or thirteen or fourteen. Ob- viously we were fascinated with these films because almost all take place in the corrupt night-world of crime, journalism, theater—the world that is a few years beyond the reach but not the imagination of an adolescent. The nervous, wisecracking men and women getting by on their courage and wit seemed so devastatingly in possession of that freedom and space which a fourteen-year-old allows as the sole superiority of adult life to his own. So we responded to the sophistication, the humor, the violence, and the American efficiency in storytelling (young people generally don't care about film technique, although, of course, they are extremely excited about actors and acting—probably more than adults are). Later on, as we saw these films again and again, we enjoyed them just as much—although we gradually began to regard their sophistication with increasing irony; perhaps *our* sophistication came to consist of a slight feeling of superiority to the movies we loved (a little backstairs snobbery being an essential element of true enjoyment).

One movie I have continued to enjoy with only the slightest change in attitude is Carol Reed's *The Third Man,* and I suppose it's my favorite film. This 1949 production from England lacked the exuberant energy of American melodrama; instead, it revealed what corruption looked like in a defeated and played-out civilization (postwar Vienna), after the party was over. Those good American melodramas I mentioned were tough-minded about sex and money, although they were often soft, in the end, on their heroes and heroines; moreover, engaging as criminality and extreme egotism might appear in the American films, these qualities were often firmly (sometimes bloodily) repudiated. *The Third Man* goes a lot further in its tough-mindedness—almost to the point of despair. Graham Greene's script sustains no illusions about anyone or anything, and although the villains are all punished, the hero is most decidedly not rewarded, and along the way the film offers about the most convincing rationale for nihilism and murder that I can recall hearing at the movies. Everyone who has seen *The Third Man* remembers the substance of what Orson Welles says to Joseph Cotten in the ferris-wheel scene, and nearly everyone, I imagine has been impressed and frightened by it.

It is of course, the supreme movie about the night-world, the ultimate example of that shining-streets-and-lurking-shadows "realism" that was so popular in the late forties. But in addition to its famous atmosphere—the knowing, world-weary people; the magnificent imperial ruins; the alternatingly menacing and ingratiating zither music—*The Third Man* sustains a mood of pessimistic irony which made an impression on me at fourteen and which seemed to reveal the nasty and permanent truth about adult experience, the truth that you could not feel superior to as you got older: life was not orderly and sane, but chaotic, sordid and dangerous; you didn't get what you wanted or possibly deserved; moral virtue, honesty and even courage might count for very little, and these qualities, as well as being useless, might make you unappealing to women and a general nuisance to everyone else. With its extravagant, almost voluptuous pessimism, *The Third Man* provides a pleasurable consolation in bad moments, a reassurance that nothing was ever meant to go right in the first place. It's so enjoyable, in part, because it gives the viewer the agreeable sensation of having confronted the worst.

Greene's characteristic pessimism and irony were reinforced in this case by producer Alexander Korda's choice of Vienna for a setting. *The Third Man* couldn't possibly have achieved the same effect if it had been set in Paris or London. In the postwar period the city of monuments and glory lies in rubble, is divided into quarters by the occupying powers, and is patrolled by military zombies in different uniforms who can't communicate with each other or the Viennese they are supposed to police. Reed and cinematographer Robert Krasker have framed the shots so that bits of rococo decoration appear in the corners of almost every composition, and Anton Karas's zither score is full of such café-repertory favorites as "Unter dem Lindenbaum" and "Alter Lied," but these traces of the imperial and gracious city are used in mocking contrast to its postwar dereliction. Perhaps the amenity of "Old Vienna" was always a bit over-elaborate, a bit sickly sweet, and with the authority of the city destroyed by war, its cultural style becomes the mere façade of decadence. The sinister "refined" manners, always such a cliché of villainy in American antifascist melodrama (as in *All Through the Night,* where the fifth columnists ran an art gallery), rings true in *The Third Man* as social description (it is also extremely entertaining). Dr. Winkel, with his collection of religious relics, and Baron von Kurtz, with his obscene little dog and his violin-playing at the "Casanova Club," are the clever survivors, the educated detritus of a cultured society bereft of economic stability or political power. Their style of ineffable weary cultivation is nothing more than a con man's charm—the false candor that hides the truth of their murderous racket in watered-down penicillin. And just as the economic center of a defeated city switches from legitimate business to black-market profiteering, the geographic center of Vienna has moved from its monuments, palaces and churches to its sewers (that most functional of visual metaphors).

Greene, the well-traveled minor novelist *par excellence,* is superb at creating characters living on the edge of desperation in some sordid or exotic milieu, and it's hard to think of a movie which has a better selection of such people than *The Third Man.* Holly Martins, the man who resists the sewer world, is the movie's nominal hero and its main source of irony. Martins is the author of pulp westerns, a well-meaning, ignorant and stupefyingly naive American. It's amusing to imagine him as Greene's nightmare image of himself—a writer who knows nothing, understands nothing and learns nothing; who is completely out of touch with the type of violent world that he writes about; who tries to live out an appropriate fantasy of solitary courage and rambunctious anti-authoritarianism, and winds up being rejected by everybody. At the very end Martins still hasn't gotten the point, he still doesn't understand that he cannot qualify as a replacement for Harry Lime—rotten bastard that he was— in the arms of Lime's mistress. Martin's courage and conscientiousness are dreadfully beside the point and at times destructive—his stumbling bravado gets an innocent man killed (Lime's porter). He's a hero who keeps searching for an appreciative audience, and everyone keeps telling him to go home. Finally he makes himself useful in the only way possible—by turning police informer and betraying his best friend.

Perhaps Martins is a warm-up for Alden Pyle, the murderously idealistic CIA man in *The Quiet American,* Greene's prescient 1955 novel about Vietnam. In this later work Greene has become extremely bitter about the stupid, well-meaning American. ("Innocence always calls mutely for our protection, when we would be so much wiser to guard ourselves against it; innocence is like a dumb leper who has lost his bell, wandering the world, meaning no harm.") Martins, of course, is far less dangerous than Pyle, even though he kills the man who fails to measure up to his ideals. We are invited to see him as a pathetic and comic figure, and Joseph Cotten makes him immensely likable. Not only do we feel protective toward him, we invariably root for him and suffer hideous embarrassment when he falls into the greedy hands of Crabbin (Wilfrid Hyde-White), the man who runs the culture racket and cons Martins into holding forth on "The Modern Novel." ("Mr. Martins, what author has chiefly influenced you?" "Grey." "Grey? what Grey? I do not know the name." "Zane Grey.")

A boy is often very confused about what makes one man attractive to women and not another; at the age of fourteen it seemed perverse to me that Anna (Alida Valli) would reject Martins at the end. Now it seems perfectly clear that if she hadn't rejected him the rest of the movie wouldn't have made much sense. For if Holly Martins has the virtue that repels, Harry Lime embodies the vileness that attracts. Harry, who knew how to "fix" things and how to get by in hard times; Harry, who made people laugh and knew where the fun was (and who also knew a quick way out—for himself—if the cops showed up); Harry, *who is an utter bastard,* gets all the love because his egotism is like an electric current—he makes things happen, he brings people alive. *The Third Man* renders homage to the dynamism of extreme self-love, and in Orson Welles it has the most famous and talented self-loving performer of the age. As written by Greene and played by Welles, Harry Lime is a man for whom all of humankind has faded into inconsequence; he has simply shut them out and found an essential gaiety in his loneliness. It is that gaiety, that American businessman's optimism, which makes him so attractive to the played-out Viennese. He may be rotten, but at least he isn't dead. In a single scene Welles takes this character through an astonishing series of moods, starting out as hearty as an auto salesman at a convention, and passing through panic, cynicism, murderousness and back to geniality again. Since we don't see Harry until the movie is two-thirds over (although everyone is constantly talking about him), his appearance *had* to be dazzling or *The Third Man* would have collapsed.

Welles's entrance is a brilliant *coup de théâtre:* we know he's there, finally there, because that cat "who only liked Harry" is seen nestling against someone's feet in a darkened doorway. Then suddenly, after Cotten has roused the neighborhood with his drunken shouting, the light from an upstairs window hits Welles like a 2000-watt spotlight (Manny Farber has complained about the falsity of this shot, but I think it's hair-raising). Very quickly, in one of the few camera movements in the entire film, the camera dollies in (as if to say, *this* is what everyone has been talking about), and we see a self-amused and wickedly sardonic smile brilliantly emerging from black clothes and a black hat rakishly tilted—and that is all. A car comes between the two men and Welles is gone, leaving behind a clatter of footsteps and a strange, teasing shadow—it reveals a man running furiously but it doesn't change its position on the wall (an effect which is achieved, I suppose, by having Welles or someone else run directly toward the light source). Harry Lime is there, but he can't be reached.

Just how unreachable he is becomes clear in the famous scene on the ferris wheel. Greene has conceded that Welles himself devised the brilliant sophistry about the Renaissance versus the cuckoo clock, but the best moment comes earlier in the scene, when Martins asks Harry if he's ever seen one of his victims. "Victims? Don't be melodramatic. Look down there. Would you really feel any pity if one of those dots stopped moving forever? If I said that you can have twenty thousand pounds for every dot that stops, would you really, old man, tell me to keep my money—or would you calculate how many dots you can afford to spare? Free of income tax, old man. Free of income tax." Greene is a Catholic writer and it's hard not to see this scene as a modern Temptation. And like all successful tempters, Harry is a psychologist of human weakness: two-thirds of human nature lies on his side of the argument. It's perfectly true, our feelings of pity lessen to nothing as we move further and further away from our victims. Harry's evil is insidious because he knows how to free himself from guilt (never look a victim in the face), and he offers the same freedom to others. Martins resists (perhaps because he lacks Harry's imagination), but he's the only one who does. Harry possesses the supreme nasty secret of the modern age which makes mass murder possible and even enjoyable, and he can't be reasoned with, he can only be killed.

The person who wants to kill him is Major Calloway, a character very much in the Conrad-Greene tradition of the man in authority whose moral passion consists of doing a rotten job as well as he can. In Trevor Howard's elegant and sardonic performance (Howard has always, *must* always, embody the bitterest truths about experience—his voice and face demand nothing less), Calloway stands between the cynical amorality of Lime and the useless idealism of Martins. He will manipulate people to get what he wants, but he's not unkind. Calloway, who knows the worst, is the pragmatic force, the professional, who tries to bring chaos under control. In the plot's final irony, Martins, rather than Calloway, finishes off Harry Lime; Martins has betrayed his best friend and finally killed him (as a last act of friendship, it is true), and although he is morally right to act as Harry's executioner, he loses the girl and possibly his soul. That cigarette he so carefully, so attentively smokes as Anna passes him by—is it not the final cigarette of someone condemned to the death of permanent isolation? It's a rather cruel punishment for his dullness and silliness, but it seems deserved; in a rotten world, no one has the right to remain an adolescent as long as he has.

Earlier I placed the word realism in quotation marks because that was the word used by some of the film's contemporary reviewers to describe its atmosphere. I think anyone can now see that in its overall design *The Third Man* is about as realistic as that eighteenth-century costume drama in which Alida Valli appears in the middle of the movie. To cite the most obvious (and overused) instance of expressive distortion, about half the shots in the movie are tilted off the horizontal axis by ten degrees or more, so that everything seems on the verge of sliding out of control. The stylization is insistent, from first to last; the term realism could only apply to the *moral* realism of Greene's story.

Possibly the critical confusion arose because *The Third Man* was one of the first British features to be shot almost entirely on location. But of course Carol Reed has turned Vienna into a vast stage set, and cinematographer Robert

Krasker has abandoned naturalistic lighting in order to produce coal-dark, glossy blacks and harshly brilliant whites. (Color film, which requires hotter general lighting, was the death of "atmospheric" melodrama.) Much of the visual style of *The Third Man* was first worked out by Reed and Krasker in their previous collaboration, *Odd Man Out* (1946). As in the earlier film, much of *The Third Man* was shot at night; both films are very dark, very black, with only occasional shafts of brilliant light, so we get an impression of a constant struggle against nothingness, against extinction. But *The Third Man* goes further with certain mannerisms, and features one of the most aggressive and persistent uses of back-lighting in the history of the medium. The main source of light is almost always deep in the shot and *hidden*—glaring at us from around a corner or under an arch or at the end of a tunnel. Thus figures are often seen in silhouette or are preceded or followed by immense shadows (some of these shadows seem to have slipped off the walls of *Ivan the Terrible*), an effect of lurking menace that carries us along from scene to scene even if we are aware how portentous and repetitive it all is.

Moreover, Reed's stage-Vienna is almost as unpopulated as the set of an absurdist play. Where are all the people? The immense, alienating crowds of the modern city (often a presence in the German expressionist films which are the stylistic progenitors of this movie) have simply been swept out of sight; the individual in this bombed-out city is now *literally* isolated—alone in the vast squares, alone when scrambling down a pile of rubble, virtually alone in a large house. There are only two sizable groups of people in the film—the crowd that gathers after the porter has been murdered and that begins pursuing Martins by mistake, and the literary society that questions him so savagely on James Joyce and Zane Grey. Both of these crowds become obscenely aggressive; it's as if experience of war had turned the survivors into gangs of predators ready to be unleashed on random victims. Besides these two groups there are only shadows and echoes. And without the general city noise which we take for granted and whose absence is oddly frightening, every voice or footstep becomes a hideous intrusion on a void.

Echoes, like shadows, reveal duplicate selves—hollow, disembodied, unreal. Yet these duplicate selves dominate the movie. *The Third Man* remains the most haunting and insidious of all night-films because we realize that Martins, the plaintive ass with fantasies of glory, stands in for us, for all fantasy-ridden moviegoers, and that this representative of inadequate ordinary decency has less personal force than the loathsome disembodied presences lurking about in the shadows of the ruined and powerless city.

"I Never Knew the Old Vienna": Cold War Politics and *The Third Man*

Lynette Carpenter
(University of Cincinnati)

IN Spring of 1948, British producer Sir Alexander Korda sent Graham Greene to Vienna to write a story for director Carol Reed; according to Greene, "Korda wanted a film about the four-power occupation of Vienna."[1] The result, *The Third Man,* is a product of Reed's and Greene's talented collaboration and of the city in which it was written and filmed, as well as of the post-war world of which Vienna was so clearly a microcosm. Released during the earliest stages of the Cold War, *The Third Man* captures the tension, mutual mistrust, and fear that characterized Western politics after the war. The film also makes a moral statement that becomes so closely identified with the depicted political reality that it translates moral values into political values.

The Third Man is not a consciously conceived political allegory; that argument would overlook the film's complex interweaving of moral, religious, and political issues. But the failure to examine carefully the film's political context has frequently led to misguided and misinformed conclusions. The specific questions of Harry Lime's guilt or innocence, heroism, anti-heroism, or villainy, and of Holly Martins' complicity or duplicity, honor or dishonor, are more easily resolved when the political attitudes and atmosphere of the time are examined.

The film asks who should be responsible for the destruction of evil. Harry Lime's organization of a deadly penicillin racket is an evil act, compounded by his unconcern for his victims, his units of profit. His best friend, Holly Martins, and his mistress, Anna Schmidt, acknowledge his guilt. But who is responsible for putting an end to Lime's operations? Anna believes that those who loved Harry, even though deceived by him, should not assist in his capture, and for a while she manages to convince Martins that she is right; he tells Calloway, "It's none of my business." But a closer look at Harry's victims in the children's ward convinces Martins that it is his business, and he agrees to sacrifice personal loyalty to social responsibility.[2] The film systematically attempts to persuade the audience to accept this decision along with Martins: by the end of the film, the audience has heard Harry talk about his victims, which Anna has not; the audience knows that Harry betrayed Anna to the Russians, which Anna does not; and the audience has "seen" Harry's victims, reflected in the horrified face of Martins and symbolically replaced on the screen by a fallen teddy bear. Anna would probably not have changed her mind if she knew all that Martins and the audience know, but the inappro-

Reprinted with permission from *Film Criticism,* Fall 1978.

priateness of her willed blindness is made evident by Martins' ironic comment, "You make it sound as if he had occasional bad manners."

Film critics in the late '50s and the '60s, most notably Andrew Sarris, often believe that Anna is right, that in a decadent world "moral responsibility is *personal* rather than *social*."[3] But this interpretation overlooks the specific political context of the film. In British public opinion, if the belief in personal rather than social responsibility had been more widespread in 1942, Hitler might not have been stopped. As it was, only America's entry into the war, a belated acceptance of social responsibility in British eyes, put an end to an expanding Nazi empire. Moreover the issue of responsibility was not settled by the war, and events in Eastern Europe, events that created the Vienna of *The Third Man,* soon reopened the question of international responsibility and commitment. Outvoted at the peace settlements by what appeared to be an Anglo-American alliance against them, and still uneasy about their vulnerability to invasion, the Russians made plans to insure their own national security by establishing a buffer zone in Eastern Europe. The alliance between England and the United States, meanwhile, was by no means as strong as it appeared to the Soviets. The British, badly drained by the war effort, saw themselves as caught between two monolithic powers, the U.S. and the Soviet Union, and in need of economic aid. When Secretary of State George Marshall proposed what came to be known as the Marshall Plan for European Recovery in June, 1947, England promptly applied for assistance, but the American Congress, fearful of isolationist sentiment and wary of such a large expenditure in an election year, balked. The situation became tense, and an angry British press condemned Americans as selfish, ungrateful, and ignorant for refusing to make a commitment to their allies. The British saw American aid to Europe as an investment in the security of the non-Communist West, and could not comprehend American reluctance to make such an investment. Thus Marshall aid to Britain, when it came, came mixed with gall.

As if to give substance to British fears, the Soviets staged a successful coup in Czechoslovakia, Austria's neighbor to the northeast, on February 25, 1948. The immediate post-war concern had been with Germany and the possibility of resurrected German militarism, and the spectre of Hitler continued to haunt Europe even after his death. But the Czechoslovakian coup sparked a fear of actual war, and the hatred and terror of Hitler found a new object in Stalin, who appeared in Western eyes as an equally despotic leader, following Hitler's plan for European conquest. Feeling a need to commit the United States to support its Western allies in the face of the new Communist threat, Congress approved the Marshall Plan three days after the Czechoslovakian coup. Four months later, in June, 1948, three months before the filming of *The Third Man* began in Vienna, the Soviets blockaded Berlin—a city, like Vienna, divided among the Allies.

When Korda sent Greene to Vienna during this period, he asked *not* for a thriller or a romance or a melodrama, but for a story "about the four-power occupation." Most of the film's contemporary reviewers considered *The Third Man* a fairly accurate portrait of Vienna, both visually and emotionally. By filming on location, Reed could appropriate the piles of rubble and the bombed-out houses, the narrow streets and mazelike sewers, and the overall dreariness and drabness of a city struggling to sustain life, using these elements of the Viennese landscape to symbolize the underlying tensions of its inhabitants, their apprehension and their desperation. Greene's story works well in this setting because the situations of most of the characters have a basis in fact. Vienna was crowded by refugees from Eastern Europe, who, like Anna, tried to obtain false papers, even false death certificates, to avoid Soviet repatriation. Nevertheless, the Soviets arrested large numbers of these refugees—360 in 1948, according to one source, or, "a man a day."[4] The influx of refugees also contributed to overcrowding and to the proliferation of black market activities, including the sale of penicillin stolen from military hospitals.

The film is exactly what Korda wanted because it is a story about the four-power occupation of Vienna told from a British perspective. Thus Anna is a Czech and Martins an American in the final version of the script;[5] Vienna is a microcosm of international politics; and the character relationships become symbolic of national political relationships.

If the film asks who should be responsible for the destruction of evil, in political terms it asks who should be responsible for the destruction of a specific political evil best termed totalitarianism. The real target of the film's criticism is the police state that Vienna has become, a state continually infringing on individual rights, restricting individual mobility, and reducing identity to a piece of paper. Yet Reed and Greene do not impersonalize the origins of this state. Some of the villains are easy to identify because they conform to cultural stereotypes of the time: the Russians, commonly cast as antagonists in Western Cold War literature and film, pursue Anna and shelter Lime. But the Russians alone did not create the police state of Vienna. Moreover Lime is the supreme villain in the story, and comes to represent all that the film condemns.

Lime embodies the attitudes from which the police state arises, and Lime best articulates them. "In these days, old man," he tells Martins on the Prater wheel, "nobody thinks in terms of human beings. Governments don't, so why should we? They talk of the people and the proletariat, and I talk of the mugs. It's the same thing. They have their five year plans and so have I." Lime is the ultimate utilitarian; he calls the people below "dots," worth twenty thousand pounds apiece. All of his personal relationships are dominated by self-interest: his friendship with Martins at school provided him with a scapegoat; his friendship with Anna provided him with a sexual partner. In refusing to think "in terms of human beings," Lime identifies himself politically with totalitarian dictators such as Hitler and Stalin, who saw "the people" as a mass to be manipulated for personal ends. He underlines this political connection in the most famous lines in the film: "In Italy for thirty years under the Borgias they had warfare, terror, murder, bloodshed—they produced Michelangelo, Leonardo da Vinci and the Renaissance. In Switzerland they had brotherly love, five hundred years of democracy and peace, and what did that produce . . . ? The cuckoo clock." [sic] Lime identifies the two attitudes, inhumanity and humanity, with two kinds of government, totalitarianism and democracy, and clearly chooses totalitarianism.

Unlike the nationalities of the other characters, Lime's nationality is not specified or emphasized; he is presumably either English, American, or Canadian, since he is English-speaking and went to school with Martins, but Welles' peculiarly unidentifiable accent and manner blur Lime's nationality. His kind of evil, his inhumanity, therefore, is not confined to a single nationality; it can gain ascendancy in various cultures at various times—Renaissance Italy, Nazi Germany, and Stalinist Russia. At present, Lime's inhumanity associates him with the Soviets, who are portrayed as equally impersonal and utilitarian. Colonel Brodsky accepts favors from Calloway that he has no intention of returning; Lime accepts sexual favors from Anna before selling her to the Russians. Like the Russian member of the International Patrol who coldly watches Anna dress when she is arrested, Lime victimizes others by his insensitivity to their feelings. However ironic he intends his use of Communist terminology, the feelings, or lack of feelings, it expresses makes his confinement in the Soviet Zone appropriate, and his necessity to remain "useful" to the Russians is an ironic comment on the nature of totalitarianism. At the time of the film's release in Vienna, the reviewer of the Soviet-backed newspaper there bitterly and energetically condemned it.

The dangers of cooperating with totalitarianism in general and with the Russians in particular are illustrated by the chief British official, Major Calloway. Calloway, perhaps the character drawn most completely from Greene's personal views, represents the good and bad in English post-war government. Calloway is good because he is on the right side in fighting Lime; his cause is a humanitarian one. Yet Calloway is not as perceptive or as clever as he pretends: the film opens with his attending the burial of the wrong man. Moreover in becoming a bureaucrat, Calloway has himself acquired a measure of Lime's inhumanity; he has become, as his name suggests, callous, and can walk through the children's ward without flinching. He also proves to be as callow as Martins in one sense, because he displays proverbial British chauvinism when he takes offense at Martins' substitution of the Irish name, Callahan, for his own; like a mischievous child, Martins baits him, and he responds in kind with childish anger and wounded dignity. The film suggests that this combination of qualities, nourished by British imperialism and strengthened by the crisis of world war, can be deadly. Calloway ultimately resorts to the most common of totalitarian tactics, the night arrest, including the search and seizure of Anna's most private possessions. The scene, like its counterpart later in the film, would have been familiar to 1949 audiences, since both Soviet and Nazi regimes had recognized the psychological advantage of surprise and darkness in arresting their victims. In the end, Calloway cooperates with the Soviets and gives them Anna's false identification papers—an act of betrayal similar to Lime's—only to discover that the Russians intend to arrest Anna, and will not help capture Lime. Like the British government of the 1930s, Calloway learns that he can neither ignore nor appease the threat of totalitarianism. Moreover, in attempting to cooperate, he must inevitably take on totalitarian characteristics.

Calloway's job would be easier if he had the help of the American, Holly Martins. With typical British optimism, he tells Martins "it won't make any difference in the long run" whether he helps or not, but his last attempt to persuade Martins by stopping at the children's hospital contradicts this statement. Martins' initial refusal to become involved is at least partly responsible for Calloway's cooperation with the Soviets, since Calloway cannot fight Lime alone. When the American finally makes his commitment, Calloway can defy the Russians by giving Anna new papers, intimating the necessity for a continued Anglo-American alliance against the Communists.

Martins' commitment to help Calloway marks the final stage of a maturing process that begins when he steps off the train in Vienna. He arrives in Vienna with all of the qualities that the British press was inclined to associate with Americans at the time, a caricature of American innocence confronting European experience (American co-producer David O. Selznick vociferously objected "for patriotic reasons"[6]). Martins is ignorant of European affairs, and views life as a third-rate Western. He has long existed on a schoolboy code of values largely assumed from Lime, a code that placed loyalty first, encouraged cheating for the sake of convenience, and emphasized "how to avoid this and that." But Lime's penicillin racket is no schoolboy prank, and Martins' growing crisis of conscience becomes critical when Lime himself violates the code by disloyalty to Anna. Martins has also come to feel a strong sense of loyalty to Anna; he feels himself losing his moral center when he begins to turn against Lime, and allows Anna to replace Lime as his mentor.

At first, Anna can easily dissuade Martins from helping Calloway because Martins' initial offer is made for personal reasons. Martins first goes to Calloway out of anger at Lime's betrayal of Anna and out of a desire for revenge. Since Anna remains Martins' primary concern, however, her anger overrules his own, and he withdraws his offer. When Martins finally acts, he does so out of a sense of social responsibility. He acts for all the maimed children in the cribs at the hospital, and all the nameless victims of Lime's penicillin whom the children represent. When he bases his decision on a sense of social responsibility, he is immune to Anna's arguments, and he is immune to desires for revenge as well. When Lime kills Paine in the sewers, Martins goes after Lime in a moment of anger; but when Martins kills Lime, he does so out of compassion for Lime's suffering. Thus his final gesture is in keeping with his awakened humanity.

In 1948, Greene wrote: "Now the State is invariably ready to confuse, like a schoolmaster, justice with retribution, and isn't it possibly the storyteller's task to act as the devil's advocate, to elicit sympathy and a measure of understanding for those who lie outside the boundaries of State sympathy?"[7] *The Third Man* advocates humanity and compassion in the face of increasing pressure to categorize, generalize, and dehumanize, a pressure that leads, when unresisted, to totalitarianism. It is important that Martins, not Calloway, kill Lime, since Calloway is an instrument of the State—a state toward which Greene, at least, feels a certain amount of ambivalence.

Perhaps the most puzzling character in the film, aside from Lime, is Anna, whose earnestness and seeming honesty often persuade viewers, along with Martins, that she is right. Yet Anna is limited both in what she knows and in what she understands. Not only is she excluded from the knowledge of certain facts about Lime that both Martins and the audience know, for example, but her confusion of Holly's and Harry's names indicates her inability to distinguish between them. She claims that Harry "never grew up" and the same might be said of Holly. Yet Harry saw the world "growing up around him," and defiantly refused to alter his childish egocentrism. Holly never noticed the world changing, and retained his childhood values out of ignorance.

Although Anna is never actually condemned for her love of Lime, the dangers of her self-destructiveness are evident. She is a born victim, and immediately falls prey to strong personalities, especially Lime, a born victimizer. She is a direct contrast to Lime, colorless, drab, and passive where he is colorful, gay, and active. She is clearly much poorer than he, and trading her beautiful theatre dress and wig for a trenchcoat and a plain hat, accompanies Martins to Lime's spacious and expensively furnished apartment, where she looks sadly out of place. Significantly, she is a woman being victimized by men and a Czech being victimized first by the Soviets, and then by the British. Her hopelessness and weakness draw her to strong personalities, just as Eastern Europe was dominated by a succession of strong personalities during the course of the century.

If the film has a real hero, perhaps that hero is none of the four central figures but Paine, whose unexpected death marks the emotional climax of the chase in the sewers. Paine, however comic he may be at times, never allows the nature of his job to destroy his compassion, and thereby remains the most likable character in the film. He is gentle and reassuring toward Anna, whereas Calloway is cold and insensitive; he is kind and polite toward Martins, whereas Calloway is deliberately harsh and uncaring. Moreover he knows and enjoys the fantasy world of Martins' Westerns, but recognizes the difference between fantasy and reality; appropriately, his specialty is distinguishing forged papers, false identities, from real ones. He dies trying to protect Martins from Lime, and his final act of self-sacrifice is a judgment on Lime's inhumanity and Martins' ignorance, as is his name. He, more than any other character, embodies what the film advocates: the choice of humanity in the face of post-war physical and moral decay. He is a minor character become major in the moment of his death, thus demonstrating the quiet heroism of the ordinary, undistinguished human life.

Critics of the film, with the exception of Sarris, have been reluctant to discuss the specific political implications of *The Third Man*. Perhaps Reed's frequent disclaimers of political intent in his films are to blame, although he was usually careful to qualify his statements on the subject: "It's another matter, of course, if the ideas are in the subject. You must always take the author's side and believe it whilst you're making the picture."[8] Earlier he had explained: "As a director I believe that my own ideas are not particularly important. What counts is the story value and characterization."[9] Yet the stories that Reed valued most, from *The Stars Look Down* (1939) to *Oliver!* (1968), were frequently stories that had political overtones if not specific political contexts. The authors he valued most were writers of political commitment, such as A. J. Cronin, Charles Dickens, and Graham Greene.

Greene, however, disavowed any political intentions in *The Third Man*, which he classified as one of his "entertainments," saying: "We had no desire to move people's political emotions; we wanted to entertain them, to frighten them a little, to make them laugh" (*The Third Man*, p. 6). But in 1948, he also wrote, concerning the author and his commitment to "public interest": ". . . with us, however consciously unconcerned we are, it obtrudes through the cracks of our stories, terribly persistent like grass through cement" (*Why Do I Write?*, p. 27). Shortly after completing *The Third Man,* Greene went to Indochina and began writing what he called his "political novels."

One reader who saw political substance in Greene's earlier work was the actor Reed wanted most for the film—Orson Welles. Welles' political commitment was emphatic during his years with the Mercury Theatre, and notorious following the release of *Citizen Kane* (a film closely related to *The Third Man* in terms of style, casting, and theme). Welles contributed more to *The Third Man* than his talented presence; he added the most famous lines in the script, the "cuckoo clock" speech—lines that translate Martins' choice between loyalty and social commitment into a specific political choice between totalitarianism and democracy.

Aside from their political liberalism, however, the three men most responsible for *The Third Man*—Reed, Greene, and Welles—shared a view of man and of the good and evil in men. For all three, the ultimate crime was inhumanity, the lack of concern for other human beings. As artists, they worked to evoke sympathy for all kinds of human beings, separating personality from morality. Greene best articulated this common goal when he wrote in 1948: "If we can awaken sympathetic comprehension in our readers, not only for our most evil characters (that is easy: there is a cord there fastened to all hearts that we can twitch at will), but of our smug, complacent, successful characters, we have surely succeeded in making the work of the State a degree more difficult . . . " (*Why Do I Write?,* p. 48). The State, according to Greene, is inclined to deal unsympathetically with people, as if they were not human at all. The artist counters that tendency whenever he or she awakens sympathy for an evil or disagreeable character, even when that character is a tyrant, like Welles' Julius Caesar in the Mercury production or Charles Foster Kane, or Reed's mine owners in *The Stars Look Down*. Greene himself suggested that "at times we are able to feel sympathy for Hitler" (*Why Do I Write?,* p. 47) because he was a fellow human. Although all three have created evil characters in their works, they have seldom created unsympathetic characters.

And just as *The Third Man* advocates humanity and sympathy in place of impersonality, it also places justice before retribution. Lime is an engaging man, who charms the audience as he has charmed Anna and Martins. He is also an evil man, and because of his evil, he must be destroyed. The audience is subtly prepared for this paradox by Reed's Mephistophelean voice at the beginning of the film ("I never knew the old Vienna . . ."), the voice of an unidentified but strangely omniscient narrator, glibly introducing the audience to the corruption and horror of the latter-day Vienna;[10] it serves as a reminder that even the devil himself can be charming. When Martins comprehends this truth, he abandons the world of his childhood, where the bad guys always wear black hats, and accepts the responsibilities of adulthood, and with them, the knowledge of good and evil.

Recent critics, such as Sarris, who condemn Martins and champion Lime are strong evidence in support of Greene's views on the nature of evil as well as a tribute to Welles' portrayal of Lime. They have been taken in, as Anna and Martins were, by Lime's charm. Moreover, they do not fully understand the political context of the film, nor how the political context supports and informs the film's moral themes. The film depicts the attractiveness of evil, and of a specific kind of political evil, even for its victims. In the West, the casting of totalitarian dictators such as Hitler and Stalin in the role of Antichrist was hardly new, yet Hitler had beguiled a nation with his charisma, and Stalin was genuinely loved by millions of Russians. Audiences in 1949 already knew what Martins learns during the course of the film: that evil can be very disarming. That critics could have forgotten, less than ten years later, the evil that charming men had done in Europe, proves that Reed, Greene, and Welles were right—charm is Harry Lime's most dangerous weapon.

[1] Graham Greene, *The Third Man and the Fallen Idol* (London: William Heineman, 1950), p. 3.

[2] In his book, *Graham Greene: The Films of His Fiction* (New York: Teachers College Press, 1974), Gene D. Phillips argues: "Greene asks his audience to take evil seriously throughout the film and not just in the hospital scene. *The Third Man* is not a spy spoof in which the moral implications of the characters' behavior can be disregarded. Greene rather develops his story in terms of a moral dilemma" (p. 71).

[3] Andrew Sarris, "The Stylist Goes to Hollywood," *Films and Filming,* 3 (October, 1957), p 2.

[4] George Maranz, "Terror in Vienna: A Man Cries for Help," *Socialist Leader,* 30 April 1949, p. 9.

[5] Anna was originally Estonian and Martins was Canadian; the Rumanian Popescu was an American named Tyler. The nationalities shifted interestingly when Reed signed Welles to play Lime. Reed apparently felt that one American villain in the film was enough, especially considering Selznick's objections that the script as a whole was anti-American, and changed Tyler to an East European, Popescu. There is no record concerning why the other changes were made, but I have tried to suggest reasons in accord with what we know of British political sentiment at the time.

[6] *Memo from David O. Selznick,* ed. Rudy Behlmer (New York: Viking, 1972), p. 386. Selznick was the American producer and distributor for the film, and his memoes concerning the script and his legal right to demand revisions provide background for the fight that eventually sent Korda and Selznick to court prior to the film's opening in New York.

[7] Elizabeth Bowen, Graham Greene, and V. S. Pritchett, *Why Do I Write?* (London: Percival Marshall, 1948), p. 47.

[8] Charles Thomas Samuels, *Encountering Directors* (New York: G. P. Putnam's Sons, 1972), p. 166.

[9] Ezra Goodman, "Carol Reed," *Theatre Arts,* 31 (May 1947), 59.

[10] This narration was added in the final stages of the editing to provide background for the story, since Reed felt that the situation in Vienna was too unfamiliar to the filmgoing public. As Phillips notes (p. 62), the voice of Joseph Cotten was substituted for that of Carol Reed in the American version. The final lines of the prologue were altered accordingly: "Anyway, I was dead broke when I got to Vienna. A close pal of mine had gotten me a job doing some publicity work for some kind of charity he was running. Anyway, down I came to old Vienna, happy as a lark and without a dime." Selznick apparently felt that the unexplained, unidentified narrator was too confusing. Although Reed might have used Cotten, who was under contract to Selznick, had Cotten still been available, he and Greene turned necessity to their advantage in composing a speech that would set the proper tone for the film. As a result, the speech seems out of character for Holly Martins; it is too glib, too ironic even for an older Martins.

P·A·R·T

TWO

FILMS
AND
EXAMINING
FILMS

PART One illustrates a few ways to examine a film and shows what might be discovered and said about it. Part Two presents many more ways to examine the experience of watching and hearing a film and to formulate informed conclusions about it in more detail. Chapter 4 attempts to make viewers more aware of the important aspects of characterization and plot in fictional films. The next, more technical chapter describes the sights and sounds of cinema. Chapter 6 describes the different major kinds of viewer responses to a film showing.

Following Chapter 6 are two lists. The first is some study questions for thought/discussion/writing that may be useful in examining a film; the second describes some exercises for examining specific, often unnoticed aspects of any film.

· 4 ·

The Story:
Some Basics

CHARACTERIZATION
People/Characters/Performers
How Filmmakers Create Characters
Characters and Conflict
PLOT
Experience and Plot
Selection of Scenes
Arrangement of Scenes

So far as we have recorded evidence, storytelling—or narration—is the oldest kind of literature. . . . Storytelling is the way a child learns the delight of the language, of the world of words, and of the bridge words build between people. Storytelling is also the way the gods have spoken, with the parables of the New Testament as a supreme example. Narration is, indeed, an overwhelmingly large part of the daily dialogues we have with each other, and we exchange narrative anecdotes as a kind of game.

William Sloane, *The Craft of Writing*

[Life is] all inclusion and confusion, and art . . . all discrimination and selection.

Henry James, *The Art of the Novel*

A few years after films were used to create the illusion of movement in the 1890s, they were used to present short, entertaining stories. So successful were they that by the teens of this century story films were increased to feature length (approximately 45 or more minutes); they drew larger and larger audiences, and they came to serve as an evening's or afternoon's pastime. To this day and into the foreseeable future, fictional films attract and will continue to attract large audiences throughout the world.[1] What exactly is a fictional film?

In fictional films characters, not people, are seen in a series of actions. The actions are presented selectively: unimportant, and often uninteresting, actions (such as every moment of a trip) are usually omitted. The actions are usually arranged chronologically and may be perceived as "happening"[2] or as remembered, dreamed, hallucinated, or fantasized, or as a blend of two or more of these five modes (as in *Annie Hall, An Occurrence at Owl Creek Bridge,* and *Slaughterhouse-Five*).

Most people see fictional films because they are interested in the character or characters (for example, the Magnificent Seven), or performer (Liza Minelli), or topic (family problems in *Kramer vs. Kramer*). Sometimes they attend because they are interested in what the film has to show about a topic, for example, love and sex. It's human interest in that most interesting of topics, human behavior. In this chapter, I'll concentrate on the basic components of stories: characterization and plot. For convenience of presentation, I have divided this chapter into those two aspects, though in fictional stories, the two aspects are inseparable: there's no story without character *and* plot.

Characterization

People/Characters/Performers

A "character" is an imaginary creation, a *fictional* person, in a fictional story (fictional film, play, short story, novel, narrative poem). In the images of film actors and actresses, characters often seem so much like people that many viewers and writers use the terms "character" and "person" interchangeably. In fact, characters give the *illusion* of life, and it is useful to employ the terms "character" and "person" to refer to two different entities (Figure 4.1).

Another important distinction is between "character" and "performer." A character, once again, is a fictional person in a fictional story. A performer is a person (actor or actress) who enacts the character. When they succeed, performers make audiences believe in the characters and (usually) forget about the performers themselves. In some cases, though, it is impossible, and in fact undesirable, to forget the performer completely. Once a performer becomes famous, for

---

[1] In the late 1970s, for instance, about 3,500 feature films were produced worldwide each year. *Journal of the University Film Association* 32, no. 3 (Summer 1980): 41.

[2] "Happening" is in quotation marks because what the viewer sees is an illusion, made up of shadows and lights, of a reenactment of a fictional or real-life event.

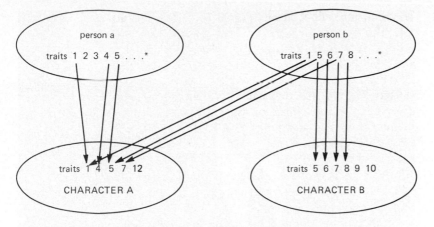

4.1 The Creation of Two Characters

Character A is based on traits from persons a and b plus an imaginary quality (#12).

Character B is based fairly closely on person b with the added imaginary qualities #9 and #10.

*Persons are far more complex than characters, thus the elipses (. . .) after the numbered traits of each person.

many in the audience the character is a character plus the performer. Usually, the performer's qualities are used to support the present role. Thus, John Wayne, who was well known for his conservative political beliefs, was cast in numerous conservative and patriotic roles. Another example of a performer's past influencing viewer responses to a character can be seen in *The Verdict*. In the early stages of the story, the central character, attorney Frank Galvin, is quite unappealing. He is self-pitying, exploitative, irresponsible. *But* the character is enacted by Paul Newman (Figure 4.2). Newman's well-known and positive image on screen and off tends to offset the extremely negative impression the character may be making, and we fairly quickly start rooting for him.

Occasionally, filmmakers cast against type and exploit a performer's well-known image to catch viewers off guard. An excellent recent example is Dustin Hoffman in *Tootsie*. But for me, the best example remains the use of a well-known performer in an Italian ("spaghetti") western. George Morris speaks for me, too, when he writes,

> In Sergio Leone's *Once Upon a Time in the West,* a homesteader and his two children are spreading a picnic in their front yard. This frontier idyll is shattered by the materialization of five menacing figures, who kill the family in cold blood. The sense of violation is exacerbated by the familiar, reassuring smile on the face of the leader of these merciless specters. It's the smile of young Abe Lincoln, Tom Joad, Wyatt Earp, and Mister Roberts, a smile which for four decades in American movies

4.2 *The Verdict,* with Paul Newman as attorney Frank Galvin. © 1982 Twentieth Century Fox. Memory Shop West.

has reflected the honesty, moral integrity, and egalitarian values synonymous with its owner—Henry Fonda.

By casting him as an almost abstract personification of evil in 1969, Leone dramatically reversed the prevailing image of Fonda, at once complicating and commenting on our responses to that image.[3]

Acting effectiveness, then, depends in part upon the audience's knowledge of the performer's life and previous roles. Acting effectiveness also depends on how well the performer can make the audience stay caught up in the character. Do we believe that the character in those circumstances would act and react as he or she does? If we do,

---

[3] Elisabeth Weis, ed., *The National Society of Film Critics on The Movie Star* (New York: Penguin Books, 1981), p. 220.

we usually judge a performance as successful. Judging a performance, however, is difficult on the evidence of one viewing of a film. A second viewing, or a comparison of the script and the performance, or various other exercises described at the conclusion of this section of the book all help viewers see the success or failure of what is usually meant to be taken for granted.

How Filmmakers Create Characters

We viewers learn about a character by its *actions:* saving a sinking ship, marrying and divorcing, writing a novel. In movies/moving pictures/motion pictures (the very words suggest how important movements are in them), actions are probably the primary means of revealing characterization. Perhaps this is so, since films are so superbly suited to single out actions, focus viewer attention on them, and show them vividly. We also learn about characters and are cued on how to react to them by how other characters in the film respond to them. Most scenes show actions *and* other characters' reactions, and numerous reaction shots intensify viewer responses. In amusing scenes reaction shots tend to intensify audience amusement. For example, in *Night Shift* actor Michael Keaton seems even funnier because of the many reaction shots of a restrained Henry Winkler. In frightening movies, such as *Halloween,* menacing actions seem more menacing when reflected in the faces of the films' characters. As in life, others' reactions often help us decide how to respond to someone or something.

We also learn about characters by their *appearances,* including looks, clothing, makeup, hair style, and possessions. Much of the character in Figure 4.3, for example, is revealed in the image of Charlie Chaplin. Here, we can see that the character dresses well: the tie, hat, cane, jacket, and vest. His mustache is trimmed carefully. He wears a flower in his lapel. Close inspection reveals, however, that the jacket is too tight, the sleeves are too short, the trousers too loose. He is not really a wealthy gentleman, though he tries to look like one. His hands, the upward turn of his eyes, and the look on his face suggest a sensitive nature. Can we imagine this character doing brutal things?

Of course, a character's *speech*—both what is said and how—is usually important in revealing what the character is like, though far less so than in plays and programs made for television. Long stretches of films have no significant dialogue, as was illustrated by the descriptions and analyses of the conclusion of *The Godfather, Part II* (Chapter 1) and of the first graveyard scene from *The Third Man* (Chapter 2).

Though used less frequently in fictional films than in most literary

4.3 Charlie Chaplin in *City Lights*. Movie Star News.

fiction, a character's *thoughts* (ideas, fantasies, dreams, hallucinations) may be revealed to viewers—by voice-over narration or by images of what presumably is going through the character's mind. As is illustrated in *Annie Hall,* subtitles may be used to reveal what characters are thinking as they mouth quite different words.

In each film, the filmmakers decide how much of each of these four sources to draw upon: action, appearance, speech, and thoughts. (Occasionally, music is also a means of revealing what a character is like.) Some films, for example, have little dialogue and never allow us to know exactly what characters are thinking, though we infer more or less what a character is thinking or feeling from actions, tone of voice, and facial expressions. Some fictional films, like *My Dinner with André* and the 1941 version of *The Maltese Falcon,* have much dialogue and few thoughts. A relatively few other films, like *Providence* and *An Occurrence at Owl Creek Bridge,* are mostly about what a character thinks.

Characters and Conflict

Stories, especially the rather long stories of feature films, would not hold audience interest if they presented only happy characters in unchanging conditions. People are fascinated with conflict, and with stories of conflict (that's probably the major reason soap operas are so popular). We learn most about a character (and people, for that matter) when we see them in conflict. We viewers like to see how others handle conflict and how it affects them and others around them. A plot summary or outline of a fictional story reveals just how much of it is made up of alternating conflicts and resolutions. Take the example of *Jaws*. Its central conflict is between the people of Amity and a giant killer shark (people versus nature). But the film shows many other conflicts between people: the townspeople and Sheriff Brody; Brody and the mayor; Mrs. Kintner, whose young son was killed in a shark attack, and Brody; Quint and Brody; Quint and Hooper. Brody is even in conflict with himself: early in the film he allows his better judgment to be overruled, and he's feeling guilty about the consequences. At the film's end, however, presumably all the conflicts are resolved. Like Captain Ahab in *Moby Dick,* Quint is destroyed by his underwater antagonist. The shark is blown up. And Hooper and Brody paddle back to the beach. The last shot of the film shows the final comforting resolution: the beach is seen in safe, bright daylight (in contrast to the opening scenes of darkness and danger).

More psychologically oriented films show conflict within a character in greater detail. In these films different aspects of the same character struggle to gain dominance over the character's actions. Again, take as an example *The Verdict*. The ineffectual, self-pitying side of Frank Galvin wars with the assertive, responsible side of his personality. Galvin's greatest enemy is not the defense attorney, Ed Concannon (played by James Mason)—though he is formidable—but himself, his attitudes about himself. Much to the audience's satisfaction, by the end of the story the nobler aspects of Galvin's personality prevail, and he wins the case spectacularly (and, in the "cold light of day" outside movie theaters, somewhat improbably): Concannon and the attractive but dangerous woman played by Charlotte Rampling are vanquished.

Plot

Experience and Plot

Writer and creative writing teacher Stephen Minot explains plot by this comparison:

> . . . [T]ake a moment to review what you did yesterday from the time you got up to the end of the day.
> Notice how naturally that chronology turned into a list of identifia-

ble events or episodes: getting dressed, eating breakfast, and, for students, attending classes, a coffee break with friends in the cafeteria, a conversation in the hall, and lunch. For nonstudents, the events would be different, but the rhythm from one unit of activity to the next is essentially the same. The point is that while the *clock* moves perfectly regularly, our *life* as we look back is recalled as a sequence of episodes.

These episodes have certain characteristics. . . . First, we often identify them by where they occurred—the setting. Second, we recall who was there—the characters. Third, such episodes remain clear long after we have forgotten what came just before and just afterward. Those unstructured periods of time which merely link one episode with the next (walking, waiting, driving, watching television, sleeping) tend to blend together and blur quickly.

Finally, we don't always remember these events in the order in which they occurred. Students complaining about bad teachers are not necessarily going to start with kindergarten . . . and a man recalling his love for a woman is not necessarily going to begin with the day he met her.

Fiction tends to imitate these patterns. What we call *episodes* in life become *scenes* in fiction. These are the basic units. And their arrangement is what we call *plot*.[4]

In selecting from episodes and observations of human behavior, inventing certain details, altering others, and arranging the actions in a significant and unified order, the writer makes a plot (see Figure 4.4).

experiences . . . a b c d e f g h i j k l . . .   Continuous and chronological; full of both significant and seemingly trivial details

plot [scene (s)] L_1 AA C_2 D_2 H_2 I K J   Not necessarily chronological; usually discontinuous; many insignificant details omitted so that significant details and patterns are highlighted

4.4 The Making of a Sample Plot
In transforming experience into scenes in a plot, the following may happen:

- New scenes without corresponding experiences in life may be made up (as in the case of AA).
- Certain experiences may not be dramatized (a, b, e, f, & g).
- Experiences may be altered as they are transformed into scenes (c, d, & h → C_2, D_2, & H_2).
- Events may be rearranged (j & k → K & J).
- Experiences may be altered and transposed (l → L_1).

[4] Stephen Minot, *Three Genres: The Writing of Poetry, Fiction, and Drama,* 3d ed. (Englewood Cliffs, N.J.: Prentice-Hall, 1982), pp. 129–30.

Selection of Scenes

In creating and revising a plot, the writer and other filmmakers can present relatively few actions taken from a long period of time, or present many actions taken from a short period of time. (Of course, innumerable options between these two extremes are also available.) As an example of the former, highly selective incidents taken from a long period of time, *2001: A Space Odyssey* probably holds the record. In forty-four or so scenes are presented events from 4 million B.C. to beyond our sense of time. At the opposite extreme are films like *High Noon* and the French film *Cleo from 5 to 7,* which present numerous scenes representing an almost continuous two-hour segment. (In some experimental films, such as *Wavelength,* directed by Michael Snow, and some films directed by Andy Warhol, a continuous action may be presented in a single shot.)

In selecting from possible actions to present, filmmakers also decide whether to present the story of one group of characters or the stories of two or more groups. Most commercial films choose the first course—probably most often because that organization is least likely to confuse audiences—and we see one set of characters during a given period of time. *The Godfather, Part II,* however, is a good example of a film that presents two stories, in this case alternating between them. The film *2001* contains the consecutive stories of four groups: the man-apes, scientists, a computer and two astronauts, and an astronaut and unseen alien(s). *Intolerance* (1916) cross-cuts between four stories set at four different places and times. As might be expected, many viewers see no unity to that film and are confused about its purpose.

Arrangement of Scenes

In addition to deciding *what* to show, filmmakers decide in what order the separate units of action (scenes) will be presented. Since most commercial filmmakers do not want to be too demanding of audience attentiveness, in commercial cinema the story is usually told chronologically, from earliest event to latest event. Fairly often, however, flashbacks to earlier action are used. In a few films, such as *They Shoot Horses, Don't They?,* flashforwards have been tried, though never very successfully in commercial cinema. Certain actions may be repeated, shown more than once, as in the Japanese film *Rashomon* or the British film *Dead of Night.* And certain actions may be paralleled with other actions. In *Cabaret,* for example, the actions of the main story—the relationship of five major characters in 1931 in Berlin—are often intercut with relevant musical numbers at a cabaret or with the emcee's expressions.

As I said at the beginning of this chapter, character and plot are inseparable. A fictional story needs at least one character doing something during a (usually) selective yet significant order of events. Otherwise there is no narrative. Most films, however, emphasize either character *or* plot. Those emphasizing characterization show one character, occasionally more than one, in detail. By the end of *Annie Hall,* for example, we know a great deal about Alvy Singer, what he does, feels, thinks, fantasizes. We even understand why he and Annie have parted, though he does not entirely.

Many other films stress plot and reveal no character in depth: the emphasis is on action. *Raiders of the Lost Ark, Star Wars,* James Bond movies, and many other adventure stories, including *The General* (see Chapter 16)—all are plot-oriented.

In stories with enough vivid detail, we viewers may trick ourselves into believing that we are experiencing a "slice of life." In fact, the characters and plots of stories are meaningful arrangements and simplifications of life's complexities and uncertainties.

> Unlike ordinary experience, which mixes the meaningful with the amorphous and random, a story's ingredients are selected for appropriateness to the story's intended effects, meanings, and structures. A story can therefore be almost free from redundancy, meaninglessness, and, especially, inexpressiveness. Stories have what electronics technicians call a high signal-to-noise ratio. Thus a story promises comprehensibility in a way that ordinary experience does not.[5]

Though simplified, not all stories are simple. Far from it. In characterization and plot some stories have a complexity, ambiguity, and subtlety approximating life. Each time those stories are experienced, they reward with new significant details, new insights, new pleasures.

Now that we have considered the basic aspects of stories, we will turn our attention to the means fictional, documentary, and experimental films use to convey stories/information/feelings and moods: the sights and sounds of cinema.

[5] Charles Eidsvik, *Cineliteracy: Film among the Arts* (New York: Random House, 1978), p. 61.

· 5 ·

Sights and Sounds

SIGHTS
Images
Edited Images
SOUNDS

If you sit and admire the camerawork of a picture the first time, there's something wrong. And the music of a film oughtn't to be admired either. Cinema is only one thing: an illusion of *many* arts working together. The minute *one* aspect begins to dominate, and subordinate everything else to it, the film is doomed.   Composer Bernard Herrmann, *Sound and the Cinema,*
ed. Evan William Cameron

As Mr. Herrmann said, the many aspects of a film are meant to contribute to the total effect without drawing attention to themselves. In this chapter I hope to help viewers become more aware of the kinds of filmic images and sounds, so that they may understand their experiences of films more completely and have a basic vocabulary to describe them. Since particular aspects of cinema's sights and sounds are usually unobtrusive, many will be noticeable only after two or more viewings or by using some exercises included later in this section.

Filmmakers—including writers, directors, art directors, cinematographers, and editors—decide what to show, how long to show it, what to present before and after. They also choose how lifelike or artificial the images and sounds will seem, through camera angles and distances, lighting, locations, editing, and so forth. The options available to filmmakers are numerous; the consequences of their decisions significant. In this chapter I'll discuss only a few basics of a topic so complex it has been the subject of entire books.

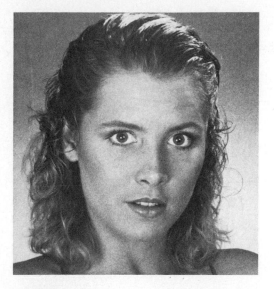

5.1 High-grain image. Photographer: Jon Terry. Model: Amie Morgan.

5.2 Low-grain image. Photographer: Jon Terry. Model: Amie Morgan.

Sights

Images

Photography has been described as "photogenic drawing, or the process by which natural objects may be made to delineate themselves without the aid of the artist's pencil."[1]

Depending on the film stock used and the laboratory work, the film's finished images may be grainy (high grain), as in Figure 5.1, or smooth (low or fine grain), as in Figure 5.2. The difference is significant, since high-grain images tend to be associated (correctly or not) with newsreels, old footage, and amateur filmmaking. Low-grain images tend to be thought of in contrary ways: controlled, often studio conditions; recent work; and professional quality. (In considering the grain of film images, remember that film copies of copies of copies may be much grainier than the original.)

Filmmakers spend an enormous amount of time and money lighting their subjects in particular ways. They do so because lighting often conveys meaning and mood in subtle yet significant ways. The importance of lighting is evident in our daily lives: on sunny days, we have sunny moods (usually, of course); on cloudy days, people tend to feel more subdued. The right light, seduction; the wrong light . . . The expressiveness of lighting is also suggested by the word "photography," which literally means "writing with light." The lighting on the subject may be hard/harsh or soft/diffused, as is illustrated in Figures 5.3 and

[1] William Henry Fox Talbot, a partial description of the world's first separate publication on photography, a thirteen-page brochure (London: R. and J. E. Taylor, 1839). From the Library Catalog of the International Museum of Photography at George Eastman House.

5.4. Some ways to light a subject by using sources from different directions are illustrated in Figures 5.5–5.10. In all these cases, the model is the same and her makeup is the same. The camera distance, lens, and angle are unchanged. But what different images! What different moods and meanings! (Note, by the way, that usually the directions and intensities of the light sources can be detected by looking at the pupils of the subject. This "catch light" is visible for all light sources that hit a subject's eyes. For another example, see Figure 2.5.)

Lighting is closely related to color, and nature's light is made up of the colors of the rainbow (Figure 5.11). Many colors are thought of as "warm" or "cool." In most Western societies, warm colors (reds, oranges, and yellows) tend to be thought of as hot, dangerous, lively, and assertive and tend to stand forward in paintings and photographs. Thus *red* traffic lights, and red clothing on sexy people. Warm-colored lights are also used to present skin in a flattering manner. Colors on the other side of the spectrum (greens, blues, and violets) are generally thought of as "cool" colors. In Europe and the United States, these colors tend to be associated with safety, reason, control, and relaxation. Examples: green traffic lights and blue or green hospital interiors (to calm and reassure). Cool-colored lights, however, give skin an unflattering tone.

In Western cultures, white—which is not, strictly speaking, a color at all but the presence of all colors—is often associated with innocence and purity, though it may sometimes imply lack of emotion, as in men's white dress shirts. Black—not strictly speaking a color but the absence of all color—is associated with experience and evil, as in the hackneyed use of black hats on cowboy gunslingers.

5.3 Hard/harsh lighting. The subject is illuminated by one direct, bright (spot) light. Photographer: Jon Terry. Model: Amie Morgan.

5.4 Soft/diffused lighting was achieved in this instance by reflecting light from a spotlight off a reflector to the subject. Photographer: Jon Terry. Model: Amie Morgan.

5.5 Back lighting. In this case the model was illuminated by a single light from behind her that reflected off the back wall. Often such lighting intensifies the sense of the subject's being threatening; thus, when we encounter someone lighted only in silhouette, we often feel uncomfortable. Photographer: Jon Terry. Model: Amie Morgan.

5.6 Top lighting. The model was illuminated by a single spotlight from above. The results: dry-looking hair, aged skin, dark, recessed eyes. Photographer: Jon Terry. Model: Amie Morgan.

5.7 Bottom lighting. As with the top lighting of Figure 5.6, the look is of dryness and age, with a touch of menace. Photographer: Jon Terry. Model: Amie Morgan.

5.8 Side lighting is often used to suggest someone with a divided personality or someone feeling contradictory emotions. Photographer: Jon Terry. Model: Amie Morgan.

5.10 Main and fill lights. Photographer: Jon Terry. Model: Amie Morgan.

5.9 Main frontal lighting. Photographer: Jon Terry. Model: Amie Morgan.

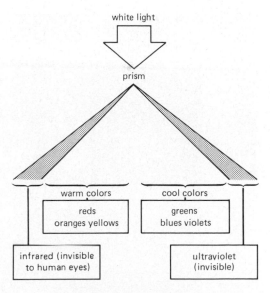

5.11 Light and colors

Filmmakers are aware of these color associations, though often, as in many aspects of filmmaking, not consciously aware. They just use certain colors in a set, costume, or lighting to add to the mood. As one example, the inside of the spaceship in *2001: A Space Odyssey* is antiseptic white. The "eyes" and "brain" of the on-board computer (HAL) are a deep red. HAL does indeed prove true to his colors: he commits violent, deadly acts.

An important factor in viewer responses to an image is how far from the subject the camera is. Camera distance determines what details will be noticeable, what details will be excluded from the frame, and how large the subject will appear. As my colleague Hope Werness reminded me, in painting (and photography) the size of the image relative to the frame can be understood as a clue to the importance of the subject. In Holbein's famous portrait of Henry VIII, for example, Henry's bulky body fills up the entire format, and one senses Henry's energy, strength of character, and power—not so much because of his facial expression but because of the close view and his dominance of space.

Figures 5.12–5.17 illustrate six camera distances and the terms usually used to indicate them. Note that in the first photograph, Figure 5.12, the surroundings seem to be the main subject. In the next two photographs, the surroundings and human subject are more in balance. In the last three photographs, Figures 5.15–5.17, the individual dominates the viewer's attention. These photographs also illustrate that the same lens used at different distances creates distortions at certain ranges. (In the case of Figures 5.12–5.17, the lens used, a normal lens, distorts slightly in close-up shots [Figures 5.16 and 5.17]. The subject is more faithfully rendered in Figure 5.15.)

When a film begins and when the story

5.12 Extreme long shot

5.13 Long shot

5.14 Medium shot

shifts to a new location, the camera often films from extreme long or long shot to present a view of the surroundings. Once viewers are oriented, the camera normally moves in closer to the subject, moving in especially close for some shots.

The camera may be positioned quite close to a performer's face, or a telephoto lens may be used to create a comparable effect without intruding into the performer's face. In close-ups, the many nuances of human feeling may be forcefully suggested. (See again Figure 5.16.) Ray Birdwhistell claims in *Kinesics and Context* that the human face is capable of some 250,000 different expressions. The eyes, which have been called the "windows of the soul," are particularly expressive. (The expressiveness of close-up photographs of people was discovered early in the development of photography. Stella Pandell Russell tells us, "Early creative photographers worked largely in the area of portraiture."[2])

Sometimes, positioning the camera far from the subject is especially effective. The camera may be placed far from the subject to create or enhance a humorous situation. Filmmaker Charlie Chaplin reputedly said close-up for tragedy, long shot for comedy, and his own films often illustrate the truth of that claim. We can also see these consequences in a sequence from *Quest for Fire*. Eighty thousand years ago, three hominids are treed by some saber-toothed tigers. Early in the sequence many close-ups and medium shots are used of the hominids scampering up the tree, the tigers at the base of the tree trunk, the hominids' faces

[2] Stella Pandell Russell, *Art in the World* (San Francisco: Rinehart Press, 1975), p. 97.

5.15 Medium close-up

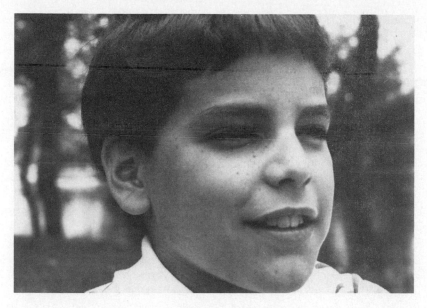

5.16 Close-up

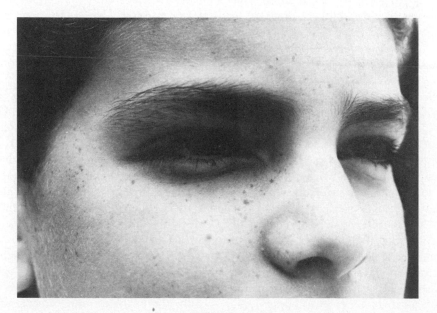

5.17 Extreme close-up

registering panic, and so forth. These close and medium shots thrust viewers up close to the actions and reactions and involve us in the danger and fear. The sequence, however, also contains three long shots and one extreme long shot showing the three large creatures in a rather small tree. In those shots, in all but one of which the hominids are seen in silhouette and thus seem even more remote, the hominids look small, pitiful, ludicrous—not so much endangered as silly.

At other times a long shot reinforces the serious mood of a scene. In a scene from *Cabaret,* for example, a male character who has been posing as a non-Jew initially pursues a Jewish character because of her wealth. He finds himself, however, falling in love with her, even though he is aware that in 1930s Berlin to fall in love with a Jew is dangerous. He goes to her house. In long shot we see him pounding on her front door. After the door is opened, he is heard saying, "I'm a Jew." Even though the character up to this point in the film is rather unappealing, it is a moving scene, in part because at this moment of vulnerability he looks dwarfed by his surroundings. Another example of a long shot contributing to the serious mood of a scene is found in *Rocky.* After Rocky angrily turns down Mickey's offer to coach him for the title fight, Mickey walks slowly down the stairs and out into the empty street. In an outdoor, long shot we see Mickey buttoning up his coat collar and walking down the street, away from us viewers. After a brief reaction shot of an angry Rocky, we see Rocky come out the door, run down the street, and catch up with Mickey. Now in an extreme long shot we may notice that Mickey shies away from Rocky (presumably he fears that Rocky is still angry and may hit him); then we see Rocky put his arm around Mickey's shoulders and talk to him, then shake his hand before parting. Again the distance from the subject adds to, rather than detracts from, the impact of the scene, in part because the viewer's imagination completes what is unseen and unheard and in part because the subjects again are so small when compared with their surroundings. The image suggests that these "small" creatures need to help each other in this large, cold, dark, empty world.

Here, as elsewhere in all stories, filmic and other, less may be more: often something shown in less detail may be more effective than a more explicit presentation. Many viewers believe that horror films are more effective when they use shadows, sounds, and reaction shots, not explicit violence, and that scenes of confrontation are more tense, more involving if the language is not too explicit for too long. Similarly, many viewers feel that a scene is most erotic when it creates a certain mood and leaves certain details to the audience's imagination, though such restraint in the presentation of violent and sexual subjects is rare in recent U.S. commercial cinema.

Images are filmed by using basically three different kinds of lenses. Often all three of them are used at different times within the same film: wide-angle, normal, and telephoto. Each kind of lens has different properties and creates different images, as illustrated in the accompanying photographs taken with a 35 mm camera from the same distance from the subjects (Figures 5.18–5.20).

Another important factor determining the expressiveness of images is the angle at which the subject is filmed. There are basically three angles: the camera above the subject, the camera on the same level as

5.18 Wide-Angle Lens (in this case, a 24 mm lens)

1. All planes appear to be farther away from the camera and from each other than is the case with a normal lens.

2. Sharp focus in all planes.

3. Compared with a normal lens, as in Figure 5.19, more of all four sides of the image is visible.

4. With very wide-angle lenses and/or with the subject close to the camera, much distortion or curvature of objects, especially near the edges of the image.

5. Movements toward or away from the camera seem speeded up.

5.19 Normal Lens (50 mm)

This lens provides minimal distortion of image and movement, though in close-ups, as in Figure 5.16, this lens distorts the image noticeably.

5.20 TELEPHOTO LENS (in this case, 200 mm)

1. All planes appear closer to camera and to each other than is the case with a normal lens.

2. Shallow depth of focus; thus, only planes very close to each other can be in focus.

3. Less of the sides of the image is visible than is the case with a normal lens.

4. Movements toward or away from the camera seem slowed down.

5.21 High angle. Photographer: Jon Terry. Model: Amie Morgan.

5.22 Eye-level angle. Photographer: Jon Terry. Model: Amie Morgan.

the subject, the camera below the subject. Figures 5.21–5.23 illustrate three positions: high angle, eye-level, and low angle. The camera, of course, may be placed at any angle above or below those indicated in these three photographs. High angles make the subject appear smaller and shut off from the surroundings. Eye-level angles are similar to the angles at which we usually meet and interact with other people and may allow us to see much of the setting. In low angles, the surroundings are again minimized, for we often see only a sky or ceiling in the background. In low-angle shots, the subject seems larger and, in many contexts, dominating and intimidating.

In subjective camera shots (often called point-of-view or p.o.v. shots) the camera films a subject from the approximate location of one of the film's characters. Such camera placements often contribute to the viewer's sense of participating in the action. As an example, consider the opening scenes of the 1932 film *Dr. Jekyll and Mr. Hyde*—where viewers see (more or less) what the character Dr. Jekyll sees—and many scenes of films directed by Alfred Hitchcock. More often in films, the camera is placed outside the action (objective camera shots), and the audience is more of a spectator than a participant (as in Figures 5.12–5.17).

During a shot, camera movement also affects the impact of images. As the camera is filming, it may glide about (dollying or tracking) (see Figures 5.24 and 5.25) or move up and down through the air (craning). Such movement may be used to allow viewers to follow a moving subject, see the subject from a different perspective, or prevent the audience from learning certain information, as is the case when the camera moves discreetly from a bed and points out a window as lovers' passions take over.

Also important is what objects are included within the frame and how they are placed in relationship to each other and to the edges of the frame. Basically, directors and cinematographers may choose to present symmetrical or asymmetrical compositions. In symmetrical compositions with only one object of interest, the object is seen in the approximate center of the frame (as in Figure 2.7). If there are two or more major objects of interest, they are seen on opposite sides of the frame and appear to balance each other out (as in Figure 6.8). In asymmetrical compositions, objects of major interest are not offset by other important objects on the opposite side of the frame (Figure 20.6).

Composition, or *mise en scène* as it is sometimes called, is another way of emphasizing or de-emphasizing certain details. Both the width and depth of the film image may be used expressively. For example, characters who are angry at each other are often positioned on opposite sides of the frame, as in Figure 14.8 from *Bicycle Thieves*. As another example of expressive composition, sometimes characters and objects are crowded into the space shown by the frame. The background to some action may be muted (for example, it may be obscurely lit and inconspicuous, or it may be out of focus and thus draw no attention to itself, as in Figures 5.16 and 5.20). Often the background is in sharp focus, and details in the background or foreground may comment on a subject in another plane. In *Citizen Kane,* for example, just before Susan Alexander Kane leaves her husband, Charles Foster Kane, we see them face to face in the background and a doll rather inconspicuously in the foreground and on the same side of the frame as Susan (Figure 15.13). That doll in the foreground subtly reminds us she has lived like a child (kept and commanded); a resolute Susan in the

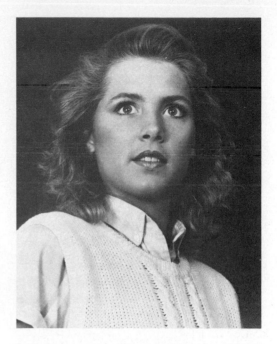

5.23 Low angle. Photographer: Jon Terry. Model: Amie Morgan.

background shows us that the situation is about to change.

Edited Images

The cliché about sculpture, that the sculptor finds the statue which is waiting in the stone, applies equally to editing; the editor finds the film which is waiting hidden in the material.[3]

The finished film is made up of "shots" and the larger units of a film, "scenes" and "sequences."

[3] Tom Priestly, British film editor, as quoted in Ralph Rosenblum and Robert Karen, *When the Shooting Stops . . . the Cutting Begins: A Film Editor's Story* (New York: Viking Press, 1979).

5.24 Dollying. Shooting on location for *The Exorcist*. © Warner Bros. Inc. Cinemabilia.

5.25 Tracking, and recording sound while shooting *Spirit of Culver* (1939). Cinemabilia.

"Shot" is probably the most useful term for film students, and it is used many times in this book, yet its precise meaning understandably often slips away from beginning students. A shot is an uninterrupted strip of exposed motion picture film made up of at least one frame, that is, an individual image on the strip of film (Figure 5.26). When projected, a shot usually depicts a continuous yet limited action, such as a hand reaching for a book. Occasionally, a shot or part of it depicts an unmoving subject. At any rate, a shot depicts something during an uninterrupted segment of time. Typically, a full-length fictional or documentary film is made up of hundreds of shots, occasionally over 1,000 shots, as in *The Birth of a Nation, Potemkin,* and *The Wild Bunch.* At the opposite extreme, some short experimental films, such as some of those directed by Andy Warhol, are made up of a single, lengthy shot.

Although "scene" is used by film teachers and writers to stand for different sections of a film, usually the term refers to a series of shots (occasionally only one shot) taken in one location during a continuous or nearly continuous time. Let's consider the first three scenes of *The Third Man.* The first, brief scene takes place in one location, a part of the Vienna train station; the action is continuous and is presented in two shots:

shot number	
1	The train is pulling into the station.
2	Holly Martins is in a train compartment. As the viewer hears the conclusion of the opening voice-over narration, Martins opens the compartment door and steps out.

5.26 One shot and the beginning of the following shot, from *(Battleship) Potemkin.*

First shot begins. When projected, this shot shows a continuous and, in this case, very limited action (less than a second long).

Frame

Cut (connection between shots)

First shot ends/second shot begins.

Second shot interrupted

The second scene consists of a single shot: Martins stops (presumably nearby) to show his passport to an American military policeman and explain the purpose of his visit to Vienna. The third scene is also one shot and is even briefer (about seven seconds): Martins approaching Lime's building (see Figure 2.4). Fictional and some documentary films stitch together scenes, usually in an unnoticeable manner. Feature films vary enormously in the number of scenes. One hundred or more seems common.

Even more ambiguous, though still widely used, is the term "sequence." Examination of various glossaries of film terms and of the usage of the term by film teachers and scholars reveals a variety of meanings. And comparison of several different published outlines of sequences for the same film reveals different "sequences." Consequently, it is best to think of a sequence as a group of related scenes, though what unifies the scenes is not always agreed upon.

How do editors combine shots into scenes and sequences and complete films? After the numerous labeled strips of film have been shot and developed, the film editor or editors, often in cooperation with the director, select(s) the best version or "take" of each shot to be used in the finished film. Often the editor shortens the shot; sometimes the editor inserts another shot in the middle of the first shot. Editors arrange shots and combine them into scenes and sequences. The whole process, which is often called cutting the film, may take months of tedious yet creative work. How shots are selected, arranged, and combined is crucial to the film's meaning and effectiveness, so much so that it is often said that a film is salvaged in editing and that a great performance is made in the cutting (or editing) room. The importance of editing can also be seen in the following, simplified example. Say that a film includes a short scene to be made up of four shots:

1. Two women are hitting each other.
2. A man talks to the two women, but we cannot hear what is said.
3. The man is smiling.
4. The two women are talking in a friendly manner.

Imagine that an editor arranges the four shots in this way:

4. The two women are talking in a friendly manner.
2. The man is talking to the two women.
1. The two women are now fighting.
3. The man is smiling.

In this scene the man seems to enjoy causing trouble.

Perhaps the editor decides on a different arrangement:

1. Women fighting.
2. Man talking to them.
4. Women now friendly with each other.
3. Man Smiling.

In this scene, blessed is the peacemaker.

Imagine yet another scene:

1. Women fighting.
3. Man smiling.
2. Man talking to the two women.
4. Women now friends.

In this scene, the man again seems to be the peacemaker, though only after he seems to enjoy or be amused by their fighting for a while (why he makes peace, we cannot tell).

Consider the consequences if all three of these imaginary scenes conclude not with a cut (instantaneous transition from the last shot of the scene to the first shot of a next scene) but with a fade-out (the image fades to darkness). Now the conclusions of the scenes have a slightly different feeling than the scenes that end with a cut. The fade-out allows us a brief moment to savor the mood and meaning of the last shot and the scene as a whole; it allows us to linger, to take a slight break from the action.

Shots may be joined in numerous ways. The most common method is to splice or connect the end of one shot to the beginning of the next shot. This transition is called a cut (see Figure 5.26), since pieces of film are cut and spliced together. This and some other frequently used transitions between shots are explained in Table 5.1.

In cross-cutting, the film shifts back and forth between two or sometimes more locations, often suggesting that different actions are taking place at the same time and that one is somehow related to the other(s). Most frequently, cross-cutting is used to show someone being menaced while someone else is on the way to help. For extended examples of cross-cutting, see the outline for *The General* in Chapter 16.

For some insight into the impact of editing, see S. Scott Smith's essay analyzing a scene from *Jaws* (Chapter 8).

Sounds

[There's] more than meets the eye.
Rudyard Kipling, "The Glory of the Garden"

Let's consider a scene from a film and see some of the ways the sound track may be utilized. On page 79 I describe the conclu-

Table 5.1
Some Common Transitions between Shots

Cut	The end of the first shot is attached to the beginning of the second shot. The most often used of all transitions, it creates an instantaneous change in one or more of the following: angle, distance, subject. See Figure 5.26.
Match or form cut	A cut where the form or shape of the image in the second shot matches or is very similar to that of the first shot. The best-known example is from *2001: A Space Odyssey,* where a bone in the air is replaced in the next shot by an orbiting spaceship of similar shape. See Figures 19.7 and 19.8, and 20.10 and 20.11.
Jump cut	A transition in which the viewer perceives the second shot as abruptly discontinuous with the first shot. Often used in films directed by Jean-Luc Godard and other filmmakers to disorient the viewer.
Fade-out, fade-in	The first shot fades to darkness (normally black); then the second shot fades in (goes from darkness to illuminated image). Often used to provide a short but meaningful pause between sequences.
Lap dissolve or dissolve	In French the term is *fondu,* which means "melted." In a lap dissolve the first shot seems to melt into the second. More precisely, in a lap dissolve the first shot fades out as the second shot overlaps it and fades in. It is often used to suggest a change of location, the passage of time, or both. In films, how much time a lap dissolve suggests is usually quite unspecific; in fiction, transitions tend to be rather specific. Lap dissolves may be rapid and nearly imperceptible, or slow and quite noticeable, creating a momentary superimposition of two images. Sometimes used in early films within a scene.
Wipe	The first shot seems to be pushed off the screen by the second shot as a line(s) moves across the frame. Not generally a common transition, but not rare either. For a "Wipe Chart" illustrating 120 kinds of possible wipes, see Roy Huss and Norman Silverstein, *The Film Experience* (New York: Dell, 1968), p. 60.

sion of one scene, then a 90-second scene in full, and the beginning of the following scene. The selection is from *The Conversation,* whose sound track was done by an acknowledged master of sound, Walter Murch. At the conclusion of the first scene, the main character, Harry Caul, a wiretapper, is seen working in his warehouse sound lab. In the following, complete scene he gets off a bus and makes a phone call to set up a meeting to deliver a tape to a client. (See Figure 5.27.)

In the complete, 90-second scene, the sound track is used in varied, expressive ways. Dialogue is employed during only approximately half of the time. As is often the case in sound films, the volume of dialogue here is different than what it would be in a comparable life situation. Indeed, we viewers are outside the phone booth yet hear clearly both Harry and the voice on the other end of the line. What is said is distinct, except for Harry's closing words. *How* the dialogue is said is conveyed with precision: Harry is hesitant and nervous; at the end of the conversation he mumbles. By way of contrast, the man in the Director's Office sounds totally confident and not at all nervous.

As is usually the case, the sound effects are the least noticeable aspect of the track, and they are used quite selectively. Here, as elsewhere, the effects are played at low volume, and often along with music and dialogue or both. For the most part, the effects subtly support the sense of being at a particular place: sounds of the bus, street traffic, phone booth door closing, phone being dialed, and so on. As is often the case, sounds off-frame enlarge the sense of a location. In this scene the most interesting use of effects is the tapping on the glass of the phone booth. After Harry goes into the phone booth, we may or may not no-

tice a man approach from the left of the frame, then stop behind the booth. The tapping sound—presumably the man tapping a coin against the glass of the phone booth because he's impatient to use the phone—is a reminder of his largely unseen presence and serves to add pressure to an already tense situation for Harry.

The music is used to support mood. Its tempo is slow and measured; its rhythms are consistent and not at all lively; its melody is repetitious and a bit melancholy or brooding. In ways difficult to put into words, the music seems appropriate for a character like Harry. For the most part, the music, not effects, accompanies the wordless action. The volume is varied for effect. As the dialogue with the man in the Director's Office is getting under way, the music decreases in volume (it eases itself out of our awareness), then stops right after the voice says, "Director's Office." It's as if the music makes way for the most important aspect of this scene, the dialogue between Harry and the man in the Director's Office. The music is also used as a bridge from the end of the first scene to the beginning of the second. And at the end of the 90-second scene the music resumes and continues into the next scene, which takes place at a different location and a later time. In both cases, using the music as a bridge between scenes seems to provide greater continuity: one scene seems to flow into the next as the music does.

Although this scene from *The Conversation* illustrates a number of uses of sound, sound may be employed in other ways, too.

In the selection from *The Conversation,* sound effects are used for the most part as background, suggesting what a location is like. Quite often, however, effects are used to intensify a mood. For example, a little later in *The Conversation,* after the selection

	VISUALS	DIALOGUE	(SOUND) EFFECTS	MUSIC
End of scene (two shots)	*Interior, Warehouse, Harry's Sound Lab, Day* Long shot of Harry and his assistant sitting at long work bench. Extreme long shot, looking toward work area; view mostly of pillars and empty space.	On tape, part of dialogue of young couple Harry and his assistants had recorded Continuation of taped dialogue but diminished volume		(Halfway through dialogue, piano solo begins.) Piano music continues.
	LAP DISSOLVE			
90-second scene (one shot)	*Street, Day* Bus pulling to stop. Harry gets off and walks to nearby phone booth. He goes in and closes door. He dials a number. Harry begins to talk. In background, man approaches booth. As Harry talks, camera dollies in slowly and stops in medium close-up of Harry. Harry finishes his conversation. He hangs up. He looks up.	Woman's voice on phone: ". . . May I help you?" Harry asks for an extension number. Man's voice: "Director's Office." After preliminaries, Harry and man set up appointment for 2:30 next day. Harry mutters he'll be there.	Street noise Bus's air brakes Background street noise Sound of door closing Street noise/dialing noise/phone ringing Coin (presumably) tapping on glass Low street noise during pause in dialogue, tapping again Low street noise Sound of phone hung up	Music continues. Music continues. Music continues. Music continues. Music diminishing. Music stops. Music resumes.
Beginning of next scene	*Residential Street, Night* Bus pulls to curb. Harry gets off. . . .		Sound of air brakes . . .	Music continues. . . . .

5.27 Sound in an excerpt from *The Conversation*

described above, Harry goes to his client's office to deliver the tapes he has made, then decides not to because the client is not there. In spite of threats made by the client's assistant, Harry leaves with the tapes. He then goes to the elevators, sees the young man he had recorded, gets on an elevator, then sees the young woman he had taped with the young man. On the elevator, the sound effects, which dominate the sound track, sound like wind in a tunnel. The sounds are loud, fluctuating, and, to me, eerie and unsettling. I could easily imagine those sounds in a horror film. The sounds add to the tension of the scene and suggest how upset and frightened Harry probably is.

Another example of sound effects used to intensify a mood is found in *Psycho*. As Marion Crane is knifed in the shower, it sounds—as one of my students observed— as if we are hearing close up a knife slicing heads of cabbage. Fortunately, I have not heard the sound of a knife stabbing flesh, but I doubt it sounds like slicing cabbage. In this scene from *Psycho,* however, the sound intensifies an already powerful scene and seems appropriate.

A final example of sound effects used to intensify a scene comes from *The Godfather*. After Michael thwarts an attack on his hospitalized father, the corrupt police captain and his men arrive at the hospital entrance. During the scene of the police arrival and confrontation with Michael, we hear thunder three times. The first time occurs as Michael pushes away Enzo, the baker's helper (presumably so he will not become involved with the police), and as policemen grab Michael. The thunder occurs a second time as the police captain gets out of his car and approaches Michael. The thunder occurs a third time as we see the police captain's reaction after slugging Michael and as Michael slumps down. We viewers *hear* this

thunder for the most part as we *see* the police in action, especially the police captain. The thunder underscores the reckless and frightening power of the police.

These three examples and many possible others illustrate how sound effects may be used not so much to suggest a location as to intensify a mood. Like light and shadow, tone of voice, and music, effects frequently add significant yet often inconspicuous nuances to a film. In these instances, the effects are not precisely true to life—the too loud wind in the elevator of *The Conversation,* the loud slicing noise in the shower scene in *Psycho,* the timely confluence of thunder and police in *The Godfather*. The effects are not so untrue to life, however, as to draw attention to themselves, especially during a first viewing.

Without attempting any systematic or complete listing, I'll just point out that music can be used in ways other than those discussed in the excerpt from *The Conversation*. In addition to being used to establish mood and ease transitions between scenes, it can help establish place and time. In *The Godfather, Part II,* for example, the music helps orient viewers. When the story shifts from the Corleone Tahoe compound to Cuba, the Latin music helps orient us right away; since the film often cuts between its two complicated stories, we viewers need all the orientation we can get.

Sometimes music is used to suggest what a character is feeling. In *Citizen Kane,* for example, Kane has his own song, and it is played at different times in the film. The first time it is played, Kane is near the height of his powers and happiness. He has just finished acquiring the staff of the rival newspaper and has set up a party to celebrate the occasion. His song is played loudly, briskly, and in a major key. After his affair with Susan comes to light and he is defeated in the election, we hear his song played softly, slowly, and in a minor, more melancholy key. Music can also suggest what someone or something is like. In *Jaws,* for example, the relentless, strongly rhythmical and accelerating bass melody suggests the shark's power and speed.

Music is used most prominently, of course, in musicals, where it often conveys mood and feelings with a force comparable to that of opera and dance. Music—which seems to draw from the same well as poetry—helps elicit feelings and moods, but even more so than with poetry, it is impossible to capture precisely in prose its meanings and moods. Irwin Edman has written,

> But just because music cannot be specific it can render with voluminousness and depths the general atmosphere or aura of emotion. It can suggest love, though no love in particular; worship or despair, though it does not say who is worshiped or what is the cause of the despair. Into the same music, therefore, a hundred different listeners will pour their own specific histories and desires . . . And the very fact that there is nothing definitive or exclusive in the emotional atmosphere of a given composition will make it all the more accessible as a means of catharsis or relief for the listener. Words are too brittle and chiseled, life too rigid and conventional to exhaust all the infinity of human emotional response. The infinite sinuousness, nuance, and complexity of music enable it to speak in a thousand different accents to a thousand different listeners, and to say with noncommittal and moving intimacy what no language would acknowledge or express and what no situations in life could completely exhaust or make possible.[4]

Sometimes a post-1930s fictional film has no dialogue; its meanings and moods are conveyed solely by its images, music,

[4] Irwin Edman, *Arts and the Man: A Short Introduction to Aesthetics* (New York: W. W. Norton, 1939).

and sound effects. Examples of short narrative films that use no dialogue yet are quite expressive are *The String Bean* and *Red Balloon*. Examples of feature-length fictional sound films that use no intelligible dialogue are *The Thief* (1952) and *Quest for Fire* (the latter film contains languages devised by novelist Anthony Burgess, but they are untranslated and only vaguely understood by audiences). Like *Quest for Fire*, the first and fourth (last) sections of *2001: A Space Odyssey* (Chapter 19) are without intelligible dialogue. *Silent Movie*, directed by Mel Brooks, has only one spoken word, and numerous short films, including many cartoons, are without dialogue. As I have illustrated a number of times in this book, many scenes in fictional films are without dialogue, yet the plot, characterization, moods, and meanings are still readily comprehensible.

Occasionally, it is effective for filmmakers to use no sound, not even the background or ambient sound we experience during all waking hours. The effect is readily noticeable—sometimes distractingly so—and tends to heighten viewer response. In *2001: A Space Odyssey,* for example, as astronaut Frank Poole goes outside the spaceship to replace a part the computer had predicted was going to malfunction, we hear his breathing quite clearly; then all sound stops. We are plunged into silence. During the next few minutes Poole struggles with his air line, then tumbles lifelessly through space. This action is cross-cut with his partner, Bowman, in the spaceship, then in a pod trying to help. The scenes of Poole are accompanied by deadly silence; the interior scenes with Bowman have normal ambient sound. A short time later, when Bowman explodes the pod door and is catapulted into the vacuum of the emergency air lock, we again hear nothing. Finally he manages to pull a switch that starts to close the spaceship's outer door, sends air surging into the entry chamber, and returns us to the normal world of sound. After the silence, the sound of the swooshing air is highlighted; it's as if we have been submerged in water a long time and reenter the world of glorious air. In these and other uses of silence the effect is comparable to pauses in music and poetry: a break in the natural flow of things, a change that can be unsettling and that can increase our desire to return to the sounds and rhythms of life.

How are such intricacies in the sound track, which we normally quite rightly take for granted, achieved? Answer: through a complicated, time-consuming, and creative process.

During filming, dialogue, effects, and music are usually recorded onto magnetic tape. After the film's visuals have been edited, the final work on the sound track is done. Occasionally, some of the dialogue has to be redone. Sometimes certain effects are unsatisfactory, and new sound effects are made up in a premix (so called because the resultant sound is blended in later in the final sound mix). As an example, imagine that the sound mixer is working on a fight scene and isn't satisfied with the sound of someone being hit, so a new sound is made up. Perhaps that "punch to the jaw is effected by striking a piece of beef, adding a fraction of a second of gunshot impact with a seashell, and dropping a wrench onto cement. Layered onto these is the squishy sound of a hook being torn from a fish and a cloth being ripped. These fragmented sounds, shortened to cover a one-second blow, convey the combined impression of impact, broken bone, mashed flesh and shock."[5] Finally, all the tracks are

collected together; then they are blended together (in the final mix) as they are synchronized with the images. At this point the sound editor may add dubbed voices, narration, additional sound effects, more music. (The recording and mixing of sound are illustrated in Figure 5.28, and a photograph of a modern mixing board is shown in Figure 5.29.)

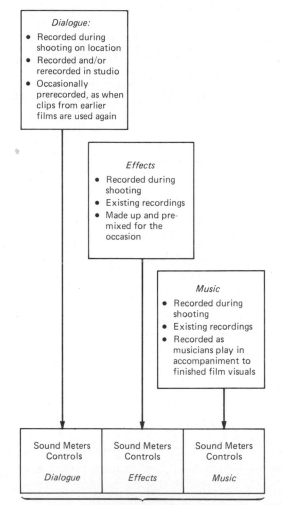

5.28 Recording and mixing sound

[5] "Hollywood Sound Effects Exploding," *American Business,* Winter 1983, p. 25.

5.29 Three-position mixing console, used to mix sound for commercial feature films. Left mixing console, for dialogue, with 20 inputs; center mixing console, for sound effects, with 20 inputs; right console, for music, 25 inputs. Courtesy of Glen Glenn Sound, Hollywood. See also Figure 2.16, a photograph of a mixing console, vintage 1940s.

During the final mix the sounds between scenes are also decided upon. Three possible ways to use sound at the junction of scenes are illustrated below.

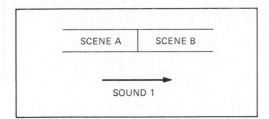

5.30 The sound from the first scene continues into the following scene.

The sound (dialogue/effects/music) from the first scene may continue into the next scene (see above). This use is illustrated by the excerpt from *The Conversation* (p.79). It is also used in *Citizen Kane*. At one point Kane applauds Susan's abysmal singing and piano playing. During the lap dissolve to the next scene, we hear continued applause, augmented since several people are now clapping for a speech Leland is making for Kane's campaign for governor.

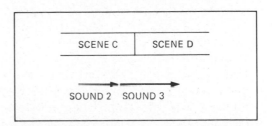

5.31 Sound from the first scene ends before the scene does; then the sound from the second scene begins.

Sometimes, especially in films from the 1970s and 1980s, as we see the conclusion of one scene, we hear the sound, frequently music, that goes with the beginning of the following scene (see Figure 5.31). In *The Godfather, Part II,* for instance, as a scene ends in young Vito's residence, we hear a train whistle. In the next scene, which begins shortly afterward, we see a train making the same sound, then see Vito's grown son Michael riding in the train.

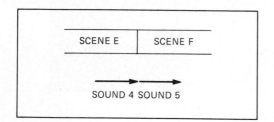

5.32 Sound ends with scene. New sound begins with new scene.

Usually, the sound ends with the visuals of one scene and is replaced by new sound as the next scene begins (see Figure 5.32). The sound ending the one scene may be similar or identical to the sound beginning the next scene (in which case the transition is similar to a visual match cut). Sometimes the sound of the first scene is quite dissimilar to the sound beginning the next scene (something like a jump cut). Depending on the similarity or difference, the result will contribute to a continuity or disruption between the scenes. Most often the new sound is different but not abruptly so.

Now that we have examined some basics of stories in the previous chapter and a few aspects of images and sounds in this chapter, we are ready to consider the different ways a film affects viewers.

· 6 ·

Viewer Responses

PACE
SENSUOUSNESS
FEELINGS
SYMBOLS
MEANINGS
FANTASIES
EVALUATIONS

"I was to a [picture] show oncet that was me, an' more'n me; an' my life, an' more'n my life, so ever'thing was bigger."

"Well, I git enough sorrow. I like to git away from it."

"Sure—if you can believe it."

Chapter 23 (two unidentified characters)
John Steinbeck, *The Grapes of Wrath,*

Nuances of feeling, subtleties of thought that practical experience keeps us too gross or too busy to observe, that words are too crude to express, and affairs too crude to exhaust, have in the arts their moment of being. For these reasons, too, for the observer, they are absorbing flights from life. But they may—in major instances they do—clarify, intensify, and interpret life.

Irwin Edman, *Arts and the Man: A Short Introduction to Aesthetics*

As viewers watch a film, complex, ever-changing reactions take place in them, and afterward they react further to the experience they have had. It is this complex topic of viewer responses that I will now attempt to describe briefly. I want to stress that word "attempt," for film scholars have not studied this subject in depth, nor is it easy to study. What follows are my efforts to sort out some of the major kinds of responses viewers may have as they watch a film and afterward as they continue to react to it and express their reactions to others.

Pace

"Pace" refers to the viewer's sense of a story moving rapidly or slowly. Sometimes viewers are aware of a film's pace. We may look at our watches and think that the film is dragging. Or, as we watch action scene after action scene in a 1980s film, many of us are feeling that the film gives us too much too soon. Pace is determined by several factors. It is determined by how much action occurs during the film and how often the action is interspersed with calmer moments. Pace is also determined by editing style. Much fast cutting (frequent brief shots)—as in *Star Wars* and *Raiders of the Lost Ark* and in the action comic books and movies that inspired them—creates a rapid, even frantic pace. Cuts or rapid lap dissolves or rapid wipes between scenes—as in all three films of the *Star Wars* trilogy—make for a more rapid pace than leisurely lap dissolves between scenes—as used, for example, throughout *Citizen Kane*—or slow fade-outs followed by slow fade-ins. Also important in determining the pace of a film are the number and length of conversations, the speed of the movements depicted, and the frequency of views of scenery. Thus, *2001: A Space Odyssey,* which has few rapid movements and numerous lingering shots of scenery, has a slow pace. Viewers are sometimes aware of pace but frequently are not. Usually we are so caught up in the film that we are unaware of its pacing. Let's consider the opening nine scenes of *Rocky.*

scene number	action
1	"November 25, 1975 Philadelphia" "Resurrection A. C." (Athletic Club) Rocky in boxing match. He wins.
2	In dressing room, Rocky puts on robe with "The Italian Stallion" on back of it. Losing fighter and Rocky get paid for the fight.
3	Credits are superimposed over the entire shot/scene: Night. Rocky approaches pet shop, taps at window, then continues on. Across street is a gym building with dirty banner: "Professional Boxing." Rocky passes youths singing at street corner. They exchange greetings.
4	Inside his apartment: his turtles (Cuff and Link), Rocky Marciano poster, fish (Moby Dick), photo (presumably) of self as boy. Rocky puts ice on his cut head and lies down.
5	Day. Pet store. Rocky talks to shy Adrian; her boss, Gloria; and a boxer dog.
6	Dock area. Collecting for Gazzo. Rocky doesn't

get full payment, yet doesn't break man's thumbs.

7   Bridge. Car stops by Rocky. He gets in. Car drives off.

8   Inside car: Rocky gives money to Gazzo, gets paid with part of it. Driver insults Rocky.

9   By sidewalk, car stops: Gazzo and Rocky get out and cross street. Gazzo unhappy with Rocky for not breaking the dockworker's thumbs as directed. Gazzo leaves. His driver shouts another insult at Rocky. Rocky shouts back, then walks away.

These opening scenes reveal Rocky's character and his situation: where he lives and works and what the people in his life are like. (As in most films, what we *see* in these scenes is more revealing than what we *hear*.) The information is presented at a varied rate: the pace does not remain the same for long. The film begins, even before the credits, with action, violent action: a boxing match and a lively crowd; then the pace slows for several scenes. The end of scene 4, Rocky comparing his present battered looks with a photograph of himself as a boy, is quiet and reflective; then the pace picks up again with the next scene. Scene 6 returns to violent action: Rocky roughing up the dockworker and collecting money. The tension subsides momentarily, then picks up again since Rocky's employer, Gazzo, seems dangerous (a gangster type?),[1] and we cannot be sure what will happen next. The driver's teasing (verbal violence) also threatens to lead to violence—but doesn't; Rocky walks off, and the pace slows once again.

Varied pacing, as in these nine scenes, can help maintain audience interest and prevent fatigue. Pacing can help deemphasize or emphasize certain actions and effects—for example, by slowing the pace to let a mood take effect or to give viewers a moment to reflect on what they've just seen. Also, pacing can be used to build and sustain tension, as in the long final fight at the end of *Rocky* and its emotional aftermath.

Sensuousness

Many films have a powerful appeal viewers frequently take for granted, their sensuousness. "Sensuousness" refers to the senses (traditionally regarded as five: sight, sound, touch, taste, and smell) and

---

[1] The actor playing Gazzo had played a similar role, working for organized crime, in both *The Godfather* and *The Godfather, Part II*.

should not be equated with "sensual" or "sexual." Of course, all films are made up of moving images and sounds—keeping in mind that even "silent" films were usually shown with musical accompaniment and sometimes with sound effects—but some films encourage viewers to luxuriate in sights and sounds more so than do others. (In commercial cinema, usually the sights and sounds are pleasurable.) The many colorful sunsets in *Walkabout* (Figure 6.1); the various views of the water, horse, and island in the first half of *Black Stallion* (Figure 6.2); and the concluding and prolonged sights and music of *Close Encounters of the Third Kind*—all are delights to eye and ear, as are sections of films that linger on or single out movements, music, textures, and colors. Figures 6.1 and 6.2 capture some of these visual

6.1 *Walkabout*. Direction and cinematography by Nicolas Roeg. A 20th Century–Fox Release. Movie Star News.

delights, though they are in black and white, not the original color, and the still from *Black Stallion* cannot capture, of course, the flowing movements of the running horse. By way of contrast, we do not often luxuriate in the images and sounds of *My Dinner with André;* its basic appeal is more mental, more intellectual, as is true of other films that rely heavily on dialogue (*Diner* and *The Big Chill,* for example). The same, I think, could be said of *The Maltese Falcon* (1941) and indeed of detective and mystery films in general. Pointing out the frequency, prominence, and function of sensuous images and sounds can help describe a film and account for its impact. Certainly we viewers respond to prominent images and sounds, but, as is often the case in film viewing, we frequently take them for granted.

6.2 *Black Stallion.* Direction by Carroll Ballard; cinematography by Caleb Deschanel. A United Artists Release. Movie Star News.

Feelings

I believe that viewers react emotionally to films for two different reasons. Let me explain by describing my own emotional reactions to two films. As I watched *Coming Home* (1978) for the first time, I thought that its characters and situations were simplistic: the characters either too admirable or too unadmirable, created more to illustrate certain viewpoints about politics and sex than to be believable characters (see Figure 6.3). Although I was unmoved *by* the film, I was moved *as* I watched it. I was moved because my mind kept jumping to similar situations and to those I love in similar predicaments. I was moved largely because, like most adult Americans who lived during the Vietnam War, the subject was (and is still) intensely painful.

My experience of *Citizen Kane* is quite different. Every time I watch *Citizen Kane,* as I see Rosebud burning in the furnace and the smoke rise from Kane's darkened mountaintop retreat and hear Bernard Herrmann's music, my throat tightens; I feel a fleeting melancholy (see Figure 15.15). The subject matter of the film is universal enough that most alert viewers will be caught up in the presentation and be moved. I am moved by the ending of *Citizen Kane* because of

6.3 *Coming Home* with Jon Voight and Jane Fonda. © 1978 United Artists Corporation. Movie Star News.

what is *in* the film: a believable character, with whom I empathize (he was, after all, raised by a bank!), whose life is one of materialism, unfulfilled dreams, and loneliness. I am also moved because the treatment is restrained: I do not feel that the filmmakers are trying to force me to respond. Instead they suggest, through glimpses of significant objects and with music, loss and finality. My response to *Citizen Kane* is to *Citizen Kane,* whereas the response I had while watching *Coming Home* was largely to the thoughts set off by the film. I say "largely" because people, of course, are complex, and what we feel as we watch a film is sometimes a blend of what the film sets off directly and indirectly.

Emotional responses to a film are often slighted in English-language analyses, perhaps in part because many undirected discussions of feelings do not lead to understanding and appreciation and in part because of the Anglo-American tradition of discouraging discussion of feelings. Feelings are too subjective, we are told. Teachers teach, usually by example, that discussions of feelings do not belong in the classroom. When I ask students how they *feel* about a character, scene, or film, they are often reluctant, especially in large groups, to speak up. Yet discussions of feelings *and* how the film set off those feelings can be helpful in understanding our reactions to a film showing. Such an examination helps us understand whether it is a well-made film that engages us, or whether we are engaged by merely the subject matter and our own private world of thoughts and memories. To be useful to other viewers, however, the feelings described need to be those that the film itself sets off, and the emphasis needs to be kept on the film's topic and treatment.

A discussion of *Citizen Kane,* or most other fictional films, might explain how the viewer felt about the characters and the actions and what in the film encouraged that response. (Pauline Kael often does so in her analyses; it's one reason I think she is a superior critic.) A full description and evaluation of a film needs to account for its topic, treatment, and effects, both conceptual and emotional.

Symbols

Sometimes objects have *meanings* to the people who see them. A flag, for example, is not merely a decorated piece of cloth. In the minds of many, the cloth stands for or symbolizes a certain place, people, history, and culture. Often, of course, that piece of cloth, that symbol evokes strong feelings from those who see it; sometimes it provokes actions.

By presenting certain objects in particular ways, storytellers can charge them with meaning. In *The Godfather* and *The Godfather, Part II,* for example, doors are sometimes used symbolically: they are not just objects connecting rooms. In the last two shots of *The Godfather,* Michael's wife, Kay, and we in the audience see Michael in his den/office surrounded by three of his men. One of them kisses Michael's hand and says, "Don Corleone"—meaning the new head of the Corleone family and its criminal business (Figure 6.4). The second man kisses Michael's hand and, at nearly the same time, the third man goes to the door and closes it. The film's final action obliterates Kay from our and Michael's view (a kind of concluding wipe to darkness) and, more importantly, blocks out both Kay and the audience from further views of Michael's criminal life. Late in *The Godfather, Part II,* Michael finds his estranged wife sneaking a visit to their two children at the Corleone estate. After a dramatic, wordless, face-to-face confrontation of about thirty seconds, Michael shuts the door in Kay's uncertain, then pained face. In both instances, the door stands for or symbolizes the barrier that has come between Michael and his wife. This symbol reinforces an important meaning of the two *Godfather* films: Michael's growing alienation from loved ones as he becomes increasingly involved in the family's criminal business.

   The Godfather contains other symbols that can be used as illustra-

6.4 Al Pacino as the new godfather. Publicity still from *The Godfather.* © 1972 Paramount Pictures. Movie Star News.

tions. At the beginning and ending of the scene where Luca Brasi (Vito's faithful strongman) is strangled to death, the camera looks into the bar through a glass window with fish etched on it. Later, dead fish wrapped in Brasi's bulletproof vest are delivered to the Corleone compound, and we learn that it is a Sicilian message that Luca "sleeps with the fishes" (that is, he's dead). At this point, some viewers will realize that the etched fish seen briefly in the foreground of Luca's murder were unexplained symbolic objects, not just insignificant decorations. (For interpretations of three symbols in *Citizen Kane*—Kane's two sleds [Figures 15.14 and 15.9] and the glass paperweight [Figure 15.8]—see Don Reed's essay in Chapter 8 and the Questions and Observations section of Chapter 15.)

Since so few viewers of *The Godfather* are likely to know the significance of the Sicilian message of fish in a vest, that symbol is explained. If we examine how symbols are used in many fictional stories, however, we will notice that symbols usually go unexplained and are subject to somewhat different interpretations by viewers. By examining how symbols are used, we film viewers discover that we become aware of symbols because certain objects are shown repeatedly or are placed in prominent locations or are seen in important scenes—or by a combination of these ways. In addition to contributing meanings to a story, symbols may intensify viewer reactions to it—as in the case of the symbol burned in a furnace at the end of *Citizen Kane*. Why, after all, would we be moved by the burning of *just* a sled? If we examine how symbols are used, we also notice that they may be obvious—for example, motorcycles in most youth films—and immediately understood by audiences. Sometimes, however, symbols in films are not at all obvious—for example, the etched glass fish in *The Godfather*—and pass by unnoticed during a first or even later viewing.

Meanings

As we saw in the previous section, symbolic objects sometimes add meanings to a story. More often, the meanings of a story—often referred to as "theme" or "themes"—are expressed mainly by means of the characters' actions and speech. Consider the following dialogue:

> "Daughter, your young man stays until a very late hour. Hasn't your mother said anything to you about this habit of his?"
> "Yes, father. Mother says men haven't altered a bit."

A simple conversation, but it's more than just amusing dialogue. It suggests certain meanings. In this exchange, the underlying point or meaning can be seen in at least two ways: *"Men tend to grow more conservative as they grow older* or *Fathers often scold their children for doing exactly what they did themselves when young.*"[2]

The above dialogue reveals at least those two slightly different meanings. Usually complete stories have more complex meanings. Consider, for example, *Jaws*. Its characters and actions imply these primary meanings: politicians are more concerned with business prosperity than public safety—a point made in a not very subtle manner during the first half of the film. (See Figure 6.5.) A macho working-class loner and a rich educated specialist bachelor both fail to solve a large problem plaguing the town. But a rather ordinary family and community man eventually destroys the beast, thereby ridding the community of its collective nightmare and at least partially redeeming himself for his earlier weakness (see Figure 6.6).

The characters and actions of *Gandhi* might be seen to suggest the following primary meanings: nonviolent philosophy and passive resistance are often met with violence and/or imprisonment, which in turn lead to moral and political pressures on the aggressors and, eventually, concessions to those living by nonviolent principles. This nonviolent strategy is effective if one has courage to be nonviolent and if the

6.5 *Jaws* with Murray Hamilton as the mayor. © 1979 Universal City Studios. Movie Star News.

[2] Both the joke and the interpretation of it are from Laurence Perrine, *Story and Structure,* 2d ed. (New York: Harcourt, Brace and World, 1966), p. 117.

6.6 The three protagonists in *Jaws* (left to right): sheriff, veteran fisherman, and shark specialist. © 1979 Universal City Studios, Movie Star News.

antagonists are sensitive to moral and political pressures. The film also shows how a character (who in fact has many resemblances to the historical Gandhi) with conviction, courage, political acumen, dedication to nonviolence, and belief in the ultimate triumph of good changes the course of history, but human nature is streaked with weakness and evil: the Gandhi character is killed by a disgruntled follower, and the Muslims and Hindus he worked to keep peaceful turn on each other (Figure 6.7).

Star Wars shows that even "a long time ago in a galaxy far, far away," when people are oppressive and evil, other people rebel. The rebels succeed mainly because of the actions of five characters: Luke, Kenobi, Princess Leia, Han, and R2-D2 (C-3PO has little impact on the film's action). The wise, avuncular knight trains the promising youth (Luke); when the time comes, the knight gives up his life in the body, yet his spirit continues to help his young charge succeed in destroying Death Star and its inhabitants. The young hero is also aided by Princess Leia, who has had the plans for Death Star stolen; by Han, who charges to the last-minute rescue; and by R2-D2, who helps in the "escape" from Death Star and assists in Luke's attack on it. Evil forces are destroyed, though not entirely (a sequel was planned, and Darth Vader escapes). Order and right are reestab-

6.7 *Gandhi*. © 1982 Columbia Pictures Industries. Museum of Modern Art/ Film Stills Archive.

lished—and celebrated during the final triumphal march and ceremony.

The film has additional, secondary meanings. For example, the story shows that people are not always what they seem to be. Like Rick in *Casablanca,* who is played by Humphrey Bogart, the young pilot (Han Solo) appears cynical, mercenary, and selfish (appropriately, his last name is Solo), but when the crucial moment comes, he helps the young man in his attack on Death Star. Through Luke's and Han's initial reluctance to fight against Imperial forces, then their actions and success, the film also suggests that good, though reluctant people must be moved to action against evil; the film shows that these two men succeed because they are willing to put aside self-interest and, in the case of Luke, to listen to the voice of past wisdom.

Another meaning implicit in the film is that life is more than just objects and actions. To some people trained in and sensitive to it, there is a "Force" or cosmic spirituality. Kenobi says to Luke, "The

Force is what gives a Jedi his power. It's an energy field created by all living things. It surrounds us and penetrates us. It binds the galaxy together." The Force can be used for good (Kenobi) or evil (Vader). In the duel between Kenobi and Vader we see an image of a kindly, cowled monk/knight opposing an obscured, armored, evil knight (Figure 6.8). Spirituality (the Force) when used in conjunction with technology is seen as more powerful than technology alone. One pilot uses a computer and misses the small, vulnerable spot on Death Star; Luke trusts the Force, turns off his computer—and makes his final run without the services of his trusty but damaged R2 unit—and destroys the evil battle station. Here Luke follows Kenobi's earlier advice: "Let go your conscious self and act on instinct. . . . Your eyes can deceive you. Don't trust them." So powerful is the Force that death itself is no threat. During his duel with Vader, Kenobi says, "You can't win, Darth. If you strike me down, I shall become more powerful than you can possibly imagine." Vader strikes. Kenobi's body vanishes—but he lives on in the Force.

These meanings and more are implied by the story's characters and actions. (In the case of *Star Wars* few adults take its meanings very seriously, since the film seems so much like an animated comic strip, has been so popular with children, and has seemingly influenced all of the kinds of products children use.) Normally, no one in a film tells viewers the meanings, at least not many of them. Instead, meanings

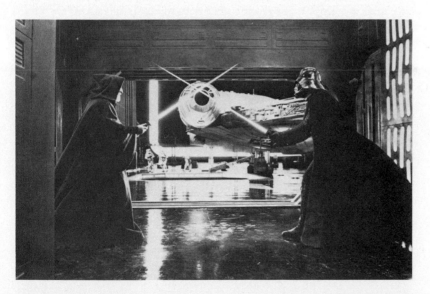

6.8 *Star Wars*: Ben Kenobi (left) duels with Darth Vader. © 1977 Twentieth Century Fox. Memory Shop West.

are suggested by actions, though most viewers, especially during a first viewing, are only vaguely aware of these implications. In the case of *Star Wars,* for example, most viewers seeing the film for the first time probably notice only that the film is about the triumph of good forces over evil. Many more meanings are implied nonetheless. In the cases of *Jaws* and *Star Wars,* indeed the *Star Wars* trilogy, the meanings are reassuring (in most commercial films the meanings are comforting): the forces of evil are destroyed, though not without sacrifice, and the forces of good succeed.[3]

In discussing meanings, as much as possible it helps to avoid using the characters' names. That way it is easier to keep the emphasis on the *significance* of the action, not the action itself. It's also a good idea to say that a story *shows* or *suggests* its meanings—not *says* them—since meanings are usually dramatized (or acted out) and implied, not stated directly. The meanings of a story may be simple or complex. Often, the meanings of a feature film are so complex that the interpretation and explanation of them are the subject of a sizable essay, and frequently two viewers will interpret the theme or meanings of a film differently. Remember the three different interpretations of *The Third Man* in Chapter 3.

An individual's interpretation of meanings is determined in part by the individual's outlook and values. Thus a Marxist will tend to see different meanings in a story than a capitalist will. Consider carefully this conclusion from a Marxist analysis of *Star Wars* (earlier in the essay many examples are given to support the generalizations that follow):

> In the end, *Star Wars* embraces by implication all the things it pretends to oppose. The Nuremberg rally scene [the last scene of *Star Wars,* which is visually quite similar to a scene from *Triumph of the Will,* a documentary film celebrating the rise to power of Hitler and the Nazis] is a fitting conclusion coherent with the film's fascination with speed,

---

[3] In *Star Wars* the evil forces are sometimes symbolically equated with Nazism. Darth Vader's helmet looks something like the helmets worn by German soldiers in World War II and the helmet-masks worn by the evil, invading Germanic tribes in the famous Soviet film *Alexander Nevsky.* The storm troopers are a more obvious reference to Nazi Germany. The fighter pilots preparing to go out for the final showdown and the dogfights complete with ball turret gunners are themselves reminiscent of World War II films featuring the air force. Part of the appeal of *Star Wars,* probably especially for older viewers, is that it allows them to relive the triumphs of World War II movies.

Star Wars is also influenced by at least three other sources: U.S. Western films (black versus white clothing, gun slinging, saloon/cantina brawls, and so forth); medieval stories (kindly wizard, good prince, endangered though feisty damsel, black knight); and probably most of all 1930s Buck Rogers and Flash Gordon serials (continuous battles of good versus evil characters in various exotic locations, stitched together by a variety of snazzy wipes between scenes).

size, violence, and with the mysticism which cloaks the film's patriarchal power structures. The romance plot incorporates sexism and racism and supports a hierarchical social system which glamorizes those at the top and literally turns those at the bottom into machines. The robots in *Star Wars* . . . are human beings turned into machines, a metallic Laurel and Hardy, the ultimate workers in a capitalist technology.

The film's commitment to excitement and speed locks it into a hard-energy weapons technology that undercuts its attempt to disassociate itself from the harmful and threatening aspects of that technology. By having no thought-out, consistent position on any of the issues he touches on, Lucas dooms *Star Wars* to repeat all the dominant ideological clichés of our society. That distant galaxy turns out to not be so far away after all.[4]

As is illustrated by this passage, Marxists tend to see a story's political implications. They also tend to see most Hollywood films as entertaining distractions from the flaws of a capitalist system yet endorsements of its values. Non-Marxists are perhaps more likely to notice the psychological rather than political implications of stories.

Understanding meanings in a film is extremely important, especially in the cases of fictional and documentary films: such understanding helps viewers see what a film shows and suggests about human experience. Understanding meanings also helps viewers realize when a film attempts to manipulate them unduly—as in propaganda films or prejudicial fictional films.

Fantasies

If a film entertains well, if many people see it, then it usually reflects the fantasies or daydreams of many in its audiences. And seeing one's fantasies on a large screen in a darkened room is usually pleasurable and reassuring.

Three cases in point would be *Rocky, Rocky II,* and *Rocky III.* Each of the three films shows a likable, good-natured individual succeeding in both his love life and in his work.[5] There are many believable happenings in the films, but they are mainly fairy tales that many viewers would like to see come true.

In *Rocky,* for example, Rocky succeeds in spite of the skill, media coverage, and intimidating showmanship of his opponent (Figure 6.9). His efforts are exhilarating and the results of his work reassuring: hard work and discipline are rewarded. But—could a *person* in

---

[4] Dan Rubey, "*Star Wars:* Not So Far Away," *Jump Cut* 18 (August 15, 1978): 13.

[5] In *Rocky,* he doesn't win, but it's too strong to say he loses: in completing the fight, he wins a kind of victory.

6.9 Rocky (right) faces his intimidating opponent, Apollo Creed, in *Rocky*. © 1976 United Artists. Movie Star News.

Rocky's situation succeed so well? Consider Rocky's big fight with Apollo Creed at the conclusion of the film. At age 30, with no previous major fights and after only five weeks of training, Rocky becomes the first man to knock down Creed; Rocky becomes the first man to go the distance with Creed (last all 15 rounds). In the 14th round, Rocky in fact seriously injures Creed, who begins to hemorrhage. Rocky very nearly wins the fight, losing only by a split decision (two judges voted for Creed; one for Rocky). Rocky achieves all this though his nose was broken in the first round! The film does not give us viewers time to dwell on these improbabilities—in fact some of the information is barely audible on the densely mixed sound track. Then, too, we viewers are so excited by the fight that we tend not to notice its improbabilities and probably don't want to do so.

Similarly—perhaps to satisfy some female fantasies—Adrian triumphs too. At the beginning of the story, she's shy, more than shy: she's crippled with negative feelings about herself. A mere few weeks later, she's an attractive, poised woman: she begins to wear brighter, more stylish clothes; she holds her head up more often; she looks people in the eye more frequently; she smiles more often; she shows a wider range of emotions; she stands up to her dominating brother. (We could argue that Adrian's triumph is another of Rocky's triumphs, since it is *his* love that seems to bring about these changes. *Rocky,* for the most part, is a replay of male fantasies.) We are seeing here in *Rocky,* as elsewhere in so many popular movies, a world of pleasant dreams that *looks* lifelike. (Probably the film was especially popular because it appeared just before the bicentennial celebrations, which reaffirmed American values.)

In the three *Rocky* films, *Jaws, Superman, Popeye,* and many other popular U.S. films, the heroes are unassuming, modest, and ordinary—yet heroic when circumstances call for it. This desire to feel heroic is widespread, and these "reel world" stories fulfill audiences' deep-felt desires usually left unfulfilled in the mere "real world." In many movies, as in our fantasies and dreams, the little guy defeats the big, bad wolf. (I suspect that commercial films worldwide—not just in the United States—most often reenact male daydreams.)

Sometimes the fantasies of foreign films are universal and transparently clear. In *Chariots of Fire* (Figure 6.10), for example, the appeal is similar to that of the *Rocky* films, though here we root for two heroes and take satisfaction in two triumphs. Sometimes, though, knowledge of a foreign culture is necessary to appreciate a film's appeal. For instance, *(Battleship) Potemkin* is not so much history as an embodiment of 1925 Soviet fantasies: in the film the czarists are totally evil; the masses completely noble, unified, and triumphant. Non-

6.10 *Chariots of Fire.* © 1981 Warner Bros. and the Ladd Company. Museum of Modern Art/Film Stills Archive.

Soviet audiences may marvel at the film's techniques yet be unmoved by its fantasy appeal.

In summary, though films usually *look* real, most popular films are best understood as reflectors of fantasies rather than precise portrayals of life outside the theater. Their meanings are not so much true to life as true to wishes.

Evaluations

As we watch a film, we often pass judgments on specific aspects of it. We think approving or disapproving thoughts. "That color is all wrong for her hat." "That music is beautiful but sad." "That character is evil." After the film is over, we almost surely pass a judgment on the film as a whole. Something like, "It's a turkey," or "It's the best film I've seen this year." If we are especially interested in the film, we may work out our judgments in greater detail. For example, we may conclude that a film is moving and engaging but its meanings no more interesting than those we find in soap opera.

In making evaluations about the successes or failures of a film, you will make certain assumptions about what constitutes a "good" or "bad" film. You may, for example, think that a film is "great," because it has lots of action. (For many viewers the amount and intensity of action are the main criteria for excellence.)

As you read reviews and analyses of fictional films, however, you may perceive that what is most often praised are the following characteristics:

1. The story holds the audience's interest as a story, and we believe in, or are willing to believe in, its characters and plot, whether they are imaginary or lifelike. The imaginary aspects, such as the plot of *Time Bandits,* are creative; the lifelike parts seem true to life.

2. The film has complexities in one or more of the following: characterization, plot, meanings. If the film concentrates on characters, at least some of them have an emotional range and richness comparable to what we find in life. Stories like "Little Red Riding Hood," for example, are simple in all three aspects. Films like *The Godfather* are not.

3. The film has subtleties and requires of its viewers attentiveness and intelligence. The film neither shows nor explains too much. It requires of its viewers active participation.

4. The film uses appropriate and normally unobtrusive techniques—camera work, sound track, and editing—to convey its story (in the case of fiction films), information (in the case of

documentaries), or emotions or sensuous experiences (in the case of experimental films). Usually, we should not be distracted, for example, by camera movement or editing, since they could interfere with our involvement in the film.

5. The film is unified. Nothing in it is unnecessary. All aspects of it work together to create its moods and meanings.

Some people might add as a sixth quality "originality," but there are so many stories and techniques adapted from fiction, drama, television, and radio that it's usually difficult to be certain about what is original.

To illustrate how these five criteria could be applied to a film, I will explain my evaluations of *Citizen Kane* (see Chapter 15).

The story is believable. As I watch it, I never think that the filmmakers are just trying to make a point rather than show a story, and I stay caught up in its story. A person like the character Charles Foster Kane could exist, as could the other characters in the film. The characters speak and act as we would expect, given their backgrounds and the situations they find themselves in.

Citizen Kane is full of complexities. A central concern of the film is Kane's true nature, which no character in the film entirely understands, nor, in my interpretation, does any viewer. As the outline in Chapter 15 illustrates, the plot is also complex: the numerous actions are selected and arranged in a complicated yet significant way. The meanings (or themes)—what the film suggests about the topics of wealth, power, love, friendship, and so on—also qualify the film as unusually complex, especially for a commercial film.

On the criterion of subtlety, *Citizen Kane* also rates highly. The film requires active, alert viewing. Most people find that each additional viewing reveals new significant details and more insights. In my opinion, however, the film occasionally and briefly lacks subtlety, as in the attempted humor at the expense of the blustering Mr. Carter and Kane's too-awkward moments just before the engagement announcement.

Applying the fourth criterion, appropriate and normally unobtrusive techniques, I give the film a mixed rating. Though the techniques—camera work, sound track, editing—are all extremely accomplished, the techniques are sometimes distracting. As one example, when Kane stands over Susan at the picnic and bullies her, his shadow falls on her face. The point of the scene is already quite clear, and the symbolism of the shadow unnecessary.

On the last criterion, unity, *Citizen Kane* again rates highly. The film has no unnecessary parts. What could be cut without loss? The film is unified in showing some aspects of a famous man's life and how some people perceived him and how someone after Kane's life tried to learn something about him. All these aspects work together to create a thought-provoking yet moving film.

These five criteria are restricted to standards used in Europe and countries whose culture has been shaped by Europe (the United States, Canada, and elsewhere) but may not apply to many places and times. I hope, however, that these criteria, though perhaps incomplete, will be of some help in reaching judicious, defensible evaluations.

In this and the preceding two chapters I have attempted to explain some of the components of film experiences: characterization and plot (in the fictional film); images and sounds; and basic kinds of viewer responses. The next two sections—study questions and exercises—may be used selectively in examining any film closely.

Questions for Thought/Discussion/Writing

The following questions are intended to help viewers become more aware of what they know about a film and how they know it. The questions may also help viewers better understand how and why they respond as they do. Not all the questions are appropriate for every film, and, of course, time, resources, and goals will determine which of the following questions are useful for a particular film. For those questions most appropriate for the film being examined, please remember: in thinking out, discussing, and writing down responses, the most frequent dangers are straying from the issues the questions raise, not answering all parts of the questions, and not giving enough specific examples from the film. Film experiences are so complex that no viewer will be able to answer all of the appropriate questions until after a second or third viewing, or after using some of the exercises following this list of questions.

Characterization and Plot

1. **a.** Who is the protagonist or main character? Why do you say so?
   b. Describe the character's or characters' physical characteristics and personality.
2. **a.** For the major characters, how is characterization revealed: actions, appearance, speech, thoughts (ideas, fantasies, dreams, hallucinations)? Which of these four methods of revealing characterization is used most often in the film? Which of the four methods is used the least or not at all?
   b. How well do you get to know and understand the major characters? What information about them is revealed? What information about them is withheld?

   c. Are the major characters convincing? Why do you say so?

   d. What are the major conflicts between characters? How are they resolved? Do any of the characters have internal conflicts (uncertainty, guilt, etc.)? If so, what are the conflicts? Are the film's most important conflicts between sharply distinguished good and evil (as in *Star Wars* and *Raiders of the Lost Ark*), or are the most important conflicts more complex and subtle?

3. A "scene," remember, is a shot or, much more frequently, a series of shots of uninterrupted action or seemingly consecutive action in one location.

   a. Are any of the scenes in the film unnecessary? Why do you say so?

   b. Are any scenes placed in a confusing order? Explain.

   c. What are the film's sequences (major *groups* of scenes)? Justify your answer.

   d. Does the film have a chronological or nonchronological structure? What are the advantages of the choice?

4. a. Basically, does the film stress characterization or plot? Why do you say so?

   b. So far as you are aware, what aspects of characterization and plot have been used in commercial television, popular fiction, comics, popular films, popular songs?

   c. How complex and subtle are the characterization and plot? Why do you say so?

5. Nearly always films present their characters and actions in such a manner that they encourage audience approval or disapproval. In the *Rocky* films, for example, audiences like Rocky enormously because of what he is like and what he does.

   a. If the film presents certain behavior or attitudes in an approving manner, in what ways does it do so? How do you know?

   b. Which, if any, behavior or attitudes are satirized or made fun of? How strongly felt is the disapproval? How noticeable is the disapproval?

6. As we consider a film, we often compare and contrast it with other films we know well. This is both understandable and desirable, for it can help us understand what is original and what is traditional in the film.

   a. In characterization and plot, does the film have important similarities to other films you know well? If so, what are the films and the similarities?

   b. In characterization and plot, what differentiates the film from the other, similar films?

Sights and Sounds

Images

7. a. Are the images high-grain or low-grain? Are both looks used within the same film?

   b. What does that look contribute to the film?

8. **a.** Where is lighting used to support or create a particular mood? What mood?

   b. Where are shadows used to conceal information? To enhance mood? To reveal what a character is like or is feeling?

   c. If a certain kind of lighting is used repeatedly, describe it and explain its effects.

9. **a.** Does the film use "cool" or "warm" colors to achieve certain effects? Is color used in a symbolic way within the film?

   b. Is color used to enhance mood? If so, where and how?

   c. How natural or lifelike is the color?

10. **a.** For an especially significant scene, what camera distances are used? To what effect?

    b. Are many close-ups used in the film? Of what? Why?

    c. Generally, does the camera stay back from the characters and show much of the setting? Illustrate your answer.

11. **a.** For some of the most significant shots in the film, what lens is used: wide-angle, normal, or telephoto? With what consequences?

    b. Is one kind of lens used frequently in the film? If so, what lens and with what consequences?

12. **a.** Does the subject tend to be filmed in high, eye-level, or low angles?

    b. Where are camera angles especially significant or effective? Why do you say so?

13. **a.** Where are subjective camera shots (point-of-view shots) used in the film? How often are they used? What effects do they have on your viewing experience?

    b. Where are camera placements used that make the audience feel like an outsider looking in on the action (objective camera shots)?

14. **a.** Generally, does the film use moving camera shots: does the camera glide about (a technique called dollying or trucking), and move up and down through the air (craning)? Or does the camera tend to remain stationary?

    b. What is the effect of the camera movement or lack of movement?

    c. Does the camera stay in one location but rotate horizontally (panning), or does it rotate vertically (tilting)? Where and with what consequences?

15. **a.** Are significant objects bunched up or spread apart? Are they in the center of the frame or off to a side?

    b. Are significant objects arranged in such a way as to balance out the composition or to create an unbalanced, asymmetrical composition?

    c. In what ways do background and foreground objects or characters relate to each other?

Edited images

16. **a.** Generally, is the film's editing characterized by frequent shots of short duration (called fast cutting) or by shots of long duration (slow cutting)? To what effect?

    b. In what scenes is the story time longer than the running time? Conversely, and much less commonly, in what scenes is the running time longer than the story time?

c. Does the editing tend to be smooth and unobtrusive or disruptive and obvious? Explain.

d. For the film under examination, where are the shots connected for a particular effect—for example, to stress similarities or differences?

e. Does the film use cross-cutting? If so, where and to what effect?

Sound

17. a. Where and why is offscreen sound used?

b. Where is sound used to suggest size and texture of the surfaces of a location?

c. How frequently is dialogue used?

d. Is the dialogue always distinct, or is some of it indistinct? Does the dialogue sometimes overlap and interrupt other dialogue?

e. Where is silence used? What effect does it contribute?

f. Where is volume raised or lowered for effect?

g. Where are sound effects used to intensify moods?

h. Where is sound used between scenes to create a certain effect? What effect is created or supported?

18. a. Where is music used? For what purposes?

b. Is the music always subordinated to the film's other components, or does it sometimes stand out on its own? Explain.

c. Can you recognize major melodies or tunes? Are they repeated? With or without variation?

d. Is the music part of the story itself, or is it played as complementary to the story, as in the case where we see characters in a lifeboat while we hear an orchestra?

e. Where does the music suggest a particular place, or time, or both?

f. Where is music used to suggest what a character is feeling?

Viewer Responses

19. a. Where is the film's pace rapid? Where is it slow?

b. What is the film's overall pace? Why do you say so?

c. How important is the pace to the film's impact on the audience? Why?

20. How do you *feel* about the main character(s) and the film's events? What is it about the film that makes you respond in that way? How do your feelings influence your overall response to the film?

21. Does the film have any important symbols? If so, what are they? What do they mean? How do you know?

22. a. What are the film's meanings or theme? Be sure to explain in some detail.

b. Are the meanings convincing or not? Why do you say so?

c. Are the meanings complex or simple? Ambiguous or clear? Explain. Are the meanings disturbing or reassuring? Why?

d. Are the meanings restricted to a particular culture or time, or are they universal? Please justify your answer.

e. Are the meanings of the film explicit or subtle? Please explain why you say so.

23. What fantasies do the film reflect? Why do you say so?
24. **a.** What does the film convey to you about the history and culture of the society it depicts?
    b. How accurate are those impressions?
    c. How do you know how trustworthy those impressions are?
25. **a.** Did you become involved in the story and stay involved in it?
    b. Does the film contain complexities? If so, where?
    c. Is the film designed for an intelligent, sensitive, attentive audience?
      (1) Where in the film is less shown—because of the script or acting, or camera work, or editing—than might be shown? Where is the audience required to use its imagination, rather than be shown certain material? What is the consequence of this restraint?
      (2) What aspects of the film demand special attentiveness from viewers?
      (3) Does the film ever show or tell us something we already know? Do the filmmakers show us too much (sex/violence) and create too shocking an effect for the overall purposes of the film?
    d. Does the film employ its techniques of photography, editing, and sound in a manner appropriate to the film? Please explain.
    e. Are all aspects of the film necessary? What unifies the film?

I hope that at least some of these questions help viewers in their examination of the complexities of film experiences. The following section may be used to discover specific, often inconspicuous aspects of movies by means of various exercises in viewing, listening, reading, and writing.

Exercises for Examining Films

The following exercises may help viewers become more aware of particular aspects of a film. For example, the sound track may be studied by listening to it with the image turned off. Some of the following exercises may be applied to any film, and many of these exercises may be used with a videodisc or videotape player (see also Chapter 10). In home or classroom, time and resources limit the number of these exercises that can be used with a film. Probably most readers will want to read the following section quickly to get an idea of the kinds of exercises possible, then at various times refer to specific exercises to examine closely certain aspects of a film. For convenience, the following exercises are divided into four kinds—viewing, listening, reading, and writing—though a number of them overlap.

Viewing

1. Run a scene without the sound turned up; then discuss what you have learned and how you have learned it. Rerun the same scene with sound

and discuss again what the visuals reveal. This exercise may be used before or after you have seen a film for the first time.

2. View a scene; take notes; then discuss your observations with other viewers and note-takers. Watch the next scene again while taking notes. Stop and discuss. Continue for several more scenes.

3. After you have seen a film in its entirety, view its opening scene again. What moods and meanings does it convey? Next, view the film's concluding scene again. What moods and meanings does it suggest? In what ways are the opening and closing of the film related?

4. Rerun a scene (if possible, in slow motion). Explain where the filmmakers show more than they might have. Show where less is shown than might have been (for instance by moving the camera back or forward, changing the lighting, using a lens that distorts the image, giving a sound for an object rather than showing it, shortening a shot or omitting shots altogether). Is the scene characterized by restraint or explicitness? To what effect?

5. Rerun a scene, if possible in slow motion. Explain what the camera angles and distances contribute to the scene.

6. Rerun a scene; pay special attention to the lighting. How hard or soft is the lighting (see Figures 5.3 and 5.4)? From what directions does the lighting come (see Figures 5.5–5.10)? What information is obscured or emphasized by the lighting? What mood is created?

7. Rerun a short scene (in slow motion, if possible). Explain how the length of each shot, the arrangement of shots, and the transitions or connections between shots all influence the scene's impact. Run the scene yet again; perhaps make an outline of its shots. Review and revise your explanations.

8. View an important scene featuring one of the major characters. For the performer playing the major role, explain how face, body build, voice, and gestures all contribute to characterization. What other roles has the performer played that influences your response to this film? Are previous roles similar or dissimilar? In what ways do those performances influence your response to this film?

9. View a scene that includes most of the major characters. Compare the scene with the comparable part of the script (preferably a cutting continuity script, which describes the finished film). Run the scene without sound; then run it without the picture but with the sound. Discuss what the performers contribute to the scene.

10. Examine the makeup and clothing of one of the major characters. What do they reveal about the character? Do they change significantly during the story? If so, how? What do the makeup and clothing reveal about the time and place of the story?

11. For a subtitled foreign-language film, view several scenes without reading the subtitles. What did you notice that you did not see during earlier viewings? What is the significance of those new details?

12. If you have access to a projector or video player with freeze-frame option, freeze-frame an expressive image; then discuss the importance of what was excluded from the frame and what was included. Next, explain the significance of how objects are arranged within the space of the frame.

Listening

13. Run a scene with sound only; then run the same scene with the picture only. Finally, run them with both sound and picture. *Or* run a scene with picture and sound, discuss the sound; run the scene again with the sound only and discuss.
    a. Discuss what the dialogue (what is said and how), sound effects, and silences all contribute to the impact of the scene.
    b. Try to identify as many different sounds as possible within the scene.
    c. Where are sounds faithful to their sources? Where are sounds unfaithful to sources?
    d. How dense is the sound mix: is it made up of many or few different sources blended together? Explain.
    See also question 17 in the earlier section Questions for Thought/Discussion/Writing.

14. View a scene without the sound turned up and try to guess what sounds might accompany the images. Replay the scene with the sound, then discuss. Play another scene without the image but with the sound track. Try to guess what images might accompany the sounds. Play sounds and images and discuss.

15. If you have access to a videotape or videodisc player, watch the film and make notes about where music is used (noting the counter). Next, play back scenes where music is employed and discuss what the music contributes to each scene. Play one or more scenes with the image but without the music, then with the music but without the image; then play the scene with both image and music.
    a. Are any of the melodies or tunes repeated? If so, with or without variations?
    b. Is the music predominantly melodic or rhythmical?
    c. How do instrumentation, volume, tempo, and key affect the music?
    d. What mood(s) does the music create during the opening credits?
    e. Is the music sometimes used to cover weaknesses in the film, such as inappropriate acting? If so, where?
    If you do not have access to a video machine, make an audio recording of the music in the film (clearance from the copyright holder or distributor may be necessary for films still protected by copyright laws). Replay the music and discuss what it contributes to the film.

16. For one short scene, make up a chart describing its visuals, dialogue, effects, and music (similar to Figure 5.27).

Reading

17. Read one or more published outlines or synopses of the same film.
    a. Where is the description accurate, clear, concise?
    b. Where does interpretation intrude?
    c. Where are evaluations made or implied?
    d. Discuss the usefulness and limitations of each outline or synopsis.

18. Read the fictional or dramatic source of the film, or at least a section of it. View the comparable section of the film. Reread the section of the fiction or play. Consider the following questions:

a. What are the major differences? In what sense are they "major"?

b. What are the major similarities? In what sense are they "major"?

c. What changes were made because of choices made by the filmmakers? (It was possible to film something or to film it in a certain way, but the filmmakers chose not to do so.)

d. What changes had to be made because of differences between the media of fiction/drama and film? (It seems impossible to do as well in film an aspect the other medium can do quite well.)

See also the section on Films and Fiction in Chapter 12.

19. View a scene or two of the film, and compare it or them to the similar section of the cutting continuity script, which describes the finished, released film.

a. Where is the script accurate?

b. Where is it inaccurate?

c. What kinds of inaccuracies does it contain: vagueness, wrong facts, interpretation of meanings, evaluation, other?

d. What uses does the script have? What limitations?

20. View a scene or two of the film, and compare it or them to the comparable section of the screenplay or shooting script (versions of the script used before and during the making of the film). In what ways does the finished film differ from the early versions of the script? How important are the changes? Why do you say so?

21. Read carefully one or more reviews of the initial showing of the film. Next, compare and contrast your responses with those of the reviewers. Where do dissimilarities result from different perceptions, assumptions, and emphases? Why do you say so?

22. After reading a review or analysis carefully and at least twice, consider the following questions:

a. What significant details in the film did the writer notice that you had not yet noted? Are certain details in the review or analysis unnecessary? Are some details confusing? Are any details incorrect?

b. What descriptions are especially useful, or skillfully phrased, or both?

c. Usually, certain terms are used repeatedly and/or prominently in an essay. How clear are they? Are more examples needed to help clarify the prominent terms? Are additional definitions necessary?

d. State the thesis (central and unifying idea): describe it as objectively as you can (without passing judgment on it). Is it stated directly (often at the beginning and/or conclusion)? Or is it implied and left for the reader to infer? Finally, how persuasively is the thesis argued? Why do you say so?

e. Is the argument amply illustrated with specific, accurate, and relevant examples from the film? Why do you say so?

f. Are the major evaluations or judgments supported with convincing evidence? Explain.

g. Is the essay clearly organized? What are its major parts? Why are they arranged in a particular order?

h. Does the analysis take into account distinctively cinematic aspects (cinematography, editing, sound track), or does it restrict itself to qualities fictional films share with literature (such as characterization, plot, and meanings or theme)?

i. Does the analysis make any generalized statements not subject to proof? If so, what are they? What are some of the assumptions about the nature of the film medium that the writer makes? Are the assumptions (or premises) reasonable or unreasonable? Explain.

j. What aspects of the review or analysis are now incorporated into your own analysis? Explain in detail.

k. In what important ways, if any, does this analysis of the film conflict with your own analysis? Please explain in detail.

l. What does the analysis suggest about its author's personality and background? How do you know?

m. If you have studied at least several analyses, explain some of the major different ways of analyzing the film.

n. What additional questions are appropriate for this particular review or analysis?

Writing

23. Immediately after seeing a film, rapidly jot down a list of the images and sounds that come to mind. From the list select the most significant ones; then explain *why* they are significant.

24. View a short scene with the sound turned up. As objectively as possible, describe the scene in writing: try to avoid making evaluations (which reveal your approval or disapproval) and inferences (which show you making certain assumptions that may not necessarily be correct). View the scene a second time, without the sound. Revise your description; perhaps divide it into shots. What aspects of the scene are especially difficult to capture in writing? Why?

25. Make an outline of a sequence or two of the film. Try to describe the action as accurately, objectively (without inferences and evaluations), and concisely as possible. Formulate headings for the sequence(s) and justify them.

a. What action is omitted that could have been shown?

b. What action is shown in detail?

c. What action is shown only briefly?

d. What is emphasized by the film's selection and arrangement of scenes?

Though time-consuming, making an outline has many advantages: it helps you decide what is important in each scene; it helps you see which scenes are merely transitional; it makes you more aware of how individual scenes are connected to form a longer story; it makes you more aware of when you are describing something and when inferences and evaluations slip in; it makes you aware that a film is more than its action and that much of the film experience is not easily captured in words. The exercise is both humbling and instructive.

26. Write and rewrite a one- or two-paragraph plot summary of the film's major actions in the order they occur. Review your draft; make the summary as accurate and clear as you can. (Assume that your reader has not

seen the film.) For a sample plot summary, although probably more detailed than the one you will make, consult the plot summary for *The Third Man* in Chapter 2.

27. After you see a film, write an analysis of an important scene; then view the scene again. (For a sample analysis, see the discussion in Chapter 1 of the last 50 seconds of *The Godfather, Part II*.) How accurate was your analysis? What did you notice during the second viewing that you missed during the first? Why during the first viewing did you miss what you noticed during the second?

28. For a film based on a novel or short story, choose a scene from the fiction and adapt it into a scene for a film; then compare your adaptation of the scene with that of the filmmakers. (Satyajit Ray of India practiced this exercise before he became a film director.)

29. Choose some film terms that you have heard repeatedly but that are not included in the Glossary of this book. (You may want to choose some terms you used in one of your essays or in class discussion.) Define each of the terms as accurately as you can. In your definitions, be sure to explain in what large category the term belongs, then what differentiates it from other members of the same category. For example, a movie projector is a machine (category) that makes possible the presentation of motion pictures on a reflective surface (kind of machine). Before you begin, you may want to review some of the definitions in the Glossary.

30. Make a set of study questions that apply to the film (and that are not merely adapted from the list of study questions included in the previous section). Try to formulate questions that draw attention to significant details and important issues. Also, try to phrase your questions so that they do not encourage or discourage any particular answer (that is, avoid leading questions). Try to anticipate how your readers could misunderstand your questions, and attempt to reword your questions to prevent this. Next, arrange the questions in a meaningful order. Finally, write answers to at least some of the questions.

31. Imagine that you have been asked by someone who has never seen the film what it is like. Write out an analysis of the film's major qualities. What important points would you make? Before you begin writing, try to organize your thoughts and feelings, and in your analysis try not to jump from detail to unrelated detail, or worse, from generalization to unrelated and unillustrated generalization. Be careful not to give much description or plot summary.

32. Go to the library; look up a review of the film in question; photocopy the review; and study it. Write a summary of the review; then explain in writing how accurate and persuasive the review is. Why do you say so?

After studying the material in Chapters 4 through 6, considering some study questions from the previous section, and doing a few exercises from this section, the viewer has gained greater understanding of a film and is better prepared to attempt a more detailed, written analysis of it. Part Three suggests some practical ways to do so and illustrates some results.

P·A·R·T

THREE

WRITING ANALYSES

STUDYING the basic components of stories (in the case of fictional films), sights and sounds, and viewer responses is helpful in understanding our experiences of films. So, too, are discussions, and exercises in viewing, listening, reading, and writing. To understand a film even more so and to express your responses to others with more insight, clarity, and force, the next step is to write an essay about the film and your response to it. It may be hard work, but it's an excellent way to deepen understanding and appreciation. The three chapters in Part Three are intended to help you write more effectively about films. The chapters include suggested steps that most writers have found useful as they write and rewrite, suggested topics to write about, and some sample student analyses that illustrate, I think, an interesting variety of responses to films, responses that both enlighten and stimulate.

· 7 ·

Rewriting about Films

To write is always hard, and to write well is often excruciating. It is said that poor writing reflects bad thinking or stupidity, but this relation seldom holds. Poor writing more often reflects what pathologists call a low pain threshold.

John R. Dunlap, *The American Spectator*, April 1981

Suggested Steps

When asked how they became successful, writers invariably answer that they read and write a lot. As Gene Olson puts it,

> Reading is to writing what inhaling is to exhaling. They're not the same but they are part of the same process; one must precede the other and co-exist with the other. Reading can do more than almost anything else to help your writing. *Almost* anything else. Finally, to learn to write, you will have to write and write some more, then do some more writing.[1]

[1] Gene Olson, *Sweet Agony: A Writing Manual of Sorts* (Grants Pass, Oregon: Windyridge Press, 1972), p. 109.

A few writers compose and rewrite one page or paragraph or sentence at a laborious time (they are sometimes called "bleeders"). Probably fewer still compose and revise in their heads, then later write down and revise slightly. If one of those methods works for you, fine. If not, you may try some variation of the approach offered below.

Most writers find that they need to alternate periods of work with rest. There's no time to do so the last few days before an essay is due. Begin the work at once. I've divided these periods of work and rest into sixteen steps. But not all of them are appropriate for every writer and every situation. The following suggestions are to be tried, in whole or part, in whatever order works for you.

1. Note-taking   After the first viewing of a film to be written about, it's a good idea to jot down observations and questions about it. Those notes should then be reviewed and revised. If you see the film a second time, note-taking is essential. If you have no adequate light source, then you need to take notes in the dark (assuming, of course, that you do not have access to video versions or to an editor/viewer). If you use a large tablet of unlined paper and do not write too many lines on a sheet, you will be able to take readable notes and to watch the screen at all times. Also useful are pen-and-penlight combinations that illuminate a small writing area. After the film showing, the notes should be read and corrected as soon as possible. The next day, it helps to review and correct them again.

2. Short gestation period   Often, before beginning an outline or first draft, it helps to think about the assignment and to jot down notes, even random thoughts or impressions. Many writers find that if they think about the topic, then do something else before writing, the outline and first draft are easier to write than they otherwise would be. This period should be short, however, so that procrastination does not displace gestation.

As you incubate your ideas, you may want to gather together the weapons you'll need in your upcoming war with words. Until word processors totally replace typewriters, the following supplies or equipment are useful in writing and revising.

- A plentiful supply of inexpensive paper for early drafts (backs of unwanted typed sheets are ideal)
- scissors and cellophane tape (to cut and rearrange sections)
- Correction fluid (a white liquid applied with small brush to cover over small typing errors)

- Correction tape (one-sixth-inch), to tape over errors longer than a short word
- Typewriter opaque film (used to strike over incorrect marks while the paper is still in the typewriter)
- Access to a photocopying machine

The next three steps (3–5) may be used in whatever order works best:

- Writing a thesis statement, or a few concise sentences that summarize the main and unifying idea of the essay and, ideally, suggest its organization into major parts
- Making an outline
- Writing the first draft

3/4/5. A thesis statement A thesis statement located early in an essay aids both writer and reader. The following two thesis statements, for example, help clarify the purpose and organization of essays they help introduce:

- Although the topics and meanings of *Grand Illusion* and *Open City* have much in common, the moods of the two films differ greatly.
- In *Citizen Kane,* shadows seem to be everywhere. Some are literal, some metaphoric; some ostentatious, some subtle.

Sometimes it is possible to formulate a thesis statement before making an outline or first draft. Sometimes, the thesis statement is so detailed that it's possible to write a first draft without first making an outline. Often, however, the thesis evolves as one works on an outline. Unfortunately, sometimes it does not emerge clearly until a second or later draft. For the essay to be unified and forceful, though, it must eventually step forward and be stated or clearly implied in the introduction and be explained in the essay itself.

3/4/5. An outline Outlines are useful for most writers most of the time, especially in writing long essays and books, but some successful writers never use them; instead, they think out the organization—major parts and their arrangement—or jot down some squiggles, or write draft after draft. Sometimes, a short outline leads to a more detailed one that is nearly a first draft. An outline is most useful when its parts are of similar importance and all relate to a central, unifying topic. To give a simple example, for an essay about the camera work in a film, the following outline may help in the writing of an early draft:

I. Introduction
II. Lenses
III. Angled Shots
IV. Distances from Subject
V. Conclusions

In outlines and early drafts, try leaving wide margins on all four sides of the lines and space between them. You'll have room to improve.

3/4/5. The first draft In the first draft most writers find it best to focus attention upon organization (what are the major parts of the presentation and in what order should they be arranged?) and upon examples (how can I illustrate my points to those who may not understand or agree?). Spelling, punctuation, even sentence structure may be done carelessly at this stage. In the first draft, one hews out rough paragraphs; in later drafts one fine-chisels sentences and words. For many people, fussing over a spelling or a word, or pausing to check a punctuation mark, or looking up a passage guarantees loss of momentum and even, in extreme cases, "writer's block."

6. Revising After you have finished the first draft, check to see that each paragraph has a clear topic sentence. Beginning with your *last* paragraph, study it and underline the topic sentence in pencil. If what you have is vague or misleading, rewrite it so that it accurately summarizes the main point of the paragraph. If you have no topic sentence, write one for the paragraph. What exactly is the main point of the paragraph? Next, turn your attention to the next-to-the-last paragraph. See that it has a clear and accurate topic sentence. Proceed until you have an underlined topic sentence for each paragraph. (I suggest you study your paragraphs out of order so that your mind cannot easily trick you into assuming that you have said what you meant.)

Now that you have underlined the topic sentence of each paragraph, underline the thesis statement (main idea of the essay); then read the thesis statement and each consecutive topic sentence. If any topic sentences do not support the thesis or if the draft does not proceed meaningfully from point to point, do some rewriting at once.

> Blot out, correct, insert, refine,
> Enlarge, diminish, interline;
> Be mindful, when Invention fails,
> To scratch your Head, and bite your Nails.[2]

Proofreading one's drafts is trying to see one's errors and—human nature being what it is—the process needs to be repeated frequently

---

[2] Jonathan Swift, "On Poetry: A Rhapsody" (London, 1733).

before the essay is completed. Unfortunately, many writers, especially inexperienced ones, proofread their drafts once—maybe twice if they want to be thorough!—and they seldom spot what to improve. Several strategies may help:

   a. Proofreading at different speeds (rapidly one time; slowly the next).
   b. Reading on different occasions (for instance, three times just after completing the first draft; twice more after a break; twice more the next day).
   c. Proofreading different times looking for a particular known weakness—for instance, once or twice for complicated, unclear sentences; twice more for ununified or unillustrated paragraphs. If you tend to write fragments (incomplete sentences), proofread from the end of the essay to the beginning, a sentence/fragment at a time. Chances are, you'll be more likely to spot any fragments.
   d. Proofreading one time silently, the next time aloud. For some writers reading a draft aloud—one time slowly, the next time rapidly, at all times clearly and forcefully—is the single best way to spot weaknesses.
   e. Asking someone to read the draft aloud as if delivering a speech but without interruptions or commentary, perhaps as you close your eyes and listen (not recommended for late in the evening).

7. Incubation period   After the first draft and repeated proofreadings and corrections, a point is reached where you feel as if nothing more is to be done. At that point further proofreading and correcting can be a waste of time. Worse, it can inject new errors. It can sap enthusiasm for the project. It's time to get away, to occupy the mind and senses elsewhere—a swim or some other exercise, a concert, reading, a snack, a conversation, whatever. If you have been working hard, often a day or two away from the draft is necessary.

8. Proofreading and rewriting   After a break from a project, writers often return to it only to be confounded by the words there. Did some malevolent spirit leave them on the paper during the night? Now one sees the writing in a less flattering light, and additional rewriting and correcting are possible.

9. The second draft   Once the first draft with its corrections becomes messy and cramped, it is time to recopy the essay, again leaving wide margins on all four sides and space between the lines for further revisions. After copying the essay, some writers check the accuracy of the transcription by reading the first draft aloud while someone else follows along in the new copy.

10. Repeated proofreading and correcting   Using all or some of the proofreading strategies suggested above in step 6, you can inevitably correct and improve the second draft. At this stage, it might also be well to check that the essay does not confuse a performer with a character, or a character with a person (see Figure 4.1). For instance, George C. Scott is not the character Patton in the film of that title—he enacts that character—and the character in the film is not the same as the historical General Patton.

At this stage it is also worth checking word choices, replacing general words with those describing specific aspects of the film(s). Words like "good," "great," "wonderful," "interesting," "terrible" can be replaced by specific references to the film(s). "Vera Miles was great in *The Searchers*" neither communicates much nor convinces a skeptical reader. Instead, use examples from the film: "In most of her scenes Vera Miles, as Laurie, shows concern, devotion, and spunk. In the scene where Martin is about to leave for the last time to rescue Debbie, she also shows vehement and convincing hatred, wrinkling her brow and biting off her words." Although this second description is scarcely a full account of Vera Miles's performance, it is an improvement over the original vague sentence.

Are some sentences still not right? You've thought about them. You've put them aside for a while. But do they still twist away from your meaning? Imagine that you are with a friend, and say aloud to that imaginary friend what the point of the sentence is; then write down that you just said. Chances are you'll be much closer to writing what you meant all along.

Now, too, is a good time to scrutinize the essay's first and last sentences. Often they're the hardest to get right. Are they clear, lively, interesting? Above all, are they clear? If not, consider chopping out the first sentence or more. At the end of the essay, consider dropping one or more sentences. If omitting at the beginning and ending doesn't help, bad news—you'll have to rewrite what you already have.

11. Rechecking materials   At this stage it may be wise to recheck certain materials (and rewrite portions of the draft as necessary):

  a. The assignment or goal and the thesis. Does the draft of the essay answer the assignment? Does it develop its thesis? Do *all* parts of the essay help explain it?
  b. The checklist (exercise 22, c–g, on page 111). How well does your draft stand up to the questions posed?
  c. The film or films under study and, if possible, reliable cutting continuity scripts for them.
  d. Printed sources, if any, cited in your essay. Beginning writers of film analyses, and especially relatively inexperienced writers,

should make no more than a few references to other sources. Otherwise, they may have trouble sorting out their own responses.

12. Adding notes   It's unnecessary and time-consuming to insert notes earlier in the writing process. Although footnoting is explained in many handbooks (such as those listed in footnote 3 on page 124), it is so troublesome that I've included a few reminders:

a. Use quotation marks around *exact* wordings borrowed from readings:

Janet Leigh "is an ideal choice [in *Psycho*] to play Marion Crane, whose breasts are especially desirable to a psychopath with an unnatural love for his mother. Then, too, she has aged just enough; her body has grown thinner, her face taken on a hard-edged, slightly mocking intelligence that is perfectly appropriate for a secretary who has been treated a bit roughly and has begun to long for security."[1]

At the bottom of the page or on a separate sheet at the end of the essay cite the source:

[1]James Naremore, *Filmguide to Psycho* (Bloomington: Indiana University Press, 1973), pp. 30–31.

b. Use a note number but not quotation marks for all ideas and facts borrowed and put into your own words. Sometimes the main point of an entire book is summarized and notated, as in the following example:

It can be argued that German films from *The Cabinet of Dr. Caligari* to the early 1930s and the rise of Nazism mirror the changing political moods of Germany.[2]

At the bottom of the page or end of the essay, cite the source:

[2]Siegfried Kracauer, *From Caligari to Hitler: A Psychological History of the German Film* (Princeton University Press, 1947).

c. A reference to a source cited earlier in the essay may be indicated in short form in a footnote: [3]Naremore, p. 4. Or it may appear in parentheses in the body of the essay: (Naremore, p. 4).

d. Unless directed otherwise, use the following, widely used formats (circles are used here only to emphasize certain details):

● Book: James Naremore, *Filmguide to Psycho* (Bloomington: Indiana University Press, 1973), pp. 10–13.
● Article in scholarly journal: William F. Van Wert, "Hallowing the Ordinary, Embezzling the Everyday: Werner Herzog's Documentary Practice," *Quarterly Review of Film Studies* 5, no. 2 (Spring 1980), 183.

- Article in popular magazine: Richard Schickel, "Woody Allen's Breakthrough Movie," *Time,* 25 April 1977, p. 70.
- Article in newspaper: Gene Siskel, "'The Godfather, Part II': Father Knew Best," *Chicago Tribune,* 20 December 1974, sec. 3, p. 1, cols. 1–6. (Since most back issues of newspapers are available only on microfilm, including column numbers saves your readers time.)

Documenting carefully suggests knowledge of and respect for others' work. It builds up readers' trust in the writer. Careful documentation also often helps readers find useful sources.

13. Final draft Recopy the draft, if necessary (it often is) and if time hasn't run out. If possible, type your final draft or get someone to type it for you. As Louis I. Middleman shows,

> Reading takes energy, and the less energy the reader has to use up in decoding a message, the more there is for understanding and appreciating it. Like spelling, punctuation, and usage, the physical appearance of a message should permit the reader to arrive at meaning without obstruction or distraction. *Doesn't this sentence take you longer to process and appear less authoritative than the one set in type before? And the handwriting isn't even so bad.*[3]

For the final copy, double space throughout, leave one-inch margins on all four sides of the writing, and use substantial, not onion skin, paper. Check again for the accuracy of the transcription.

14. Proofreading and making minor corrections On the final copy, check repeatedly and correct as necessary for each of the following.

a. Spelling and word choice:

- If you are a poor speller, proofread the essay backward, a word at a time, last word first.
- Look up words that cause you any doubt.

---

[3] Louis I. Middleman, *In Short: A Concise Guide to Good Writing,* p. 90. Other useful, short books on writing are Quentin L. Gehle and Duncan J. Rollo, *The Writing Process;* Gene Olson, *Sweet Agony II: A Writing Book of Sorts* (1983); Ken Macrorie, *Telling Writing,* 3d ed.; John R. Trimble, *Writing with Style: Conversations on the Art of Writing;* William Strunk, Jr., and E. B. White, *The Elements of Style,* 3d ed.; and A. M. Tibbetts, *To the Point.*

- Look up all words you use infrequently in writing.
- Make certain that you copy correctly from the dictionary.

b. Punctuation: Any of the many recent writing handbooks will help guide you. Be especially careful to check uses of the colon (:), semicolon (;), and dash (—).

c. Notation format: Not only check each note but also check to see that all similar notes, such as for books, are done in the same way. Be sure to use the same source for footnote formats throughout your essay.

d. In most publications, film titles are italicized rather than put in quotation marks. In a paper written out in longhand or typed, titles of films would be underlined.

e. When discussing action, use the present tense; for instance, "Michael Corleone then goes to the door . . ." (not "went").

15. Incubation period   Now you think you're finished; you hope you are—but experience tells you that you are not. This is the time to spend a day or two away from the final draft.

16. Final proofreading and correcting of minor errors   using techniques suggested above. To insert added or missing words, draw a caret (˄) *below* the line to show where the addition belongs, and write the correction above the line. Most teachers and publishers do not mind a few minor corrections on the final draft, particularly if neatly made. Then, also, to recopy an entire page to try to eliminate a few minor errors often injects new, more distracting errors.

Few writers do all of these sixteen steps and in the above order, nor do writers generally follow the same steps for every essay. People are too various and writing is too complicated for that to happen. Nonetheless, many writers use at least some of the above steps, and effective writing demands more time, patience, and care—a higher "pain threshold"—than is often recognized or expended.

Processing Words

All of the above sixteen strategies—gathering material, organizing it, writing, revising, incubating, revising further, etc.—apply to working with a word processor, a kind of computer programmed to aid in writing, revising, and printing. A word processor makes reluctant writers less reluctant because it banishes a lot of the messiness and interruptions of writing any other way. No more hitting the carriage return at the end of each line. No more changing sheets of paper after every 250 words or so. No more correcting errors with tapes and fluids, scissors and cellophane tape. With word processors you can add material, delete it, rearrange individual words or large blocks of words, and always have legible copy. And you'll make fewer trips to the not-always-reliable photocopying machines. A word processor makes proceeding through the steps of writing and rewriting faster, more efficient, less grueling. As two experienced word-processing writers have expressed it,

> [F]or the vast majority of working writers, these tools offer ease, productivity, and new insights into creating worlds with words that far outweigh the nuisance of learning a slightly different way to work.
>
> The main lesson we've learned as word processing writers is that these machines do exactly what we ask of them. When we give them an instruction, they carry it out instantly and obediently. (This total responsiveness is just what many people find intimidating at first.) When they do foul up, it's usually because we've given them the wrong message—not because of some mysterious event or electronic foible. Word processors are as reliable as television sets, use less electricity than many light bulbs, and don't smoke, drink, or sass back.
>
> For us, the rewards have indeed been worth the effort of applying this new technology. We've doubled or tripled our writing production; been able to design and dress up our manuscripts; stayed away from pastepots and copying machines; and—most exciting—have become better writers because we can easily and painlessly revise and reprint until we're truly satisfied with our work.[4]

Topics

Many kinds of topics are possible, but for beginning film students the best topics are usually those on one aspect or those that compare and contrast a major aspect of two or three films. As in all writing, the best topic is usually one you are very interested in.

One Aspect

No short essay (500–2,000 words or 2–8 double-spaced typed pages) can fully analyze a feature film. The experience of seeing and hearing a feature is too complex to capture in less than a book, as studies devoted to describing, interpreting, and evaluating a film or a few films, such as Robin Wood's book *The Apu Trilogy,* demonstrate. A

[4] Andrew Fluegelman and Jeremy Joan Hewes, *Writing in the Computer Age: Word Processing Skills and Style for Every Writer* (New York: Anchor Press, Doubleday, 1983). This book explains the options available on word processors and gives some sensible strategies for writers. Two other books on the topic I have found useful are Laurence Press, *Low-Cost Word Processing* (Reading, Mass.: Addison-Wesley, 1983) and Dan Poynter, *Word Processors and Information Processing: A Basic Manual on What They Are and How to Buy* (Englewood Cliffs, N. J.: Prentice-Hall, 1982).

short essay is wisely restricted to one aspect, often of a single film, particularly if you have little experience in writing about films. Possible aspects of one film to examine and write about include photography, composition, editing, sound, script, costumes, sets, structure, characterization, mood, and meanings or theme. It's extremely difficult to discuss acting or directing on the basis of one film, and without some training in music, it's hard to write very convincingly about it. Sample topics include "In and Out of the Dark: Lighting in *Citizen Kane*," "Contributions of the Music in *Psycho*," "Different Uses of Sound in *Mr. Hulot's Holiday*," "Putting It All Together: Editing in *The Third Man*," "Home and Wilderness in *The Searchers*," "Man and Woman in *Knife in the Water*," and "Father and Son in *The Godfather, Part II*." By restricting yourself to one aspect of one film, stating so clearly and early in the essay, and by explaining many examples from the film, you help both yourself and your readers.

Comparison and Contrast

You may study films in pairs or groups, or you may discuss two aspects of the same film, comparing and contrasting to learn what is shared and what is distinctive to each. Two or more films could be considered under one of the following topics:

technique
Camera work (distances, angles, and lenses)
Lighting
Color
Composition
Acting (same performer in two or more films)
Editing
Sound
Music (Usually, only someone with training in music should
    attempt this subject.)

subject
Insight into culture(s)
Character studies
Crime and punishment
Film and ideology (political outlook)
Men in action
Images of women
Men and women together

other topics
Nontraditional film forms
Genres (such as western, musical, horror)
Satire of human behavior

Portraits to admire
Films written by the same person
Films directed by the same person

The list of topics could easily be longer.

In comparing and contrasting two or more films, it helps readers if you use the same pattern throughout the essay. For example, for an essay comparing and contrasting the editing of *Potemkin* and *Mother,* the following organization would help readers follow the presentation:

I. Introduction, concluding with a thesis statement that the essay will discuss the length of shots, their arrangement, and the transitions between shots in *Potemkin* and *Mother*
II. Length of shots in *Potemkin*
III. Length of shots in *Mother*
IV. Arrangement of shots in *Potemkin*
V. Arrangement of shots in *Mother*
VI. Transitions between shots in *Potemkin*
VII. Transitions in *Mother*
VIII. Conclusions

After stating the order of discussion in the thesis, it is important to follow it: in the example above, for instance, discussing transitions (VI and VII) before length of shots (II and III) will invite confusion. Discussing the lengths, arrangements, and transitions in *Potemkin* and *then* the same aspects in *Mother* is also risky, since essays so organized tend to divide into an essay on one film, then another essay on the second film, without making quite clear what similarities and differences the writer perceives.

Throughout the essay be sure to point out similarities and differences. Do not ask your readers to guess what you think are the similarities and differences. Frequently use transitional phrases (such as "Unlike X, Y is . . ." *or* "Both X and Y have . . . in common").

Sample comparison and contrast student essays—on two films and on two aspects of the same film—are reprinted in Chapter 9.

Writer and Reader: Four Considerations

Probably because most people spend so much more time in life talking and listening than writing and reading, the relationship of writer to reader is often misunderstood. It is wise to bear in mind the following four considerations.

1. Writing is only words on paper, and it lacks the tone of voice, gestures, and eye contact of spoken language. If communication between writer and reader breaks down, no warning signs appear, no frowns, no dazed looks.

2. Compared with speech, writing demands greater planning and more careful execution, and readers need more reminders about the material that is being covered and that will be covered. Thus, a thesis, careful organization, and transitions are crucial. So, too, are conciseness, specificity, and illustrations. The student essays I've read with too many examples could be counted on one hand. Consider as one model the following paragraph:

> What movies do is make perception easier. The darkened theater cuts out the claims of peripheral vision. The large images on the screen open up the perceived world for analysis . . . and allow [viewers] to see details simply not available in ordinary experience. Because film makers can further assist perception by careful lighting, lens choice, and camera placement, and can guide expectations and discriminations in a thousand more subtle ways, they can radically enhance the efficiency of seeing. For example, Murnau, in *The Last Laugh,* brings us in close to his central figure, giving us details of skin texture and posture well beyond what we could see in everyday life. . . . Murnau brings the camera in low, letting us see the man's face and eyes; he lights the face to emphasize the wrinkles and destitute expression; he highlights posture so that the viewer gets the full message of dejection and fatigue projected in the image. Virtually every device in the repertory of cinematography is similarly designed to enhance perception, to help us see. And, in a sense, the film maker can make the viewer more intelligent perceptually, at least while the film is running. Movies use perception in ways that make being "perceptive" remarkably easy. That is one reason why they are so involving.[5]

3. Writers need to ask themselves continually what their readers are likely to know and then to plan accordingly. Thus, if the reader is the teacher in a course that has just viewed a film, it is unwise—indeed uninteresting for the reader—to recount much of the film's plot (description of major characters and actions). To take another example, if an essay is written for a magazine read by the general student population, all film terms need to be made clear by context or defined.

4. Writers do well to keep inconveniences for readers to a minimum. Although the early drafts of an essay are for the writer's eyes, the final draft is for others and should be as free as possible from distracting errors, such as misspellings, inappropriate words, mispunctuations, and ungrammatical sentences. Consider the following paragraph:

> In The seven Samurai, Kikuchio is the best. He reconcils village and samurai after their arrival. He is the one who see close, when he recount's the plight of farmers. He is the one who is allowed to dominate a scene for so long, when he is drunk and trying to catch Katsushiro.

[5] Charles Eidsvik, *Cineliteracy: Film among the Arts* (New York: Random House, 1978), pp. 21 and 23.

He enjoys women and children. He has a sense of humour. He is a feirce, untiring and brave fighter. He morns the loss of others, sitting on the grave. Sprawled out on the bridge, mud washing off buttocks in the rain, we admire him. He is very unique; a triangle on a banner of circles, a jazz tune set against the relentless bandit drums. One of the great creations of cinema.

Although this paragraph contains some interesting observations and helpful detail—in fact, it is the kernel of an excellent essay about the character of Kikuchio—it makes for slow, often annoying reading. Its unillustrated generalizations, spelling or typing errors, punctuation, sentence structure, wordiness, and word choices would be acceptable in an early draft, but in a final draft they expose a writer who did not put enough time and effort into minimizing distractions for readers.

Benefits to Writer

Perhaps the most important benefit of careful writing is that it always leads writers to greater understanding of their topic: it helps them to sort out ideas and impressions, organize them, and test them. What on first response seems like a reasonable observation about a film often gets retracted or qualified during the examination that writing brings to it.

Careful writing brings a satisfaction of more exact and more complete communication with others than is possible with speech.

Compared with speech, writing has greater permanence and a wider audience: it can have an effect longer and on more people than discussions, which usually dissipate with the wind. The best writers have the satisfaction of knowing that people of distant times and places may learn from and enjoy their writing. What Carl Sagan said about ancient books applies as well to all writings that are preserved and read:

> [O]ne glance at . . . [a book] and you're inside the mind of another person, maybe somebody dead for thousands of years. Across the millennia an author is speaking clearly and silently inside your head, directly to you. Writing is perhaps the greatest of human inventions, binding together people who never knew each other, citizens of distant epochs. Books break the shackles of time. . . . If information were passed on merely by word of mouth, how little we should know of our own past. How slow would be our progress. Everything would depend on what we had been told, on how accurate the account. Ancient learning might be revered, but in successive retellings it would become muddled and then lost. Books permit us to voyage through time, to tap the wisdom of our ancestors.[6]

[6] Carl Sagan, "The Persistence of Memory," Program Eleven, *Cosmos* (PBS series). The wording is from the television program, not the book based upon the series.

· 8 ·

Student Analyses:
One Aspect

Deborah Helfman Kaufman: *Clothing in* Little Caesar
Leslie Ellen Olson: *Visual Presentation of Character in* Grand
   Illusion
Don Reed: *The Significance of "Rosebud" in* Citizen Kane
S. Scott Smith: *Editing to Create Suspense in* Jaws
Jan E. Kitchen: *Limitations of Cutting Continuity Scripts*

[W]hat marks a critic is not what he rejects so much as what he applauds—
and why.   Roy Huss and Norman Silverstein, *The Film Experience:*
Elements of Motion Picture Art

AFTER examining some of the complexites of the film experience,
the best way to deepen your understanding and communicate your
responses with precision is to write an analysis. In this and the following chapter are reprinted some student analyses. All but one were
written by my former film students. The exception is Hollis Chacona,
who was a graduate student at the Universty of Texas when she wrote
the essay on *The Seven Samurai* in Chapter 9. I include her essay to
demonstrate how an advanced student can blend readings of history
and culture with close viewings and analysis in an illuminating way.
In all the essays the observations and examples are the students' own.
I have revised the essays only slightly. I am grateful to these students
for allowing me to edit and publish their work so that other students
may gain a better understanding of film analysis. I hope you enjoy
their essays and find them enlightening. I do.

Clothing in *Little Caesar*

Deborah Helfman Kaufman

THROUGHOUT *Little Caesar* clothes indicate Rico's self-image and status and in many scenes foreshadow either his progress in obtaining power or his decline—which eventually comes as a result of his tremendous vanity.

In the opening scene of the movie Rico is wearing ordinary, middle-class clothes and a hat which covers part of his face, showing him to be a common bandit, of no unusual wealth or status, and a man who feels the need to hide, if only behind a hat brim. The first conversation of the film is about clothes, immediately demonstrating the differing ambitions and attitudes of Rico and Joe. Joe would like nice clothes simply for their own sake, for the glamour. Rico is not interested in clothes, money, or other luxuries, but rather in power. He later shows, though, the enjoyment he gets from clothes, not in themselves, but as a symbol of his status, as a sign of the power he has over other men.

After reading an article in the newspaper about a banquet held in Pete Montana's honor, Rico becomes determined to ascend the hierarchy himself, to "be someone." His first step up occurs when he meets Vitorri and easily assumes both his position and his pinstripe suit. Rico subtly takes on the garb of each new adversary just prior to conquering that person's territory. He proceeds to take on the stick pin of Little Arnie and later the suit and ring of Pete Montana. He reaches his original goal when a banquet is held in his honor, similar to the one held for Montana which first inspired Rico. The only difference is that Pete Montana had no photos of himself in the paper, but because of Rico's vanity, he allows the photos to be taken. He further demonstrates his pride by buying ten copies of the paper containing this picture. At this point in the film Rico starts wearing a derby hat. It is different from his former hat in that it shows off, rather than conceals, his face. He is proud of himself, his advancement in status, his appearance, and he no longer feels he has any need to hide his position like a common thief. As he saunters down the street, he is feeling at his peak, newspapers in hand, coat open, fancy suit, gold watch, and bowler—all the trappings of the status he had obtained displayed upon his body.

In previous incidents Rico readily took on the clothes of each new character, between the scenes, and without any mention of the changes. But the transition is obvious when Rico self-consciously tries on the "monkey suit" that Big Boy wears in a later scene, to see how it feels. Rico accepted the other clothes easily and without forethought, but this suit is first tested and self-consciously inspected by him. His vanity is shown as a weakness by his ludicrous posing in front of the mirror.

When Rico appears at Big Boy's house, he immediately seems out of his element. He is awkward and subservient, completely different from the tough and confident behavior he displayed in earlier scenes. He drops cigar ashes on the floor, sits self-consciously in the chair, and stares boyishly at all the luxury around him. He and Big Boy are wearing identical suits, down to the bow ties around their throats, but Big Boy's outfit seems to suit him, whereas Rico's doesn't quite seem comfortable, thus foreshadowing the fact that Rico could never take over Big Boy's position as he took the others, despite his later boasts. It is now seen that Rico doesn't have the qualities to fit in at Big Boy's level.

In the last scene Rico has on the clothes of a bum and makes literal the figurative statement in the newspaper that "He rose from the gutter and returned to it." His hat is similar to the hat he wore in the first scene, again concealing his face. He cannot tolerate the insinuations in the paper about his lack of strength and power, and his pride prompts him to foolishly reveal himself to the police. Rico falls from power not because of Joe's betrayal of him, but because of his own doing, because of his vanity.

Visual Presentation of Character
in *Grand Illusion*

Leslie Ellen Olson

A fascinating part of *Grand Illusion* is the visual presentation of the characters. The film explores the attitudes of different men from different classes toward each other and toward life in general. All four of the main characters merit discussion—the career officers who have so much in common, de Boeldieu and Rauffenstein, and the noncareer officers, Marechal and Rosenthal. The career officers are formal, emotionally detached, and devoted to duty; the noncareer officers are informal, demonstrative, and casual in the performance of duty. By contrasting Boeldieu and Marechal, one can demonstrate Renoir's techniques of visual presentation of characters.

In the opening scene in the officer's mess, Marechal's attitude is presented visually. Renoir shows him first with his hat pushed jauntily back on his head, his jacket unbuttoned, and his scarf loose; he is listening to music and probably thinking about a woman. Within a few more shots Renoir introduces Captain de Boeldieu. He arrives with an official air and haughty manner; he is meticulously dressed according to regulation and is shown adjusting his monocle; his mind is on his job—checking the accuracy of some aerial photographs. He scoffs at Marechal's casual attitude toward the photographic assignment. Their difference in outlook on life is apparent immediately.

In scene after scene the film shows the differences between these two characters. Boeldieu is shown again and again off in his own section of the frame, sometimes in his own tidy corner of the room playing patience (a form of solitaire). In a dining scene in the prison camp he is jovially slapped on the back by another man; Boeldieu puts on his monocle and looks at him with near contempt. This demonstrates how he separates himself from other people. Marechal, on the other hand, is shown in the midst of fellow prisoners smoking and chatting with them. In one scene another prisoner washes Marechal's feet (Marechal had been wounded). This simple, caring act demonstrates Marechal's accessibility and his acceptance of his fellow men.

The separateness of Boeldieu and Marechal is demonstrated definitively in a scene during roll call in the prison yard. A German guard is in the foreground, seen slightly out of focus, but cutting the frame in two distinct parts. Boeldieu is on the left, impeccable in dress and demeanor, and Marechal is on the right, slouching, jacket over shoulders with hat again pushed back on his head. There is no pertinent dialogue with this shot. What Renoir wants to say about these men he says visually.

The script supports this strong visual characterization. For example: in another scene a visibly frustrated Marechal is talking about wanting out of prison to fight for himself and his country. His emotions are running high. Boeldieu, in typically cool aristocratic fashion, says that the emotional question of fighting does not apply to him, that just as a tennis court is for playing tennis on, a prison camp is for escaping from.

True to his noble blood and sense of duty, Boeldieu offers to be the distraction so that Marechal and Rosenthal can escape when the time is right. He is not doing it as a personal favor for Marechal and cuts Marechal off when he tries to express his thanks (thus cutting off any emotional exchange). Renoir conveys the impression that Boeldieu is merely acknowledging "noblesse oblige."

Boeldieu shakes Marechal's hand in a gentleman's farewell then faces the camera, straightens his white gloves (another sign of his formality), and with great dignity prepares to go act as a decoy. Marechal and Rosenthal escape and Boeldieu is shot; true to his precise nature, he looks at his watch before he falls to assure himself that he has done his duty—that he has given his men time to escape.

Through mostly medium shots which are not distracting, Renoir allows the viewer to scrutinize the characters. Some of his shots are up to a minute long, and the film uses no extreme angles and few close-ups. Still the film manages to present the characters with great visual impact because of the way they are arranged within the frame. Boeldieu and Marechal are memorable largely because of the effective way they are presented visually.

The Significance of "Rosebud" in *Citizen Kane*

Don Reed

A delicate crystal globe rests in the massive hand of Charles Foster Kane. Inside the globe a tiny house is lost in an eternal blizzard. We see Kane's lips move. We hear him utter a single word: "Rosebud." The sphere slips from his grasp and falls to the floor. As it shatters, Charles Foster Kane—millionaire, newspaperman, builder of castles—dies, and the secret of Rosebud dies with him.

Who or what was Rosebud? What could be so important that it would occupy the final thoughts of one of the world's most important and powerful men? These are central questions in *Citizen Kane*. The audience learns, in the final scenes, that Rosebud was the name of the sled Kane played with as a boy in Colorado. However, by accident or design, the significance of Rosebud was never directly explained in the film.

We can find many possible explanations for the significance of Rosebud. The simplest explanation would attribute it to the random mutterings of a dying mind. Rosebud may also represent the simplicity of Kane's childhood or his lost childhood innocence. However, because of the events occurring in Kane's life at the three times Rosebud appears or is mentioned, I think that the best explanation is that Rosebud represents Kane's helplessness at the hands of fate when he is unable to control the most significant losses in his life: his removal from his family, his wife Susan's departure, and his own death.

The audience sees the sled, Rosebud, for the first time when young Kane is faced with the prospect of being taken from his home and family. He uses the sled as a weapon in an attempt to dissuade Mr. Thatcher, the banker, from taking him away. However, Kane's mother, who has a power far stronger than Kane's boyhood fury, has already made the decision, and Kane is helpless to prevent the events that will lead him to so much sorrow.

The other times Rosebud is mentioned, the sled is not actually present. At these times the spirit of Rosebud, the sense of irretrievable loss at the hands of fate, is represented by the glass paperweight. The tiny house surrounded by artificial snow is like the boarding house scene re-created in miniature.

The second time we encounter "Rosebud" is when Kane's selfishness has finally driven his second wife, Susan, away. Kane attacks her room in a manner similar to his attack upon Thatcher. When he encounters the paperweight, his violence stops and his anger turns into resignation. The scene from his childhood has apparently reminded him of the earlier instance, and he may realize that he is just as powerless to stop Susan from leaving as he was in stopping his mother from sending him away.

With his dying breath Kane once more speaks the word "Rosebud." He is faced, for the final time, with a situation over which his money and influence give him no control. This time, however, Kane does not fight. Perhaps he now sees the futility of fighting. More likely, he has simply lost the strength and will to fight.

Rosebud appears once more, in the final scene of the film. Overlooked by the newsmen, the sled is thrown into an incinerator by a workman simply doing his job. The sight of the small wooden sled burning creates, in my opinion, the most powerful image of the entire film. This scene says to me that no man, no matter how rich or powerful, can avoid his fate. And that, I think, is why Rosebud touches us so deeply.

Editing to Create Suspense in *Jaws*

S. Scott Smith

In 1975, Universal Pictures released one of the top moneymaking films of all time—*Jaws*. Since that time the movie has brought menace and terror to millions of viewers. A key reason for the popularity of *Jaws* is the film's suspense, created in part by the masterful editing skills of Verna Fields. One important section of the film—the scene on the beach, revolving around the shark attacking Alex Kintner—contains numerous illustrations of how the editing of a film can be just as important as directing in creating suspense. In the following paragraphs I will discuss in particular the manipulation of the length of shots and the use of reaction shots to convey various degrees of suspense and terror.

A popular editing technique is the manipulation of the length of shots in a particular scene. The scene of the shark attack upon Alex Kintner opens with the longest shot of the entire scene, over thirty seconds (see the description of shot number 1 in Table 8.1). It is this exceptionally long shot that establishes a base mood of calm and stability on which the editor builds the suspense and terror, layer by layer. As the scene progresses toward the inevitable shark attack, the length of shots decreases from an average of two or three seconds to as little as one thirtieth of a second (in a video version, less than one twenty-fourth of a second of film) almost prior to the actual attack. To be exact, the first nineteen shots, excluding the first shot, run an average of two or three seconds, up until the first "false alarm" that Brody observes. As Brody recovers from his scare and relaxes back into his beach chair, the editor once again extends the shot to twice as long as the previous eighteen to ease the audience back into its own sense of security (shots 15–20). After this, the shots resume their two- or three-second average until once again coming to a lengthy shot of sixteen seconds (shot 22). The shot following this explains the extra length in that we are shown Alex Kintner floating on his raft, from exactly the same angle as we will later see him attacked. By preceding this shot with an unusually long one, the editor has once again established a false sense of security in the viewer and related that security to Alex on the raft; Alex is now much lower on the viewer's list of probable victims. After an old man chides Brody about his fear of water, we see a one-and-a-half-second shot of Brody's two boys running along the beach, followed by the last lengthy shot before the shark attack (shots 29–36). In this shot several stratagems are used to ease the viewer's tension before assaulting him with the actual attack: a romantic song is heard on the sound track, Ellen massages Brody's neck, and the shot extends to a relatively leisurely eight seconds. Immediately after this shot is an establishing shot of a group of swimmers in the ocean, followed by a close-up of an individual swimmer that runs one thirtieth of a second (one frame)—the shortest shot possible in any film (shots 37 and 38). This in turn is succeeded by five rapid shots of other swimmers splashing in the water, thus creating a frantic feeling in the viewer (shots 39–43). After two shots of a boy calling for his dog, which is nowhere to be seen, and one of a stick floating in the water, the viewer is at last certain of impending violence. And finally, after toying with the viewer's emotions for over two and a half minutes, the attack is suggested in a long shot duplicating the earlier one of Alex on his raft (shots 28 and 49).

Another technique used in this scene to create suspense is the inclusion of shots of the actors' reactions to certain events. The primary character used in these shots is Brody. In fact, before the actual shark attack there are at least two distinct instances when Brody reacts to false alarms, thus exciting the viewer to the possibility of violence. One of the false alarms occurs while Brody is peeking at the ocean over a friend's shoulder. A scream is heard from the beach; nothing out of the ordinary in a crowd of swimmers, but the moment is intensified as Brody jumps from his chair and stares out at the ocean. The origin of the scream, a couple playing in the water, is not shown until after Brody reacts, thereby allowing the audience to imagine all sorts of terror just by looking at the expression on Brody's face. When the actual attack occurs, one of the most powerful reaction shots in contemporary American cinema is used. Much of the impact was achieved by the skills of the director: the shot uses a camera that tracks backward while zooming in, thus creating the illusion of pulling Brody out of the background. However, it was the skills of the editor that structured the entire scene in such a way as to make this reaction shot have the power it did. In this way the two false alarms that Brody experiences (see shots 17–20 and 22–25) serve only to heighten the terror when he finally does view the real shark attack.

It is clear from just these two aspects that editing plays an important role in the making of a motion picture. And it can be used to intensify not only feelings of terror, but also many other feelings and moods. It has been said that the editor can make or break a film, and in studying the editing in just this three-and-a-half-minute scene of *Jaws,* it is easy to understand why.

Table 8.1
Shot-by-Shot Outline of Beach Scene
based upon a laser videodisc version of the film
(30 frames per second)

Shot Number	Description	Frames/Seconds
1.	Obese swimmer enters water. Alex Kintner comes up beach to mother, passes Brody. Close-up of Brody.	969/32.3
2.	Person floating in ocean. Boy running along beach and throwing stick.	73/2.4
3.	Closer shot of boy throwing stick, front view.	27/.9
4.	Couple playing in water. Dog swimming out into water.	85/2.8
5.	Mrs. Kintner reading. Alex runs past.	44/1.5
6.	Alex paddling raft away from shore.	103/3.4

Shot Number	Description	Frames/Seconds
7.	Dog swimming with stick in its mouth. Man swims by and grabs at the dog.	136/4.5
8.	Obese woman in ocean.	88/2.9
9.	Alex floating on raft.	65/2.2
10.	Boy grabbing stick from dog on beach.	39/1.3
11.	Close-up of dog running alongside boy.	99/3.3
12.	Brody watching beach, medium shot. (wipe)*	39/1.3
13.	Brody watching beach, medium close-up shot. (wipe)	46/1.5
14.	Close-up of Brody watching beach.	56/1.9
15.	Obese woman floating in ocean. (wipe)	90/3
16.	Brody watching beach, medium shot. (wipe)	78/2.6
17.	Closer shot of obese woman floating in ocean. Dark object swimming toward her. (wipe)	93/3.1
18.	Brody watching beach, looks up, concerned.	51/1.7
19.	Obese woman in ocean. Dark object emerges from water—old man's bathing cap. (wipe)	71/2.4
20.	Closer shot of Brody relaxing.	166/5.5
21.	Man walking toward Brody; he kneels and talks to him.	117/3.9
22.	Close-up of Brody looking over man's shoulder.	65/2.2
23.	Brody's p.o.v. (point of view) of ocean.	97/3.2
24.	Scream. Brody jumps up, looking at ocean.	18/.6
25.	Couple in water—playing.	68/2.3
26.	Man still talking with Brody.	35/1.2
27.	Side view of Brody sitting down; Ellen in background. Ellen moves next to Brody.	488/16.3
28.	Long shot of Alex on raft; swimmers in the foreground.	146/4.9
29.	Old man sitting down by Brody and drying off.	39/1.3
30.	Brody looking around old man to ocean.	44/1.5
31.	Side view of old man drying off.	32/1.1
32.	Closer shot of old man talking to Brody.	142/4.7
33.	Brody reacting to old man.	51/1.7
34.	Old man getting up and leaving.	44/1.5
35.	Michael and Sean, Brody's sons, running on beach.	46/1.5
36.	Ellen moving up behind Brody and rubbing his neck and back.	239/8
37.	Long shot of swimmers in ocean.	89/3
38.	Close-up of swimmer—lots of water spray.	1/.03
39.	Close-up of another swimmer.	11/.4
40.	Close-up of another swimmer—less spray.	13/.4
41.	Close-up of another swimmer.	10/.3
42.	Close-up of another swimmer.	13/.4

*I use " wipe" to refer to the technique of having a person walk in front of the camera and momentarily blot out the image; after that person has passed, the next shot begins.

Shot Number	Description	Frames/Seconds
43.	Close shot of two swimmers playing.	16/.5
44.	Sean on beach building sand castle.	70/2.3
45.	Long shot of boy calling for dog.	87/2.9
46.	Closer shot of boy calling for dog.	115/3.8
47.	Close-up of stick floating in water.	87/2.9
48.	Underwater point-of-view shot of swimmers—tracking to an extreme close-up of legs kicking.	462/15.4
49.	Long shot of shark attacking Alex.	52/1.7
50.	Man pointing to shark—Mrs. Kintner in the near background.	48/1.6
51.	Another long shot of shark attacking Alex.	50/1.7
52.	Underwater shot of Alex being pulled under. Blood mixing in with air bubbles.	91/3
53.	Brody sees attack—track back/zoom in.	60/2
54.	Group of swimmers reacting to attack by panicking.	81/2.7
55.	Man and woman pointing at ocean. Brody running past; swimmers on beach in panic.	125/4.2
56.	Mrs. Kintner getting up amid commotion.	35/1.2
57.	Brody running back and forth through crowd.	60/2
58.	Another angle of Brody in the crowd.	61/2
59.	Swimmer in water, pulling out children.	44/1.5
60.	Ellen grabbing Michael out of water.	36/1.2
61.	Close-up of Sean on beach.	59/2
62.	Swimmers running out of the water.	55/1.8
63.	Brody on beach with crowd.	111/3.7
64.	Closer shot of frantic swimmers on beach. Mrs. Kintner walking from the crowd to the shoreline and calling "Alex."	326/10.9
65.	Torn and bloody raft floating up out of ocean.	200/6.7

Limitations of
Cutting Continuity Scripts

Jan E. Kitchen

In considering the advantages and disadvantages of cutting continuity scripts, which describe the finished film, two disadvantages keep surfacing: (1) film experiences are subjective and therefore cannot be entirely captured by the script, and (2) many aspects of the film are portrayed through techniques peculiar to film, and these techniques cannot be demonstrated by the script. I am aware that cutting continuity scripts have advantages: they can be a useful resource for studying films, but I will limit my discussion to the disadvantages of these scripts. The disadvantages of a cutting continuity script will be illustrated by reference to the movie *Blow-Up* (directed by Michelangelo Antonioni).

As film experiences are subjective in nature, when we read a script of a film, we are reading *one* subjective interpretation of a film which was intended to be interpreted by the viewers. If the person reading the cutting continuity script has not seen the movie, he will not be able to discern which parts of the script are the writer's interpretation and which parts are objective; indeed, the writer himself may not be aware of this in all cases. For example, in the Simon and Schuster script for *Blow-Up* the description of the relationships of some of the characters in the film is a subjective interpretation by the script writer. The script refers to Bill and Thomas as friends, and to Patricia, the woman seen with Bill, as Bill's wife. In the movie, it is never made clear exactly what the relationship is between either Bill and Thomas, or between Bill and Patricia. The script has blurred the point made in the film that relationships are ambiguous. If one had merely read the script and not seen the film, the point the film makes about the ambiguity of relationships would have been missed entirely.

In the scene where Thomas walks in on Bill and Patricia making love, we have another example of the subjectiveness of the film script. The script says that Patricia motions for Thomas to stay and watch and that she watches Thomas until she reaches orgasm. In the movie it is not at all clear that this is what is taking place. This particular scene has been interpreted in a number of ways: Patricia is motioning for Thomas not to bother them; Patricia is acknowledging him, but letting him know they were busy and not to be bothered; and Patricia is simply waving hello. Given the ambiguities apparent in the different interpretations of this scene, it must be viewed by the individual so that he can form his own interpretation(s).

The second disadvantage in cutting continuity scripts—that aspects of the film are portrayed through techniques peculiar to film and thus are only subjectively attainable—means, of course, that these aspects cannot be captured in the script (if they are captured in the script, we get back to the first problem: that of having them interpreted by someone else). An example from *Blow-Up* of an ambiguity not captured by the script is the confusion about Thomas's photography studio and his apartment. In viewing the film, it is never clear where Thomas lives, where he works, or what, if any, is the relationship between the two places. This confusion has an impact on the movie as a whole: it is one more ambiguity in a film full of ambiguities. To give a physical description of Thomas's studio (and apartment?) does not convey the confused feeling we get when viewing the film. In reading the script, therefore, this ambiguity is missed.

By reading the script and not viewing the film we would miss much of its force. For example, we would miss experiencing such contrasts as that of Thomas's behavior when he is taking pictures and his behavior when he is not taking pictures. It is essential to realize that Thomas is emotional when he is taking pictures and unemotional when he is not relating to the world through his camera.

A great deal of what is expressed in a movie is expressed through nonverbal techniques: the speed of the action, the lighting, the sound, the camera angles, and the arrangements of shots and scenes. Obviously these techniques have visual impact and thus cannot be entirely captured on the printed page. By not viewing the film, that is, by not experiencing these techniques peculiar to film, we would miss much of its impact and, thus, much of the message of the film itself.

Although scripts can be useful, we need always to be aware of their limitations: scripts cannot capture the essence of film.

· 9 ·

Student Analyses:
Comparison and Contrast

Edward De Vries: Invasion of the Body Snatchers (1956) *and* Seconds
Russell L. Bianchi: Fat City *and* Blue Collar
George V. Vinson: It Happened One Night *and* Carnal Knowledge
Susan Watkins: *Brigid in the Book and 1941 Film Version of* The Maltese Falcon
Hollis Chacona: *The Samurai and Villagers in* The Seven Samurai

COMPARISON and contrast essays point out similarities and differences between two objects or experiences. In doing so, they often make readers aware of qualities in each entity that close but separate study of each might not reveal. The comparison and contrast approach to studying film often yields surprising, interesting insights.

The only problem is that comparison and contrast essays require of their writers special attention to organization and a keen awareness of what their readers are likely to understand. Too often, attempts at comparison and contrast essays result in two separate essays that make the reader guess at the similarities and differences the writer had in mind. Two ways to avoid these pitfalls are to discuss a similarity or difference within the same paragraph or in consecutive paragraphs—not in separate sections of the essay—and to use a generous supply of transitions, such as "similarly," "likewise," "on the other hand," "by way of contrast." The following five essays make clear to the reader some major similarities and differences.

Invasion of the
Body Snatchers (1956)
and *Seconds*

Edward De Vries

---

*I*NVASION *of the Body Snatchers* (1956) and *Seconds* can both be considered science fiction movies. Though *Invasion* takes place years ago, it is science fiction because it concerns an "invasion" of a small town by other-worldly organisms. On the other hand, *Seconds* is not other-worldly at all, for it takes place entirely on Earth with no extraterrestrial intervention. But what makes this film science fiction is its futuristic stance: though the time is depicted as present day, there is to date—as far as we can know—no such organization which can transform a Mr. Hamilton into a Mr. Wilson. In contrast to *Invasion*'s somewhat other-worldly problems, then, *Seconds* is science fiction because of its futuristic—if plausible—course of events.

Both films, to a certain extent, take a look at relationships. In *Invasion* it is the romance between the doctor and Becky. In the film's short time span they grow intimate and become the final two holdouts for humanity in the town. But near the end Becky, too, falls to an alien organism and becomes a virtual zombie. When Miles realizes this, he runs away in fear. This is not the first time a relationship has ended for either, though, for the film makes it clear that both have been divorced. *Seconds* presents an equally dismal view of the inevitable end of relationships between men and women. Hamilton and his wife have become distant from each other over the years; as his wife later states, they lived in a "sexless truce." There is nothing to keep him from apparently "dying" and becoming the new Tony Wilson. As a new man, love blossoms anew with a young and carefree Nora, but even this is doomed to failure, for Nora is a company employee. Thus they split, crushing Wilson, eventually contributing to his failure as a "reborn" and leading to his death.

The two movies differ greatly in their meanings. Each, though, has something important to say. *Invasion*'s basic meaning is that mankind had better beware lest it lose all capacity for love, joy, hate, fear, etc., and become unfeeling creatures. This is what happened when the alien pods transformed themselves into existing people: the individuals lost all their emotions. And this loss is also what the doctor and Becky feared most. The central meaning of *Seconds* is much different. This movie suggests that although most people may want to change, do things differently, or start all over again in life, this change has to come from inside or it will be in vain. Hamilton tried changing as the company dictated he would to begin anew, but he failed, for he was following someone else and not himself. And the film made it clear that the company had a high rate of failures, that many more returned than were successful. *Seconds* shows that change, or beginning as a new person, is something which must be done with motivation and power from within the self as the key.

In a technical sense also, these films have some important similarities. Both pictures make excellent use of different shades and lighting. Both pictures emphasize the shadowy dark areas, lending kind of an eerie and other-worldly—or futuristic—quality to the images. Only in the more romantic moments, such as the doctor and Becky eating a cheery breakfast together in *Invasion*, or in Tony's and Nora's blooming but short-lived love in *Seconds*, do the shades lighten and become more open and airy. Also, most scenes of both movies are shot indoors in confined areas such as rooms, hallways, caves, cars, airplanes, etc., creating a sense of confinement and imprisonment in the situations the characters are in.

Both films also make effective use of the musical sound track. In *Invasion* the score becomes harsh, dissonant, and clashy when an important and potentially shocking scene is near or upon the screen, but more light and easy in the more cheery and romantic scenes. In *Seconds* also is a light and tinkling undercurrent of music weaving in and out of the scenes of Wilson's better moments. But when the prospects change for the worse, the music becomes loud, eerie, harsh, and dominated by a pipe organ. Music, then, is effectively used to underscore the visual images and create the proper mood for the viewer in both films.

The two films are, however, paced very differently. *Invasion* is fast-paced and quick: it seems as if someone's always in a hurry, always running or driving fast to get somewhere, or always being chased or chasing. The movie itself jumps quickly from event to event as the pod takeover spreads. The movie is exciting, suspenseful, and seems to fly to its conclusion. On the other hand, *Seconds* is paced much more slowly and much more leisurely: few hurry anywhere. This is effective in conveying a sense of despair which many people have about their lives and in portraying seemingly tedious drudgery. This slow pace also works in drawing out the shock and terror in the viewer until the very end. Thus, compared with *Invasion, Seconds* may seem to drag by, and might be considered boring by viewers used to more action-packed films.

In view of these similarities and differences, one can still be led to the same conclusion about both films: both are scary. This is not to say that they are scary in the common spooky and ghostly sense, but rather they are frightening in what they portray and warn against. Who wants to live in a world without feelings and emotions? And who wants to see the existence of such a company with total disregard for the value of human life and moral values?

Fat City
and *Blue Collar*

Russell L. Bianchi

T HE most striking feature and similarity between these two serious and excellent films are their themes of inexorable desperation and futility which plague the major characters throughout their daily lives. The stories unfold through the conflict which erupts in the struggle these characters wage against their environment, their misfortune, and their weakness as they attempt to grasp some fulfillment in otherwise meaningless lives.

In addition to almost identical themes and basic conflicts, the cinematography of the dark and dirty environment is also very similar. The photography of grayed and subtly colored buildings, as well as the deep, low-keyed tones of the bars, has a depressing but oddly beautiful quality to it which mirrors the overall emotional nature of the two films. They are also similar in that they share a strong linear story line with a definite exposition, complication, climax, and resolution.

Aside from the fundamental similarities, each film portrays its theme differently. Most noticeable is the much more internal, personal, and isolated struggle of the characters in *Fat City*. Tully and Munger fight their battles, both physical and psychological, against opponents and situations which, to a large degree, they have chosen themselves. Jerry, Smokey and Zeke, on the other hand, struggle together against a problem which is imposed upon them from the outside. Even the lyrics in *Fat City* express an internal dialogue, whereas the score of *Blue Collar* reflects the externally observable rhythm of machinery and the noisy ambience of a factory.

The means with which the characters of each film seek relief from their troubles is also quite different. In *Fat City,* when Tully attempts to escape the futility of his life, he does so in the more isolated activity of drinking. Even when he is drinking with Oma, we never get the feeling that they understand or share in each other's burdens. Jerry, Zeke, and Smokey, however, find escape in the camaraderie of parties at Smokey's apartment. The secondary characters in *Fat City,* such as Earl, Lucero, and Ruben, also reflect a more isolated condition. We are shown in detail Lucero as he gets off the bus alone and spends his time alone in the almost complete silence of his hotel room. The same sense of separateness is true of Ruben's condition to some degree when we see him talking to his wife about the hopes he has for Ernie's future, and she is turned away, ignoring him completely. In *Blue Collar,* however, we get a sense of unity in the somewhat corrupt motivations or clandestine dealings shared by such lesser characters as the union representative, Miller and Eddie Knuckles.

The main characters' relationships to women also illustrate *Fat City*'s consistently more dismal approach to the theme. Tully's wife has left him and, in his loneliness and longing for her, he starts a relationship with Oma. Because of her odd nature and alcoholism, however, Tully is never able to maintain their association, and they soon break up. She even berates him viciously when he returns to claim his clothes. Similarly, Ernie's marriage is based, for the most part, on Fay's pregnancy, and we are inclined to believe they are never very close. In *Blue Collar*, however, there is a genuine feeling that Jerry and Zeke are close to their wives and are concerned for the welfare of their children despite occasional parties with Smokey. This is illustrated toward the end of the film when we see the extent to which they are willing to go in order to ensure the safety of their families.

The point thus far has been to demonstrate that in *Fat City* the major conflicts manifest themselves largely as internal or psychological actions and are worked out separately by each individual character. In *Blue Collar*, though, the conflicts are often of a more external nature and are dealt with collectively by different groups of characters, although at the end these groups are redefined.

Another interesting similarity is that in both films the main characters base their hopes on the success of risky or somewhat unrealistic plans. Although they have worked in an honest and straightforward attempt to obtain a better life for themselves and their families, all their efforts seem destined to fail. It is in view of this seemingly immutable situation that they are drawn to the belief that becoming a champion or pulling off a big heist is the only possible way out.

Both films paint a bleak picture of lonely, frustrated people caught between circumstances and inabilities which combine to strangle them. Our belief in their plight—or more important, our sympathy for their plight—comes about because each film makes a valid statement on contemporary life.

It Happened One Night and *Carnal Knowledge*

George V. Vinson

*I*T *Happened One Night* and *Carnal Knowledge* may be lumped together superficially as love stories, but here any similarities, general or specific, end. *IHON* is a brilliant realization on film of the classic boy-meets-girl topic, and a Hollywood milestone of the genre. It is witty, adult, and in several ways, which were innovative at the time, realistic. Its realism is displayed in its use of colloquial speech, in its portrayal of the discomforts of bus travel and the life of tourist camps, and in its depiction of recognizable U.S. character types.

Carnal Knowledge, as its title suggests, focuses almost exclusively on sex. The opening offscreen dialogue between Jonathan and Sandy, the sexual fencing in the conversations between Jonathan and Susan, the way they dance together, the ensuing conversations and reunions between the men, their choice of bedmates, Jonathan's idea of a slideshow, their fantasies about the woman skater in white, the bedroom scenes, Jonathan's developing fears of impotence—virtually everything in the film develops a pessimistic view of the separation of love and sex in modern society, and the difficulty of achieving love.

One feature redeems *CK* from vapid pessimism: its psychological truthfulness. Although it is not true to life because of its very narrow focus on sexual relationships, the film nevertheless appears very true and familiar to us who have had to undergo similar sexual and emotional experiments and who have no doubt carried on conversations with both sexes which are practically identical to many of those in the film, in the process of growing up. The choices of mates which the men make in the film are entirely compatible with their personalities. Their developments according to type are inevitable and correct. Their moralities are thoroughly modern and recognizable. It is psychologically sound that Jonathan finds his roommate's girlfriend desirable and tries to steal her, that Susan stays with Sandy because of his vulnerability and dependence on her, and that Jonathan remains fearful of entering into marriage. It is reasonable that Jonathan and Sandy are willing to exchange bedmates for an evening (they both see them as sex objects), and that Bobby wants Jonathan to marry her more and more desperately as he retreats from her (she cannot face rejection).

While *It Happened One Night* is also concerned with sex, it deals with this subject in a far more restrained and witty fashion. The intimacy between Ellie Andrews and Peter Warne develops more subtly and naturally into love. It grows out of and is subordinated to a rich interaction between two very strong and self-assertive individuals. Their intimacy is foreshadowed by Ellie's sleeping on Peter's shoulder in the bus. It continues to grow as they fight, as Peter lectures Ellie on humility and calls her Brat, and as they come to trust each other and value each other's company. They *are* attracted to each other. The " walls of Jericho," as Peter calls the blanket partition in their cabin, won't stand a slip and other feminine underapparel hanging over it, as Peter comments: "It's tough enough as it is." Moments before, Ellie has joked weakly, "You haven't got a trumpet by any chance, have you?" Peter finally makes the hint of a proposition at the close of the cabin scene: "You've had a pretty tough break at that. Twice a Missus and still unkissed," to which Ellie refuses to respond. Peter pursues: "I'll bet you're in an awful hurry to get back to New York, aren't you?" Whereupon Ellie cuts him short with a "Good night."[1]

Whereas Jonathan and Bobby live together briefly without getting married, Peter and Ellie begin to act as though they were already married even before the detectives give them reason to pretend. Their role-playing is conscious and deliberate. I don't feel that the sexual roles which the characters in *Carnal Knowledge* adopt are conscious in the same way; their roles arise out of their emotional dependencies and lack of self-knowledge, out of frustration rather than self-assertion. On this same theme, we admire Peter's aggressive role-playing to protect Ellie from Shapeley and the fact that he doesn't try to seduce her at any time. Shapeley's facile come-ons compare with Jonathan's puerile and deceitful ploys to seduce Susan, however, in that they both earn our amused contempt.

There are many other thematic contrasts between these two films. For example, good and evil are sharply differentiated in *IHON,* with its thieves, phonies, and good-hearted denizens, while in *CK* the characters operate in a moral limbo. *IHON* qualifies as a modern fairy tale with Ellie as its rich princess, Peter bearing the facetious title of "King" or "Great One" bestowed on him by his cronies, and trials sufficient to test the sincerity of their love. There are even parallels with the medieval romances: Peter as Lancelot sets out to deliver the bride to *King* Westley, but ends by falling in love with her and carrying her off for himself. *CK* offers no such romantic antecedents; Jonathan does not measure up to Faust, nor Sandy to Siddhartha.

In the cinematography of the two films there is a paradoxical contrast. *IHON,* though shot in black and white, is rich in "local color," that is, in realistic scenes of the Depression, in a bevy of minor but colorful characters, in shifts between locales where the rich live and the poor live, and in dramatic action. In contrast, *CK,* while shot in color, is photographed in narrow interior sets with a limited cast, presented repetitiously, and with the narrowed focus on sexual relationships which I have already noted. The respective points of view developed by means of these techniques are, of course, organic to each film, but the stark contrast of the optimistic faith in love in *IHON* and the pessimistic estrangement and despair in *CK* is thereby made only more clear.

[1] Reference for quotes: John Gassner and Dudley Nichols, eds., *Twenty Best Film Plays* (New York: Crown Publishers, 1943).

Brigid in the Book
and 1941 Film Version
of *The Maltese Falcon*

Susan Watkins

THE differences between Brigid in the book and in the 1941 film version of *The Maltese Falcon* are cosmetic and unimportant when compared with the similarities in the characters' behavior. John Huston kept scrupulously close to the words and mannerisms of Dashiell Hammett's avaricious bunch of thieves. In both, Brigid is the same amoral storyteller, a bundle of nervous mannerisms who uses men to get what she wants.

The film's Brigid is considerably older than her counterpart in the novel. It is a surprise at first to see Mary Astor's thirty-plus years, since by 1940 she had begun to play mothers of teenage daughters in other films, and the Brigid in the book seems to be in her twenties. When she relates the disappearance of her fabricated seventeen-year-old sister, she mentions that the girl is five years her junior. Of course, since she lies about having a sister, and lies about everything else, then it is possible that she is also lying about her age. There are enough references to her youth, however, to believe that she is somewhere in her early twenties. The change in age in the film works to its advantage. It seems much more plausible to see a sadder-but-wiser woman manipulating assorted men with her physical charms and heart-wrenching stories. Her portrayal blends the qualities of sensuality and pretended innocence that make Brigid the expert conniver she is.[1]

She is a different physical type in each version. In the novel "She was tall and pliantly slender, without angularity anywhere. Her body was erect and high-breasted, her legs long, her hands and feet narrow." The problem of presenting a tall and slender Brigid in the film version is apparent when one looks at the physical stature of Humphrey Bogart as Sam Spade. It is a picky difference, and the movie Brigid carries off her high-fashion wardrobe without the ranginess of a Conover model.

It is not the physical appearance of Brigid O'Shaughnessy that is important. Like all the other thieves and liars who weave the plot of *The Maltese Falcon*, she remains the same amoral, self-concerned, and greedy user.

Swathed in fur in the opening scene of the film, Brigid's eyes avoid Spade's as she unfolds her story. Only when she is desperate to ensure his cooperation does she look directly at him. Insisting her "sister Corinne" is in danger, it is necessary to do this; he must be hooked. In her autobiography Ms. Astor gives the secret for her downcast eyes amid a tangle of lie-telling: not once as she recited her story did she say anything she was thinking at the time, mostly trying to hold one unrelated thought as she begged Spade to help her.[2]

In the corresponding scene in the novel, Brigid's nervousness is depicted vividly with "a startled hand to her mouth" or "shaping her words with nervous jerkiness" but not as effectively as the film Brigid's fidgeting and labored breathing (achieved when Mr. Huston had the actress run around the set prior to a scene).[3]

At various points in the novel Brigid blushes, and this could almost lead one (at least for a while) to believe there is a touch of innocence left in her. Could a true villainess conjure up a blush on command? In the movie version it is easier to see through her elaborate fabrications and see that any embarrassment she might experience is over being caught in one of her lies. This is much more evident in Mr. Huston's claustrophobic scenes as she trips herself up in a lie, admitting it to be false, switches gears and stories, and continues, assuring Sam Spade that *this* time it really is the truth. If that one fails, she finds another.[4] She's "really good," as Spade suggests. In both film and novel she is recognized as the consummate liar she is because a person of equal ability is able to read her signals.

In both versions of *The Maltese Falcon,* Spade sees through Brigid's overblown verbiage, and he calls her on it every time. He doesn't buy her appraisal of him as a "godsend" or her outpouring over Archer's death (only yesterday he had been "so solid and hearty"). She draws back momentarily when he catches her, but she keeps on going.

In the novel Brigid offers her body as payment to Spade, whereas in the film it seems more his idea, one with which she might comply. In the film we can only guess as the camera pans to the window, curtains blowing. This alteration (one of the few from book to script) must come because of the film industry's self-censorship of that time, as did the omittance of the scene in which she undresses at Spade's insistence to prove that she did not take money from him. Innocence is no longer an issue as she does what is necessary to gain what she wants. In the 1940s, writers were free to express sexual situations to a greater degree than were filmmakers. In these instances Brigid's character, or lack of it, is shown in more detail in the book.

Because Mr. Huston follows the novel so closely, leaving out only excess baggage and those things that could not pass the front office, Brigid is basically the same character in both book and film. She can turn out more stories than the Brothers Grimm, plead them with the ability of a Duse, and use up men like a box of Kleenex while committing acts she could not possibly identify as evil because the concept has no bearing on her. She uses her sexuality as she does her theatrics, to achieve an end. Her means are basic and effective.

Is she incredulous at being sent to prison because she thinks there has been love in her relationship with Spade or because for once, her manipulations have failed her? In both the novel and the film as she begs him to spare her, she tries to convince Spade that she really cares for him. In the book, when the police arrive, he merely turns her over to them as "another one for you," only paling later as some sign of emotion over what he has done. We are left not knowing whether Brigid feels anything at all, whether in fact her story of love is just that, another story.

At the end of the film, Brigid is seen through the bars of the elevator, foreshadowing the bars of prison. She has indeed "always had a bad life" and been a liar, as she admits. She has used Archer and Thursby at the cost of their lives but loses when she attempts to use Sam Spade. She can't wriggle her way out. In both versions of *The Maltese Falcon* she has been around, and just once too often.

[1] William Nolan, *Dashiell Hammett: A Casebook* (Santa Barbara, Calif.: McNally and Loftin, 1969), p. 103.
[2] Mary Astor, *A Life on Film* (New York: Delacorte Press, 1967), p. 160.
[3] Jon Tuska, *The Detective in Hollywood* (Garden City, N.Y.: Doubleday, 1978), p. 285.
[4] Nolan, p. 85.

The Samurai and Villagers
in *The Seven Samurai*

Ms. Hollis Chacona

. . . The *samurai* is an incredibly complex figure in Japanese culture. In its purest form, the *bushido* (the tacit code of ethics for the *bushi* warrior) represents the noblest of attitudes—total self-sacrifice, altruism, and loyalty. A good *samurai* is a paragon of Japanese manhood. A good *samurai,* performing his duty, is also the harshest of oppressors, indispensable to the overlords in maintaining their feudal hierarchy. The villagers in *Seven Samurai* are almost as afraid of the *samurai* as they are of the brigands; they disguise their women and hide what valuables they possess before the *samurai* reach their village. Their fears are not unfounded, for *samurai* are the peasants' natural enemy. They have absolute power over the villagers and, during the Tokugawa reign, were granted *kirisutogomen,* the sanction to kill without warning any person of low caste whom they felt had in some way offended them. To the villagers, the *samurai* are little better than the brigands (several of whom sport topknots, the distinguishing mark of *samurai*) and are sought only in a last desperate attempt to save the village.

The *bushi* whom the villagers encounter on their mission are for the most part swaggering brutes, openly contemptuous of the villagers' petitions despite the fact that they themselves are hungry and unemployed. The number of *ronin* (literally "men on the wave," or masterless *samurai*) the villagers see testifies to the radically fluctuating political structure of the times. The *ronin* roam the countryside, their purpose in life disintegrating along with the once powerful clan system. With the outbreak of civil war in the 19th century, many clans were abolished, leaving in their wake scores of retainers who, without masters to constantly test their loyalty or command them, were truly men adrift in an increasingly unfamiliar world. It is in his depiction of these *ronin*—as opposed to a much embellished portrait of the grand *samurai* of the folk legends—that Kurosawa is able to transcend the platitudes of the oversimplified *chambara*. The focus of *Seven Samurai* is on the plight of real men, not mythical heroes.

Kanbei, the leader of the *ronin,* embodies that spirit that made the *samurai* institution great. The ambiguity with which Kanbei is introduced reflects Kurosawa's attitude toward the *samurai* throughout the film. We first see Kanbei as he is about to cut off his topknot. There are only two interpretations for

From *CinemaTexas Program Notes* 14, no. 4 (25 April 1978). Reprinted by permission of Hollis Chacona and CinemaTexas, Department of Radio-Television-Film, University of Texas, Austin, Texas 78712. *CinemaTexas Program Notes* also include credits, filmography, and bibliography.

this act in Japanese culture: either he is being publicly humiliated or he is joining the priesthood. The shaving of his head that follows seems to suggest that he is preparing to take his vows, but after only a moment's uncertainty it becomes clear that Kanbei has no intention of "leaving this world." We (along with Katsushiro, a young *ronin,* and Kikuchiyo, a self-fashioned *bushi*) realize that Kanbei has a completely different though equally lofty reason for his action. The young Katsushiro is awed by the noble courage of the rescue, while it is the apparent unselfishness of the act that intrigues Kikuchiyo. Deeply impressed by the deed they witness, both men become emotionally bound to the quiet *ronin.* The other *ronin,* too, are drawn by Kanbei's noble presence. "I know what the farmers have to put up with," Gorobei tells Kanbei, "but it's not because of them that I accept. It's because of you—you fascinate me." Shichiroji, an old friend of Kanbei's, is willing to fight "once more" out of a feeling for old times. Gorobei enlists the aid of Heihachi, a cheerful *ronin* ready to make the best of any situation, and finally of Kyuzo, the master swordsman who "is not interested in killing, only in perfecting his skill." Individually the men are decent, hardworking *ronin,* but as a group they comprise the very essence of the *samurai:* the harmonious blending of wisdom and prudence, innocence and trust, inquisitiveness, loyalty, cheerfulness, respect for martial skills and a desire for justice. Kurosawa's *samurai* are not individual supermen, but combining their various skills, the seven are able to defeat the band of forty brigands. Ironically, Kurosawa emphasizes the importance of the cohesive unit which will ultimately lead to the decline of the *samurai.*

In contrast to the *samurai,* the peasants seem hopelessly ineffectual and ignoble. Their attempts to deal with the imminent danger posed by the brigands is marred by self-interested disputes and petty squabbling. Even Rikichi's adamant stand against the brigands is prompted by the sheerly personal motive of revenge for the rape of his wife. It is only through the patient and stern leadership of the *samurai* that the villagers can group together to work for a common interest. Once the battle is in progress, the villagers gain a confidence in their individual abilities which rekindles the collective consciousness that lay dormant for so many years beneath the crushing tyranny of the feudal system. Though the *ronin*'s motives for helping the villagers are purely altruistic, Kurosawa illustrates through Kikuchiyo's speech (in what may be the most passionate scene of the film) why the farmers cannot feel the gratitude these noble men probably deserve:

> Farmers are miserly, craven, mean, stupid, murderous! You make me laugh so hard I'm crying. But then, who made animals out of them? You! You did—you *samurai*! All of you damned *samurai.* And each time you fight, you burn villages, you destroy the fields, you take away the food, you rape the women and enslave the men. And you kill them when they resist. You hear me, you damned *samurai*?

For all their honorable intentions, the seven *samurai* are placed in a position of making amends for the injustices imposed by their society upon the peasants. Ironically, the long years of injustice have forced the villagers to cultivate a totally individualistic will to survive which allows them to adapt to the changing times. But it is clear from the last scene that Kurosawa questions the merits of a society in which the noble values of the *samurai* tradition have no place. The regenerative capacity of the villagers is reflected in the seedlings they are planting, while a slow upward tilt frames the remaining *samurai* with the burial mounds of their fellow *bushi*. "We've lost again," Kanbei tells his friends. "The farmers are the winners. Not us." We are left to mourn the three remaining *samurai*, the ghosts of a dying tradition.

P·A·R·T

FOUR

ISSUES
IN
ANALYSIS

As viewers practice viewing and analyzing films, certain problems and issues emerge. Part Four addresses some of these issues. Part Four describes the advantages and disadvantages of viewing and studying films and video versions of films. It also explains some problems caused since many films are shown in different versions. Finally, this part of the book includes a chapter about additional issues in film analysis, such as the usefulness and limitations of scripts and evaluating a film and its source fiction.

· 10 ·

Film and Video: Presentation and Study

OBTAINING, EXAMINING, AND DOCUMENTING FILMS
USES AND LIMITATIONS OF VIDEO VERSIONS
USING FILM AND VIDEO

ALL film studies teachers—I would imagine—fantasize about their film students being able to view again many different films at their convenience, to check particular sections quickly, and to cite sections for the reference of others. Film students—in this collective fantasy—would each have a genie, a high-resolution, large-screen home computer terminal hooked up to an enormous film library. In a more modest version of this fantasy, students own a large library of inexpensive and compact film cassettes or discs. But in fact, films, especially many fictional films, are not readily available for study, nor are they easy to examine closely and document.

Obtaining, Examining, and Documenting Films

Features especially are expensive to make and market, and understandably their owners want to maximize their income from their investment. Thus, most major fictional films are protected by copyright laws, and feature films tend to be expensive to rent or lease. More than 20,000 titles in 16 mm are available for rental in the United States, but many are costly ($200 and more), and normally they are available for only a few days for each rental fee. Only a small proportion of all theatrical fictional films are available for purchase from recognized dealers, and 16 mm prints—all in all the most useful format for film presentation and study—cost at least several hundred dollars each.

Once the film student has acquired a print of a film, there are three ways to study it closely and to document it. One can take notes while projecting the film repeatedly, or while using an analyzer projector (see Figure 10.1) or a flatbed editor/viewer (see Figure 10.2). The repeated projections and notetaking, though quite helpful, are usually slow, particularly if the viewer wants to return to a specific scene. Very few projectors have a frame or footage counter. Analyzer projectors are time-consuming to use, especially for locating a particular part of a film, since they lack standardized index counters; in fact, most have no index counter. Flatbed editor/viewers are easy to use, easy on film, and enormously helpful for close examination and documentation, especially since most have an index counter. Unfortunately, their price tag of $12,000 or so limits the number of people who ever get a chance to study a film on them.

10.1 A 16 mm analyzer projector: 224-ES Motion Analyzer, which runs at 1, 2, 4, 6, 8, 12, and 24 frames/second in forward or reverse and has still-framing and a frame counter. Courtesy L-W International.

10.2 A 16 mm flatbed editor/viewer, with two picture tracks, two sound tracks, two adjoining screens, frame counter, and many more features. Courtesy of Steenbeck, Inc.

Uses and Limitations of Video Versions

Although film has been less accessible and more difficult to check, cite, and document than literature, art, and music, the situation is changing. With the marketing of various home videotape and videodisc systems in recent years (see Figure 10.3), many film students now can use a tool for closer, more precise examination of some aspects of many films than at any other time in film history (see Table 10.1). Video players are useful for examination of the sound track (dialogue, music, sound effects, and silences), editing (running time of shots and scenes, their arrangement, and transitions between shots), and, to a much lesser extent, the film's visuals (color, grain/focus, lighting, and composition).[1] Table 10.2 (pages 164–165) points out major advantages and disadvantages of film and video for presentation and study.

---

[1] On television, only close-ups have much visual impact, and television is less of a visual medium than many people realize; in fact, it is not entirely fanciful to call television illustrated radio. Usually, a TV's continuous vocalizings—not the images—do most of the communicating. To test this claim, try watching a typical TV program—not a theatrical film shown on TV—without sound to see how much is understood. Then listen to a comparable television program without looking at the image.

10.3 Laser videodisc player. Courtesy Pioneer Video, Inc.

In many ways videotape and videodisc presentations are superior to broadcast and cable TV. Videodiscs and prerecorded videotapes have sharper resolution and wider variation of gray tones than many films seen on broadcast and cable television (in part because films shown on TV tend to be in limited shades of gray and to lack rich blacks and "clean" whites), and they are usually without scratches and splices. Laser videodisc, stereo CED disc, and VHS Hi Fi and Sony's Beta Hi Fi videotape players all have excellent stereo sound capabilities, much better than broadcast and cable TV; even, in some cases, better than some LP records and audio tapes.

Nonetheless, many of the limitations of watching a film on television apply to watching videodisc and videotape versions of films. All video tapes and discs are played through a TV set or monitor, so the

Table 10.1
Recording and Playback Capabilities

	Playback Only	Recording and Playback
Audio Equipment	Phonograph Record	Magnetic Audio Tape
Video Equipment	Videodisc	Videotape

image is grainier than the original film, and the lighting and color are less subtle. Night scenes especially suffer. The composition is affected because the shape of the original filmed image and sometimes the content are altered—on occasion, drastically so—when a film is shown on TV (see the next chapter). The size of the image relative to the viewer is invariably decreased. To date, TV remains "smaller than life"; film "larger than life." As student Alice Heineman wrote, "When a picture from a big screen is restricted to 19 inches, many of the possible effects for initiating certain emotions are lost. For example, in *Psycho* when Marion is driving on the road at night and I get a point-of-view shot of oncoming traffic, my viewing experience seems more real and involved on a big screen than on a small screen where I feel farther away—less involved." Video sound is usually much inferior to theatrical sound. VHS and standard Beta videotape players, for example, are incapable of high quality sound, and most video versions end up being played through a TV set or monitor with one small, inadequate speaker. Finally, usually the TV viewing environment (semilighted and somewhat noisy, perhaps very noisy) is more distracting than a theater.

In spite of the limitations of seeing theatrical films on a television screen, video versions have many useful features for film students. In fact, video makes most options of the expensive flatbed editor/viewer accessible to many more people. Many video players, for example, have visible fast forward. Now home viewers can skim visual material for the same reasons readers do—to preview, check a detail, or review. (Visible fast forward, however, imparts a comic mood to much action, whereas skimming in reading rarely does.) All video players have index counters, and many have still-framing, fast forward, and fast reverse, so rapid access to specific parts is possible. By using various controls, the viewer can easily make a detailed and accurate outline and/or notes about a film on disc or tape. Then, using the search buttons or index numbers and the outline or notes, the viewer can return to any scene in a matter of minutes or, with videodiscs, even seconds. (In preparing this book I often rechecked details by using video versions.)

An outline of the film's source in literature or history may be compared with a similar outline of the film. One could also compare individual parts of the source with the comparable parts on the video version, noting how the film treatment visualizes, connects, abbreviates, expands, or omits material. In the case of films based on fiction (or fiction based on films), the words describing sounds may be compared with the sound track. The images of literature (words that represent sensory experiences) can be compared to the visuals of video viewed at normal speed, slow motion, or still-frame. The point of view of fiction can be compared with the camera angles and distances.

Table 10.2
Four Formats for Film Presentation and Study[1]

| Format | Presentation | | | | Study | |
	Environment	Image	Sound	Continuity	Access	Documentation
16 mm film	Dark theater or large room; large to small audience	Large; sharp; often unaltered aspect ratio	Good, but usually less faithful than theatrical presentations	Uninterrupted regardless of length if two projectors are used	• 20,000 + features for rent; 100s for sale • Re-viewing of a particular part is time-consuming • Limited slow motion • Still-framing with some models	Quite inexact. Most projectors have no counter (footage or frame), although one, made by L-W International, has a frame counter.
LV Laser Videodisc (Magnavox, Pioneer, others)	Semidark room; small audience	Small; somewhat grainy, but best of video versions; often altered aspect ratio	Good if external speaker is used; stereo possible with some discs	Change discs every 15–60 minutes[2]	• 600 + titles for sale • Re-viewing rapid and easy; fast forward & reverse visible with 30-minute discs, not 60 • Variable slow motion on 30-minute discs • Still-framing with 30-minute discs	Precise. By frame number on 30-minute discs, but by minute on extended-play discs (up to 60 minutes per side).
CED Grooved Capacitance Videodisc (Hitachi and Toshiba)	Semidark room; small audience	Small; somewhat grainy; not as sharp as laser discs but sharper than videotape; often altered aspect ratio	In recent models, good; stereo available with some models	Change discs every 30–60 minutes	• 1,200 + titles for sale • Re-viewing rapid; visible fast forward on some models • Limited slow motion • Still-framing on a few models	Fairly precise. By minutes.

| Video cassettes (in VHS or Beta)[3] | Semidark room; small audience | Small; somewhat grainy; often altered aspect ratio | Fair, except for Beta Hi Fi and VHS Hi Fi systems; some VHS & Beta models have stereo | With highest-quality recordings, tape is changed every two hours or so | • 4,500+ titles for sale or rent
• Re-viewing fairly rapid
• Slow motion on some models
• Somewhat fuzzy still-framing on more expensive models | More precise than CED discs but less so than 30-minute laser discs. By counter number. |

[1] The information in this table is based upon information available as of Winter 1984.
[2] Standard-play (SP), also known as CAV, discs play up to 30 minutes per side. Extended-play (EP); a.k.a. CLV, discs play up to 60 minutes/side.
[3] Each year *Video Review* magazine publishes a guide to video cassette recorders (VCRs), including a table listing the major features of the numerous VHS and Beta models.

Using Film and Video

As Table 10.2 reveals, for film *presentation,* film is far superior to video, but for outlining, re-viewing, and documenting, video is far superior to film. Consequently, the following strategy would be ideal in studying a film:

- study of background material (if available)
- first viewing (film)
- examination (video and perhaps film clips)
- second viewing (film)
- reassessment (perhaps with double-checking of a video version for certain details)

Once again in film history (as in the case of 16 mm, 8 mm, super 8 mm, analyzer projectors, flatbed editor/viewers, and television), a new technology has developed because it appears to be profitable to distributors and manufacturers, and the technology influences the ways in which we view and contemplate films originally released in theaters. Video versions will help film studies approach the accuracy, insight, and reliability of other studies, although for a film in smaller than 35 mm format, or a videodisc or videotape, the setting and film experience differ from theatrical conditions. With video, though, for the first time versions of many films can be quickly and repeatedly compared to written or musical sources, and many of their components can be easily rechecked, analyzed, and documented.[2] (For an example of an analysis based on a video version, see S. Scott Smith's essay on the editing of a scene in *Jaws,* Chapter 8; for examples on how to use video players to examine a film, see the viewing and listening exercises at the end of Part Two.) For the immediate future our analyses of particular films will be made more accurate and persuasive. And, in the not-so-immediate future, our understanding of the film medium and of its relationship to other studies and other media will grow. With the increasing use of video, the fantasy of film studies teachers is becoming fact.

[2] Unfortunately, as of this writing few foreign-language films with subtitles are available in any video format, in part because it is difficult to read subtitles on TV screens.

· 11 ·

Film Versions

Problem

IMAGINE turning to an art history book to see a reproduction of a beautiful oil painting; instead, you find a black-and-white newspaper-quality photograph. Or imagine that an editor's introduction to a copy of a Faulkner novel says that it may have fifteen, sixteen, or seventeen chapters; the copy in your hands has fifteen.

Happily, these examples exist only in imagination. Usually accurate, inexpensive copies of works of art, literature, and music are available for close study. In film studies, however, situations comparable to the examples above are commonplace. Many films are now seen in other than their original condition, and reliable prints for many films are unavailable to most film students.

Take as an example *The Birth of a Nation*. In spite of the film's offensive depiction of black people, most film scholars throughout the world agree that film technique was advanced more completely by this film than by any other fictional film ever made, and it has been frequently shown, discussed, taught, and written about. Yet today, we do not see the film with its original running time (the director, D. W.

Griffith, and others kept tampering with the film) and appropriate projection speeds (using hand-cranked projectors), its intended live orchestra music, and original tinted scenes (dyed different colors). Evidently, we see only a shadow of the original, yet almost without exception writers assume that the versions of this and many other films are complete and available to all.

Some Causes

Various factors affect how well—if at all—an older film is preserved. Until the early 1950s, most movies were printed on nitrate stock, which begins its irreversible decomposition immediately after its creation, and innumerable films made on nitrate have decomposed or caught fire. Others were melted down for their silver. Sometimes the original negative, master positives, and safety or duplicate negatives are lost or damaged (see Figure 11.6).

Numerous films undergo some form of censorship. Most frequently, offending footage is deleted—a simple act in the case of films. Redoing parts of dialogue is also common.

Often for commercial reasons the original film is different from the film that audiences see. Sometimes, as in the case of *Lawrence of Arabia,* a film is shortened so that it may be shown more times within the theater's operating hours (drive-in theaters in the United States frequently do this) and thus generate more revenue. To increase income after its initial release, a film is frequently shown in less expensive, more marketable, less complete forms: television, half-inch and three-quarter-inch videotape, videodiscs, and 16 mm, super 8 mm, and 8 mm film.

Components of the Problem

The viewed film may be different than the original film in many ways. Probably the following are the most significant aspects: its shape, resolution and brightness, color, sound effects and music, translations, and length. Each of these aspects will now be discussed in order.

Shape

Theatrical showings Inside the can of the first reel of the French feature film *Grand Illusion* was found the following letter from the director to the projectionist:

Dear Sir,

This appeal is from one technician to another. You're going to show my *Grand Illusion*.

This film is still in good shape despite its age: 22 years. But it still has a few characteristics which were in style in 1936. One of these is that it is designed for an aspect ratio of 1.33 × 1. I have composed each image to fill up this surface and leave no empty space. I have arranged details both at the top and the bottom of the frame. By projecting my film on a screen of enlarged dimensions, you would risk eliminating these details that I feel are important and also cutting off part of the heads of the actors, which seems to me inesthetic.

I ask you to help me to present my work under the best conditions, that is to say, on a screen with dimensions that will suit it.

Thanks in advance.

Regards,

Jean Renoir[1]

Renoir had reason to be concerned, because many films shown since the introduction of various wide-screen formats in the 1950s have been presented in other than their original shape by using an inappropriate aperture plate (a rectangular metal plate that determines the shape and area of the light emitted from the projector). In Renoir's case, he was concerned that the projectionist would use a wide-screen aperture plate, which would give the picture more of a wide, modern look at the expense of blocking out some of the top and bottom of the image.

Showings of pre-1950s films with a wide-screen aperture plate are fairly common and often distracting. A more frequent problem is showing 1960s and 1970s theatrical films in less than their original widths. Thus, to give an extreme example, instead of seeing an image nearly three times as wide as it is high, viewers see one that is only one and one-third times as wide as high (see Figures 11.1–11.3A). When so much of the sides of an image is chopped off, the results can be distressing. In the Italian film *L'Avventura,* for example, early in the film the characters are scattered across the wide frame at various depths of field and facing in different directions. The sense of estrangement and rootlessness is decreased if less than the original aspect ratio is shown, for one loses a sense of distances between characters. Indeed, some of the characters are cut right out of the picture. In some films characters may be diminished by a nose, an ear, or some other part. Also distorted are films conveying the expanse of a locale, whether it be a meadow or outer space.

---

[1] Jean Renoir, *La Grande Illusion: Decoupage intégrale* (Paris: Edition du seuil/Avant-scène, 1971), p. 6. This letter was translated and brought to my attention by Fred Simeral, Jersey City State College.

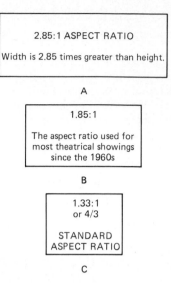

2.85:1 ASPECT RATIO

Width is 2.85 times greater than height.

A

1.85:1

The aspect ratio used for
most theatrical showings
since the 1960s

B

1.33:1
or 4/3

STANDARD
ASPECT RATIO

C

11.1 Three sample aspect ratios (drawn to scale: all the same height)

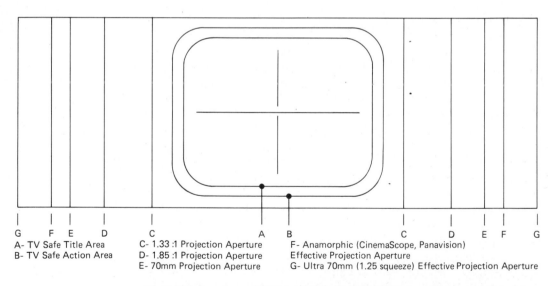

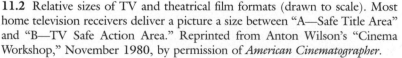

G F E D   C   A B   C   D   E F   G

A- TV Safe Title Area   C- 1.33 :1 Projection Aperture   F- Anamorphic (CinemaScope, Panavision)
B- TV Safe Action Area   D- 1.85 :1 Projection Aperture   Effective Projection Aperture
                               E- 70mm Projection Aperture   G- Ultra 70mm (1.25 squeeze) Effective Projection Aperture

11.2 Relative sizes of TV and theatrical film formats (drawn to scale). Most home television receivers deliver a picture a size between "A—Safe Title Area" and "B—TV Safe Action Area." Reprinted from Anton Wilson's "Cinema Workshop," November 1980, by permission of *American Cinematographer*.

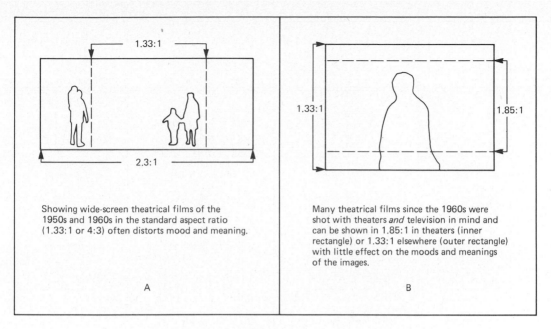

Showing wide-screen theatrical films of the 1950s and 1960s in the standard aspect ratio (1.33:1 or 4:3) often distorts mood and meaning.

Many theatrical films since the 1960s were shot with theaters *and* television in mind and can be shown in 1.85:1 in theaters (inner rectangle) or 1.33:1 elsewhere (outer rectangle) with little effect on the moods and meanings of the images.

A

B

11.3 Showing films in altered aspect ratios

TV showings   All films on television are shown in 1.33:1 aspect ratio, but the television frame masks out (blocks out) part of the edges and corners (see shapes A and B in Figure 11.2). When watching the opening credits of a film shot in the standard aspect ratio of 1.33:1, the viewer can often sense how much of the image is being blocked off, since words on the edges are incomplete. This cropping, however, is so slight that it rarely distorts the original picture significantly.[2]

Wide-screen films shown on television, however, are cropped much more, often creating major distortion. In extreme cases—those films originally intended for theatrical presentation in a 2.85:1 aspect ratio, such as *Spartacus* and *Lawrence of Arabia*—less than half of the original image remains when the film is seen on a television set or monitor[3] (see Figures 11.2, 11.3A, and 11.4D). For some televised showings of wide-screen films, a technician—not the film's editor or director—decides what part of each image will be seen by the audience (Figure 11.4D). In these scanned prints the camera often *seems* to pan to the

[2] Occasionally a film is shown on television in the 1.85:1 aspect ratio by blacking out the top and bottom of the image, but such broadcasts often lead to viewer complaints: where's the rest of the picture?

[3] At least one can usually read all the credits for anamorphic prints seen on television, since they are usually broadcast squeezed (without anamorphic projection). See Figure 11.4D.

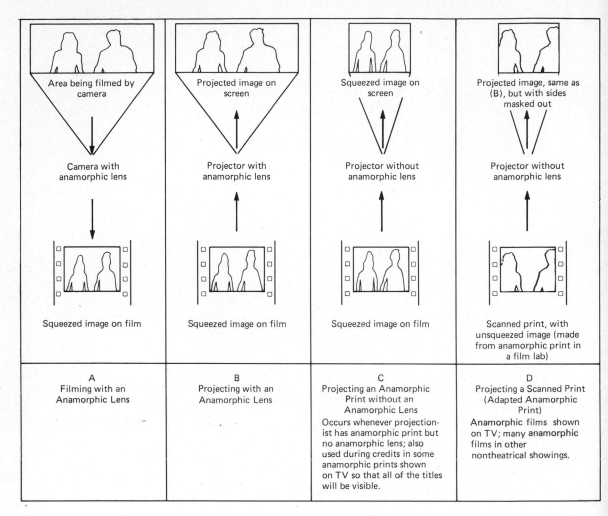

A	B	C	D
Area being filmed by camera	Projected image on screen	Squeezed image on screen	Projected image, same as (B), but with sides masked out
Camera with anamorphic lens	Projector with anamorphic lens	Projector without anamorphic lens	Projector without anamorphic lens
Squeezed image on film	Squeezed image on film	Squeezed image on film	Scanned print, with unsqueezed image (made from anamorphic print in a film lab)
A Filming with an Anamorphic Lens	**B** Projecting with an Anamorphic Lens	**C** Projecting an Anamorphic Print without an Anamorphic Lens. Occurs whenever projectionist has anamorphic print but no anamorphic lens; also used during credits in some anamorphic prints shown on TV so that all of the titles will be visible.	**D** Projecting a Scanned Print (Adapted Anamorphic Print). Anamorphic films shown on TV; many anamorphic films in other nontheatrical showings.

11.4 The anamorphic lens (not to scale)

right or left within shots to show us what is happening on the sides. To trained viewers, however, these horizontal movements are often distracting, since they do not usually occur when and in the way that panning movements would in theatrical films.

For some years now filmmakers have known that their films will eventually be shown on television and have composed their images so that no important details are beyond the standard aspect ratio frame line. Those films can be shown in theaters at 1.85:1 or on television at 1.33:1 with comparable results (Figure 11.3B).

Resolution and Brightness

The viewed version may also differ from the release print in its resolution (or sharpness) and its brightness. The kind of film stock, projection light (carbon arc, xenon, incandescent, tungsten halogen, etc.), the speed and focus of lens(es) through which the light is projected, as well as the reflective qualities of the screen, all help determine the image's sharpness and brightness.

For film students studying 16 mm prints, the resolution and brightness are also often influenced by the gauge or width of the film and the number of generations between the release print and the screened print (see Figures 11.5 and 11.6). In Figure 11.6, print 1, a theatrical

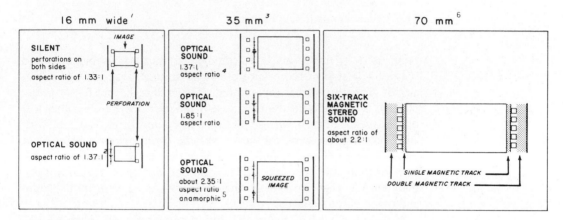

11.5 Widely used film formats

[1]Used by some small commercial theaters, airlines (though less so now that more airlines are using videotape), TV, industry, military, education. Also available are 16 mm magnetic, adapted scope prints with 1.85:1 aspect ratio, and anamorphic (squeezed) prints with aspect ratio of 2.3:1 when projected with an anamorphic lens.

[2]When projected through an aperture plate, the image has an aspect ratio of 1.33:1.

[3]This film is the same width as the microfilm used in libraries and the film used in most still cameras. Most commercial theaters, major TV showings, and major university presentations use 35 mm prints. With Dolby sound prints, stereo is possible with optical sound prints. Many other 35 mm formats are available, including with magnetic sound, but these three are probably the most often used.

[4]When projected through an aperture plate, the image will have a 1.33:1 aspect ratio. Currently, this image shape along with a wide-screen aperture plate are used for many 1.85:1 showings in theaters.

[5]When projected through an anamorphic lens, the image is unsqueezed and doubled in width.

[6]Nonanamorphic (unsqueezed) image, currently the premier projection format. It is available only in some large commercial theaters. In the U.S. and Western Europe, films shown in 70 mm are shot on 35 mm and blown up, or are filmed in 65 mm and printed on 70 mm stock.

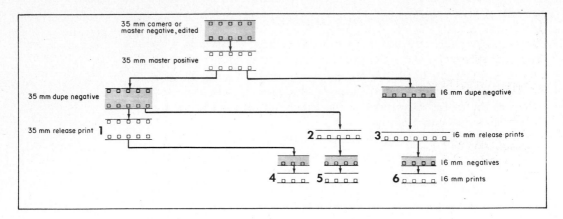

11.6 Common duplicating formats

print used in nearly all U.S. commercial theaters, is brighter and sharper—or at least more faithful to the original filmed image—than any of the other prints represented. (Generally, the master or safety positive is stored as insurance in case the master negative becomes lost or damaged.) Print 6 will be the least sharp and bright—again, with all other variables kept constant—and the other prints will range in between as numbered. Often prints 4, 5, or 6 are the only ones available for close and repeated study. Although far less sharp and bright than print 1, they are usually much superior to super 8 mm, 8 mm, and many video versions.

Consider what happens to resolution and brightness when *Citizen Kane* and *Psycho* are shown on a television set or monitor. The 35 mm release prints of those two films have sharp, bright images. But when those two films are shown on television, the results are grainy (since video images have less definition than film images). The lighting is without subtle shades of gray, and in shadowed areas details tend to get lost because TV has less range of tones than film[4]; thus, many details in night scenes are especially difficult to see. As a consequence, many television viewers are likely to miss such details as the significant glass paperweight in Susan Alexander's apartment on the night Kane

---

[4] In most European televisions there are 625 scan lines per inch (one French system has 819 lines per inch); in North America, Central America, part of South America, Japan, Taiwan, and elsewhere, 525 is the standard. The 625 scan lines per inch produce somewhat better resolution than the 525. Currently in development is High-Definition TV (HDTV), which would have more than 1,000 scan lines per inch. When HDTV is eventually marketed, and probably transmitted via satellites and cable, it is likely that the resultant image will be comparable to theatrical films, and wide-screen formats will probably also be available.

first meets her (Figure 15.12) or the whiskey bottle he finds in her room in Xanadu after she leaves him, or the meaningful fleeting triple superimposition of the last shot of *Psycho*. These details are also scarcely noticeable in some 16 mm prints, such as those too many generations removed from the release print. See print 6 in Figure 11.6, or imagine a scruffy offspring of number 6, an embarrassment to its family. Prints of such heritage are contrasty and grainy. They blur detail. We can see this loss of detail if we compare Figures 15.8–15.15, which unfortunately were made from a 16 mm print, with Figures 16.3–16.14, which are photographs of individual frames from a good 35 mm print.

Color

Several factors determine the color quality of film versions we see. Many so-called black-and-white films were hand-colored (each frame was painted different colors with small brushes) or tinted (usually whole scenes were dyed a particular color). Today, viewers rarely have an opportunity to see such prints. Also, most prints of color films, including those for theatrical release, vary in quality since most are mass-produced. And the colors of most older film prints, especially for films made since 1949, fade and shift; usually they become reddish. In these instances the moods and meanings of the color are altered.

Sound Effects and Music

Like shape, resolution and brightness, and color, the sound track is frequently changed between the release print and the viewed print. As I have pointed out several times, strictly speaking there were few silent films, since even the earliest films were shown with some kind of musical accompaniment to cover the noise of the projectors and the audience, as well as contribute to continuity and mood. Many early film showings were also accompanied by sound effects. Some re-releases, however, include distracting, inappropriate music and sound effects. Some of Chaplin's early short films have suffered this fate.

Since the adoption of the standard optical sound track along the film's edge, filmmakers have decided what sounds accompany what images. Before that time, however, exhibitors often chose the music and sound effects and supervised their presentations. But learning the original music and sound effects or even the *kind* of original music and sound effects is impossible for most early films.

Even for many recent films, it is difficult to *hear* the original film. Movies have been released in a wide variety of sound tracks, including six-track magnetic (see Figure 11.5C) and four- and six-track Dolby stereo. But projection facilities in most theaters deliver less than is possible. Many theaters are like monophonic phonographs playing quadraphonic recordings, and most television sets and monitors have only one small speaker and mediocre sound. In some theatrical and all TV presentations, the moods the music supports may lose impact.

Translations

Nearly all filmgoers are aware of the problems with subtitles in foreign-language sound films, especially in older films, and I'll take space to stress only that there is no completely satisfactory solution. It is, of course, desirable to get a full, accurate translation, but such prints are costly to make, and a complete set of subtitles for many films would turn viewers into readers. It's ideal to see the film, read a complete dialogue continuity, then see the film again, but viewers rarely have that option.

Many people prefer dubbed prints, but they, too, present problems. The major drawback of dubbed prints, in which the voices of foreign performers are replaced by the voices of native ones, is that dialogue can never be completely synchronized with lip movements. Another disadvantage is that dialogue can be altered, dropped, or added by the distributors. In some dubbed prints all of the sound track is redone, and the original music, sound effects, resonances, intonations, and synchronization of sound and source are changed or distorted. In many dubbed prints, only the dialogue is changed; the effects and music tracks are the same as in the original.

Length

One more major aspect remains, and perhaps it is the most troublesome and the most significant aspect as far as film analysis is concerned—the length of the filmed story.

Occasionally, after a film has been released theatrically, it is issued in a longer version. Examples from recent years are *THX 1138, American Graffiti,* and *Close Encounters of the Third Kind.* Quite a number of films shown on television are stretched out by adding out-takes (rejected footage) while trimming some of the original footage. One of the most notable instances would be the more complete version of *The Godfather* and *The Godfather, Part II.* (TV versions also often include closer shots and alternate takes with slightly different dialogue to soften the strong language theatrical films tend to have.)

Much more often, a film is shortened after its original release. Most viewers are well aware that feature films are usually shortened on commercial television, but for theatrical and nontheatrical films, finding a complete version of a film is also often a problem. Two examples that spring to mind are *Lawrence of Arabia* and *The Wild Bunch.* Probably foreign films are especially difficult to locate in complete versions.

Films of one culture are often shocking or unsettling to people of a different culture, especially in moral and political matters; thus, many films have been altered when shown abroad. To hold down production costs and increase the chances that a film will be widely seen, producers and studios have sometimes intervened to shorten a film. In some cases, though, and the classic American silent film *Greed* is a glaring example, much of the original film is lost, and film students cannot see the complete, original version. (In these cases, whether or not the original would be judged superior by current standards is unknowable.)[5]

Conclusions

Often the changes made after a film is released are of little consequence to viewer responses to the film. However, sometimes the changes *are* significant, probably especially in the following ways:

- *Shape of projected image*. If altered drastically, the original compositions are changed significantly.
- *Resolution and brightness*. If changed, significant details are often blurred and lost.
- *Color*. The color may be unlike the original color. It may even have changed so much that it is distracting.
- *Sound effects and music for "silent" films*. These are often omitted altogether. If supplied, they may be inappropriate and distracting.
- *Translations* in the subtitles or dubbing may be incomplete, inaccurate, distracting.
- *Running time*. Not all of the original shots may be included. On the other hand, new material may have been included (as in some TV broadcasts and occasional theatrical re-releases).

Such considerations may serve to remind you that other versions, perhaps other quite different versions, of the same title exist, and the film you are analyzing may not be the film your readers or listeners saw.[6]

---

[5] Usually, cutting continuity scripts fail to discuss the source or reliability of the film version described. For example, the introductory page of Theodore Huff's extremely useful 1961 shot analysis (cutting continuity script) of *The Birth of a Nation* says only that it is "based on a 16 mm print of the original 12-reel version, circa 1939." Unanswered are questions about the relationship of the print described to the 1915 versions. For another example, the Simon and Schuster script of *M* says nothing about the numerous different versions of that classic German film.

[6] I am grateful to Mr. David Shepard for his constructive criticism of an earlier draft of this chapter.

· 12 ·

Film Analysis:
Further Considerations

SCRIPTS
FILMS AND FICTION
FILMS AND FACT: THE REEL WORLD AND THE REAL
  WORLD
BUSINESS AND ART
FILMS AND FILMMAKERS
SOURCES OF ANALYSIS

As you analyze films and think about the process of analyzing films, certain issues usually come up. Some of them are discussed in this chapter.

Scripts

For a small proportion of all films, a script has been published. As in other aspects of filmmaking and film study, however, various, sometimes confusing terms are used. Thus a script may be called a "screenplay," "scenario," "treatment," "treatment outline," "shooting script," "continuity," "cutting continuity," or something else. Unlike plays, which are usually published in a uniform format and almost always in the final draft, published scripts tend to be of three different kinds:

1. *Preproduction:* The screenplay (or scenario) is an early version of the film story. Usually, it varies considerably from the finished film. Examples of published screenplays include Ingmar Bergman, *Four Screenplays* (1969), and Carl T. Dreyer, *Four Screenplays* (1970).
2. *Production:* The shooting script (or continuity) is used during filming. Because of changes made during shooting and editing,

the shooting script usually does not accurately describe the final film. An example of a shooting script is Graham Greene and Carol Reed, *The Third Man,* published in 1968.

3. *The Finished Film:* The cutting continuity is a description of the completed, released film. Often, it is divided into shots and includes such technical information as camera distances, angles, and shot duration. Examples are found in *The Citizen Kane Book* and *Films of Tyranny: Shot Analyses of "The Cabinet of Dr. Caligari," "The Golem," "Nosferatu."*

Comparisons of the first two kinds of scripts, the screenplay and the shooting script, with the finished film are useful in studies of the making of a film. Such studies sometimes help reveal, for instance, the contributions of the writer(s). Close study of the third kind of script, the cutting continuity, sharpens memory of the finished film and reveals patterns and details. For foreign-language films, fuller and usually more accurate translations are given than in the film itself.

No version of a script, however, can re-create the experience of watching a film. As Jan Kitchen shows in her essay in Chapter 8, cutting continuity scripts often include subjective interpretation, and they cannot re-create the experiences that film's techniques make happen. The editing, sounds, moving images, and environment of theater and audience all contribute to the experience of seeing a film. And most viewers find that reading any kind of script before seeing a film is tedious, and unsatisfactory as literature or cinema. Many scripts, too, are carelessly published and abound in errors. However, a reliable script, read shortly after the viewer has seen the film, rewards with insight and pleasure.

Films and Fiction

Let's look at a passage of fiction, then see how it is rendered in a film. The passage below is from the end of chapter 12 of *The Woman in the Dunes,* Kobo Abé's novel about a man trapped in a large sandpit with a woman who lives there:

> The woman sidled up to him. Her knees pressed against his hips. A stagnant smell of sun-heated water, coming from her mouth, nose, ears, armpits, her whole body, began to pervade the room around him. Slowly, hesitantly, she began to run her searing fingers up and down his spine. His body stiffened.
>
> Suddenly the fingers circled around to his side. The man let out a shriek.
>
> "You're tickling!"
>
> The woman laughed. She seemed to be teasing him, or else she was shy. It was too sudden; he could not pass judgment on the spur of the

moment. What, really, was her intention? Had she done it on purpose or had her fingers slipped unintentionally? Until just a few minutes ago she had been blinking her eyes with all her might, trying to wake up. On the first night too, he recalled, she had laughed in that strange voice when she had jabbed him in the side as she passed by. He wondered whether she meant anything in particular by such conduct.

Perhaps she did not really believe in his pretended illness and was testing her suspicions. That was a possibility. He couldn't relax his guard. Her charms were like some meat-eating plant, purposely equipped with the smell of sweet honey. First she would sow the seeds of scandal by bringing him to an act of passion, and then the chains of blackmail would bind him hand and foot.[1]

The comparable section of the film version runs about 45 seconds and consists of the conclusion of one shot and three additional shots (dialogue is from the subtitles of a print, not the published script):

shot number

1	. . . At the end of this lengthy shot, the woman, carrying a pan of water and a rag, approaches the man—who is lying on his back, naked from the waist up—and kneels beside him.
	WOMAN: How do you feel?
2	Man turns his head slightly away from her and groans.
	MAN: Not too bad.
	WOMAN: I'll wipe you down.
	As she turns him on his side, he lets out some more groans. The camera pans slightly to the left, and we see and hear her rinse and wring the rag in the metal pan; the camera pans right, and we see her begin to wipe his back with the damp rag. She turns the rag over.
3	Extreme close-up of part of his back and side. Camera follows her hand as she slowly wipes near his side. With a finger, she thumps/tickles his side.
4	Medium close-up of man's head and shoulders. He giggles, then quickly turns his head back toward her.
	MAN (angry and loud): Stop it!
	With a serious look on his face, he lowers his head and faces forward again.
	WOMAN (off-frame): It hurts?
	MAN (still serious): Yes!

[1] Kobo Abé, *The Woman in the Dunes,* trans. E. Dale Saunders (New York: Alfred A. Knopf, 1964).

Obviously, there are many differences between the experience of reading the passage and seeing and hearing the comparable section of the film. Some of the changes result from choices of the filmmakers. For example, the filmmakers chose to have the man laugh, then catch himself and become brusque, whereas in the book the man shrieks and the woman laughs. For another example, the filmmakers chose to supply more dialogue than is in the fiction.

Many of the differences, however, result from differences in the two media. At least three aspects of the passage are not usually translatable into film. The fiction gives many of the man's thoughts, including a memory, but attempts to render these mental states in a film might result in distortion and viewer confusion. Look again at the last two paragraphs reprinted from the book. How can film accurately convey what those words do? Without *words* how do you convey accurately and concisely "Her charms were like some meat-eating plant, purposely equipped with the smell of sweet honey. First she would sow the seeds of scandal by bringing him to an act of passion, and then the chains of blackmail would bind him hand and foot"? The figurative (or nonliteral) language is not convertible into visual images and sounds and music. Similarly, neither images nor sounds can convey well the experiences of smell, taste, feeling. Thus, "A stagnant smell of sun-heated water, coming from her mouth, nose, ears, armpits, her whole body, began to pervade the room around him" is not translatable into film.

Other differences between fiction and film result from some of film's characteristics. In 45 seconds, the film gives us viewers an excellent sense of location, shape and volume, textures, and sounds. For example, we see the forms and sizes of the man and woman; we see the texture of the man's skin; we hear his groans and the tone of voice of the man and woman. Most of these details are not rendered in the comparable passage of fiction. To do so would require enormous space and slow the story to a crawl, and even then the images in the reader's mind would be less precise than the images and sounds of the film. The movie camera can select actions and render them with clarity and force (as in the second shot where the camera pans left, then right); it can capture superbly movements and gestures and their meanings (the man's spontaneous laugh, then quick suppression of it). Film can convincingly show places, real and imaginary. Through editing, it can juxtapose objects more quickly than the blink of an eye. It can present visual texture and details. It can show us faces.

Letting others know how you feel is a basic part of communication. No creature in the world does so more eloquently than man, and no organ is more visually expressive than his face. Even in repose the human face sends a message and one that we tend to take for granted. Each face proclaims individual identity. In teams, recognition of other members is of great importance. A hunting dog in a pack proclaims its identity by its own personal smell. Primates, with their reduced sense of smell but their very acute vision, do it by the infinite variety of their faces. We have more separate muscles in our faces than any other animal. So we can move it in a variety of ways that no other animal can equal, and not only convey mood but send precise signals. By the expression on our face we can call people and send them away, ask questions and return answers without a word being spoken.[2]

Film can also capture well the nuances of sound and music. Prose is hard pressed to compete with cinema in presenting what can be seen and heard and in making us feel that we are there.

Yet films are often based on fiction, usually novels. (Sometimes, especially in recent years, a novel version of a film is published to help market the film and to profit from the publicity the film generates. Usually, those novels are not accomplished fiction and are of little interest to students of film or literature.) As illustrated with the example from *The Woman in the Dunes,* fictional films rarely re-create the source fiction very faithfully. Passages of characters' thoughts, descriptions of characters' backgrounds, analysis by the author, and a more or less consistent point of view or means of perception are uncommon in film storytelling. Nor does the fictional film, even the feature film, usually re-create all the characters and action of a novel. *Greed,* the 1920s film classic, attempted to do so, but the initial cut or version reportedly ran nine and a half hours, which was quickly judged too long to be commercial. The experiences of reading fiction and seeing film are quite different, because each medium has its own techniques, potential, and limitations. Perhaps the basic difference between fiction and film is that fiction requires its audience to visualize and subvocalize from words printed on the page, whereas film presents images and sounds more directly.

In light of the differences between fiction and film, it is not surprising that a film of a novel is not the novel. As a consequence, it is misleading, though common, to judge a film by how closely it re-creates a novel or, more accurately, the novel you visualized as you read it. Instead, the film is something related, yet new and separate: an imaginative creation that got its beginning from a writer's words.

Instead of evaluating the film by comparing it with its source—which is like trying to compare an apple pie to an apple tree—it is more helpful to compare the film version with other, similar films (and to compare the fiction with other, similar fiction). Nevertheless, a

---

[2] David Attenborough, "The Compulsive Communicators," *Life on Earth,* Program 13 (BBC Bristol © 1979). The wording is from the television program, not the book based on the series.

close comparison of a film and its fictional source can be instructive, revealing what the two story forms share and what is distinct to each. Also, such comparison usually gives insight into the process of transforming print into moving pictures and sounds, for instance by revealing how much of the original author's work remains in the finished film and how much is pared away or changed.

Far less frequently, films are based on plays. The same argument holds: the two media are cousins, and comparison of a drama and a film can illuminate the qualities of each medium but should not be used to evaluate the film's (or play's) effectiveness and value.

Films and Fact: The Reel World and the Real World

In most cases feature films need to attract large audiences in order to recoup the fortunes required to make and market them. Consequently, feature-length fiction films do not usually aim to teach facts: such strategy tends to be unprofitable. (That is why, I believe, so few full-length documentaries are released theatrically.) When a film deals with history, filmmakers usually omit or change historical details in order to make the film more entertaining, or to give it different meanings, or both. (For centuries novelists and playwrights have done the same.) The resulting films, such as *Gandhi, Patton,* and *Silkwood,* are imaginative blends of fact and fiction. *Gandhi,* for example, captures something of the person's life and influence, but is quite inadequate history, as its opening dedication concedes. To cite an example of omission: the film shows little of the last fifteen years of Gandhi's life when, in general, his influence was slipping. To cite one example of a change: the historical Gandhi was not as effective a speaker as the cinematic one. Although not history, the best of these films based on history present entertaining, sometimes complex characters and plots.

Yet the subjects and titles of films based on history often suggest factuality, as in the cases of *Gandhi* and *Patton;* frequently their publicity does, too. Films such as *The Birth of a Nation, The Battle of Algiers,* and *Gandhi* use intertitle cards or narrators or subtitles to cultivate the impression of factuality. And so compelling is the illusion of reality filmmakers may create that viewers easily forget that film characters and plots are not people and history. (Even many history teachers forget this.) In fact, films are rarely reliable history of the events they presumably re-create. They sometimes capture the spirit of the times and events but rarely provide the correct details and acceptable historical interpretations.

So impressive are large, bright, moving images presented without interruption that often a film looks like what we believe does or did exist. But fictional films (and documentary films to a lesser extent) are posed life. They look "real"; they *seem* like what we think we see in the world. In fact, that look and sound are artificially achieved. Sounds are selected, amplified or diminished, and electronically blended with other sounds. Crowds are carefully rehearsed beforehand and move in a shot with *studied* casualness. Lights and colors are carefully selected and arranged; on first glance, they look natural; on second or third glance, we sense that in a similar situation in life they would look slightly different. Products, such as Coca-Cola, are placed in conspicuous locations (it's one way filmmakers raise money or trade for services or goods). The events depicted may seem just like life, so "real," but the plot leaves out many boring, insignificant actions, such as every moment of a trip or long conversation.

> A film always transforms, surpasses, or recreates reality while it is recording it. Film is a medium and, because a medium expresses by means of its own qualities and colorations and has its own strengths and defects, it inevitably transforms what it attempts to represent. Cinema presumes a certain trust in the world as it is. Yet contrary to the old saw, the camera *does* "lie": it moves unexpectedly; it reduces dimensionality; it changes the natural size of an object or places it into an artificial context of juxtaposed or superimposed shots; it heightens a form by painting it with an unreal luminescence or beclouding it with an unreal darkness. Far from being impassive, the camera must—if it is to maintain our interest—maintain a fluidity of space and time, which is often lacking in "reality." These devices and effects may be "lies," but they are some of the ways of art, and the means to improved perception.[3]

Pablo Picasso said, "Art is a lie which makes us realize truth." That's true of films, too.

Those who say film is well suited to depicting conscious waking life—the world outside the theater—are right. The director Luis Buñuel is right, too:

> In the hands of a free spirit the cinema is a magnificent and dangerous weapon. It is the superlative medium through which to express the world of thought, feeling, and instinct. The creative handling of film images is such that, among all means of human expression, its way of functioning is most reminiscent of the work of the mind during sleep. A film is like an involuntary imitation of a dream. Brunius [Jacques B. Brunius, a French writer] points out how the darkness that slowly settles over a movie theater is equivalent to the act of closing the eyes. Then, on the screen, as within the human being, the nocturnal voyage into the unconscious begins. The device of fading allows images to ap-

---

[3] Roy Huss and Norman Silverstein, *The Film Experience,* pp. 7–8.

pear and disappear as in a dream; time and space become flexible, shrinking and expanding at will; chronological order and the relative values of time duration no longer correspond to reality, cyclical action can last a few minutes or several centuries; shifts from slow motion to accelerated motion heighten the impact of each.

The cinema seems to have been invented to express the life of the subconscious, the roots of which penetrate poetry so deeply.[4]

Film can seem both "real" and "unreal." The potential to express the external world we perceive in our waking hours is most fully realized in documentary films. The dream or subconscious potential of film, the interior world we see and hear as we sleep, is most fully depicted in some experimental films (see Figure 1.1), which of all kinds of films share the most in common with poetry.

Business and Art

For years each M-G-M film began with an image of a roaring lion, the words *Ars Gratia Artis* (Art for art's sake), and the words "Metro-Goldwyn-Mayer." Was Leo the lion a company stooge? Some people argue that feature films—the kind usually used as examples throughout this book—are not art but commercial events and public entertainments designed primarily to make money by appealing to large audiences with elementary intelligence, limited discrimination, and blunted sensitivity. Others argue that at least some films re-create something of the human experience, demand attentiveness, sensitivity, and intelligence of their audiences, and are esteemed beyond their initial run. There are many other variations of those two views and many definitions and assumptions about what is art. These two viewpoints, however, may stand as measurements; many films will be judged entirely as products of an entertainment business; others as artistic creations; many as a combination of the two.

Films and Filmmakers

It is well known that feature filmmaking is a collaborative undertaking. What one person could create a feature film? To script, costume, direct, light, perform, photograph, edit, score—not to mention finance—a feature film is beyond the powers of a single mortal. Nonetheless, many reviewers and writers of analyses are inclined to credit

[4] Luis Buñuel, "Poetry and Cinema," in *Luis Buñuel,* ed. Ado Kyrou (New York: Simon and Schuster, 1963); reprinted in Joan Mellen, ed., *The World of Luis Buñuel: Essays in Criticism* (New York: Oxford University Press, 1978).

and blame one person, usually the director, for the various aspects of a film. Sometimes, a viewer may partially discover or figure out who did what in the making of a film. By comparing various versions of the script, one may discover some of the contributions of the writer or writers. Often one may study the films of an influential director and note recurrent meanings and techniques (this is what is usually meant by the phrase "*auteur* theory").

In the case of a fiction writer or painter, assigning responsibility to a single creator is reasonable enough—although those endeavors are often not as solitary as might be believed. With films made by many filmmakers, however, it is often difficult to say with certainty which filmmaker contributed exactly what aspect to the finished product, and in most cases it is difficult to believe that the director is responsible for the creativity of *every* aspect: photography, sets, costumes, editing, scoring, and so on. Did the writer, director, star, or producer suggest a rewrite of a crucial scene? Did the writers, director, editor, star, or studio head insist that certain scenes be dropped? Examining the film or other films involving the same personnel usually yields no answers to these and many other questions about creative contributions, and reliable publications about such information are rare. Many questions about specific contributions to the finished film remain unknown and unknowable. To compound the problem, screen credits often inaccurately report who did what. It is better, therefore, especially for beginners in film analysis, to concentrate upon the film experience itself and neither credit nor blame any one person involved in the production.

Similarly, associating only one name with a film, by saying, for example, "W. C. Fields's *The Bank Dick*" or "Hitchcock's *Psycho*," suggests that only one person created and/or owns the film (as is more nearly the case in literature, musical compositions, and art works). Yet, to continue with the example of *Psycho,* although Hitchcock planned films in detail and retained strict control over their production, it is not entirely accurate to identify *Psycho* as "Hitchcock's *Psycho*." A reading of the source novel and the cutting continuity script reveals that author Robert Bloch and scriptwriter Joseph Stefano deserve partial credit for the shape and texture of the finished film. Many of the performers—especially Anthony Perkins, Vera Miles, and Martin Balsam—do more than adequate work. The music of Bernard Herrmann contributes to every scene where it is employed: view any section without the music, and its absence is pronounced. Even the title work by Saul Bass at the beginning and end of the film is unusually imaginative and appropriate. Doubtless, Hitchcock deserves much credit for supervising and coordinating all those and other efforts and for his own creativity. Various techniques and the subject matter itself also suggest that *Psycho* is a film directed by Hitchcock. Nonetheless, to label the film "Hitchcock's *Psycho*" disregards the contributions of many other accomplished filmmakers, without whose talents and creativity no director could succeed as well.

Sources of Analysis

Filmmakers are often interviewed and frequently have written about their knowledge, experience, and views. Their interviews and writings are often useful and interesting, especially in supplying background information—although the reader or listener has to beware of self-interests and failing memories. But filmmakers' *analyses* of a film, although sometimes helpful, should not be considered the final word. Why? For at least two reasons.

First, many filmmakers lack the skill or inclination to analyze films and to express themselves clearly and persuasively. (Conversely, many people skilled in those analytic traits lack the practical and imaginative talents to make successful films.) In the first chapter of his *Studies in Classic American Literature,* D. H. Lawrence wrote, "Never trust the artist. Trust the tale. The proper function of a critic is to save the tale from the artist who created it." Although Lawrence overstated the case, the analysis of a person who makes something is often unpersuasive.

The second reason is that it's difficult to analyze one's own work, especially during its making or shortly after its completion. Virtually all creative people—poets, painters, and playwrights, for instance—find this a fact of the creative life.

Some people assume that once they have read or heard about what a filmmaker *intended* to achieve, they have discovered *the* meaning or value of a film. Once again, one must be cautious, for results often do not match intentions (and films often have more than one plausible analysis). In addition, many filmmakers do not analyze their works, at least not for public consumption. Other filmmakers, such as Alfred Hitchcock, often analyze their work in an evasive, ironic manner. Instead of trying to determine the filmmaker's intentions, it is more productive to study closely the film itself, then compare notes with those more practiced in analyzing films.

Reviews are usually most useful as consumer guides; a sample of them can help you decide whether a film is worth your time and money. After seeing the film, you might want to reread the reviews carefully or seek out an analysis. Reading about the film is like talking to another thoughtful viewer. With practice, you will be able to understand sophisticated analyses, to see that analyses shed light upon both the film and the person analyzing. You will also come to a fuller understanding and appreciation of the film and, with more practice, of the film medium itself.

P · A · R · T

FIVE

SOURCES
FOR
EIGHT
FILMS

Selections

IN making the difficult decision about which films to feature in Part Five, I have used four criteria: current usage in U.S. colleges and universities; availability, including rental and/or purchase costs; variety; and difficulty for beginning film students. The list includes foreign and domestic, silent and sound, black-and-white and color. Yet it is made up exclusively of classic U.S., Japanese, Soviet, Indian, and European fiction films. No contemporary titles are included, since they are not readily accessible (many are distributed by only one company and are costly to rent). Furthermore, there are no South American, no African, no Australian films. Some countries with sizable film industries are not represented. These omissions are not meant as evaluative. Nor should the selection of films be interpreted as representative of any national cinema or film history. A few films reveal little about such immense subjects.

The films included in Part Five were all made for showings in a commercial theater and only later were shown nontheatrically (by film clubs, campus groups, church gatherings, etc.). Movies made for television are excluded. Generally, they are difficult to obtain for showing and close examination. And usually less money, time, and effort are put into their making. For these reasons, TV movies are rarely studied in U.S. colleges and universities. (If more accessible, these films would be an excellent source for studying the changing preoccupations of large groups of people who watch and enjoy them.)[1]

The background information, combined outline and frame enlargements, questions, observations (quotations from critics), and bibliography supplied for each of the following eight films are meant to help viewers know more about a film's background, its structure, its images, some major issues in analyzing the film, and readings about it. The following sources also reveal the kinds of material that are available or that can be devised. By pointing out certain details, these chapters may also make students more aware of the many significant choices filmmakers face.

---

[1] U.S. TV movies were first made in 1967. In recent years more than a hundred of them have been made and aired each year. Some foreign films—such as *The Sorrow and the Pity, Fellini's The Clowns,* and *Fanny and Alexander* (directed by Ingmar Bergman)— were originally made for TV, then shown in theaters in their native countries, then in theaters abroad.

Background

All of the following eight films were made for people of a different time and place than the readers of this book. Thus, background information, including photographs on the making and marketing of films, can help viewers better understand and appreciate these films. For these eight films I have attempted to make this background material as noninterpretive as possible, so that viewers will not be encouraged to respond in a particular way.[2]

Outlines

The outlines for each of the films that follow are meant to aid viewer memory, to help the viewer perceive the film's structure and editing, and to free viewers taking notes from the demands of capturing the rapid and relentless flow of action. Each outline attempts to describe only a small part (locations, what the characters do and sometimes say, and—often—transitions between scenes) of a complex and dynamic experience. To save considerable space minor action is omitted and indicated by ellipses (. . .). For each of the eight films, excluding *Annie Hall* and *Citizen Kane*, I have attempted to describe briefly the action of most scenes,[3] to number the scenes consecutively, and to group them under possible sequence headings. (Sometimes it's impossible to know when an action shifts to a new location or different time; thus, some scene divisions are my interpretations, which other viewers will dispute.)

I have described and numbered the scenes in *Annie Hall* but could find no sequence headings that clarify that film's complex structure. Given the complexity of *Citizen Kane,* the approach so useful for most of the other outlines would obscure that film's intricate structure; for its outline I have chosen a more involved and less linear, but I think more appropriate, format.

---

[2] Throughout this book, the date of a film refers to date of first release in its native country, as far as I have been able to determine.

[3] "Scene" in a film usually means a shot or (more often) a unified series of shots of seemingly consecutive action in one location.

Frame Enlargements

Frame enlargements are blown-up photographs of individual frames from the film, as distinguished from publicity stills, which are still photographs usually taken during the making of the film to advertise it. Frame enlargements can aid memory and convey some of the film's visual style, although they are limited, as are photographs of a dance, and are sometimes scratched. Some of the enlargements hint at the expressiveness, power, and indelibility of certain images. Others reveal flitting, frequently unnoticed details. Finally, the frame enlargements are often coordinated with the questions that follow in order to help readers discover qualities of the images and sometimes the relation of image to image, in cases where frame enlargements are used from consecutive shots.[4]

Questions and Observations

Most film viewers find at least some questions and observations interesting and useful. They help direct attention to certain details, patterns, and issues, and they can help readers reach a persuasive, judicious, and reasonably complete analysis. They also convey a sense of how others respond to a film. Occasionally they can stimulate the viewer to reexamine the film and his or her responses to it, though the questions and observations are by no means comprehensive.

Suggested Readings

Contexts

Knowing the contexts of a film can increase viewer enjoyment, understanding, and appreciation. The readings under "Contexts" include fictional and dramatic sources, film history, history, filmmaking, and filmmakers.

---

[4] I am pleased with the number and quality of the frame enlargements I have been able to provide. I only regret that I could not get access to 35 mm prints in all cases, that some copyright holders make it so difficult and costly for writers to illustrate (and publicize!) their films, and that the cost and difficulty of obtaining faithful color frame enlargements have resulted in the substitution of black-and-white for color in the cases of *Annie Hall* and *2001*.

Scripts and Outlines

Cutting continuity scripts, which describe the finished film, are especially useful, for they sharpen memory of the film and reveal patterns and details. Screenplays and shooting scripts are helpful in studying the evolution of a film.

I have listed published outlines in the section with scripts, because outlines are, in effect, more concise forms of cutting continuity scripts. They likewise can aid memory and reveal patterns.

Analyses: Others' Views

Analyses can also increase viewer enjoyment, understanding, and appreciation. They can make the viewer more aware that plausible, worthwhile analyses can be made from various perspectives. And the number and variety of published analyses listed throughout the book—although only a minute fraction of all published analyses—suggest how many people at different times and places have observed films carefully, examined their reactions to them, and attempted to communicate their responses to others.

· 13 ·

Annie Hall

13.1 Original advertisement for *Annie Hall*

Background

Country of Production: U.S.A.

First Release: Spring 1977

Process: DeLuxe color; 1.85:1 aspect ratio

Approximate Running Time: 93 minutes

Versions: So far as I am aware, 16 mm prints available for rent and video copies for sale are all identical.

Production: Ten weeks' filming at Pathe Studios in Manhattan; various locations in Manhattan; locations in Brooklyn, including Coney Island; Long Island; and a New Jersey suburb. Two weeks' filming in Los Angeles.

Selected Credits:

- Producer: Charles H. Joffe
- Director: Woody Allen (1935–   ), writer, stand-up comedian, actor, and director of *Take the Money and Run; Play It Again, Sam; Love and Death; Interiors; Manhattan; Zelig; Broadway Danny Rose;* and others
- Scriptwriters: Woody Allen and Marshall Brickman
- Design: Mel Bourne
- Costume Designer: Ruth Morley
- Cinematographer: Gordon Willis (*The Godfather; The Godfather, Part II; All the President's Men; Zelig;* many others)
- Editor: Ralph Rosenblum (six Woody Allen films, *The Pawnbroker, Fail Safe,* others)
- Music: "Seems Like Old Times," "It Had to Be You," "A Hard Way to Go," "Christmas Medley," and "Sleepy Lagoon"
- Sound: James Pilcher and James Sabat

Major Characters and Performers:

- Alvy/Max Singer: Woody Allen (actor in *Take the Money and Run; Play It Again, Sam; The Front; Manhattan; Zelig; Broadway Danny Rose;* others)
- Annie Hall: Diane Keaton (1946–   ) (the two *Godfather* films, *Looking for Mr. Goodbar, Reds, Shoot the Moon*)
- Rob/Max: Tony Roberts (New York theater experience, *Play It Again, Sam,* others)
- Tony Lacey: Paul Simon (professional singer)
- *Rolling Stone* reporter: Shelley Duvall (*Brewster McCloud, Nashville, Three Women, The Shining, Popeye*)
- Allison: Carol Kane (*Carnal Knowledge, The Last Detail, Hester Street*)
- Mom Hall: Colleen Dewhurst (extensive New York theater experience and ten or so films)
- Alvy's second wife: Janet Margolin (*David and Lisa, Enter Laughing, Take the Money and Run*)
- Duane Hall: Christopher Walken (*Next Stop, Greenwich Village; The Deer Hunter; Heaven's Gate; The Dogs of War; The Dead Zone*)
- Marshall McLuhan: himself
- Dick Cavett: himself

Six co-stars with WOODY ALLEN and DIANE KEATON pictured above are (from the upper right, clockwise): COLLEEN DEWHURST as Mom Hall; CAROL KANE as Allison; TONY ROBERTS as Rob; SHELLEY DUVALL as Pam; JANET MARGOLIN as Robin; and PAUL SIMON as Tony Lacey, an L.A. pop star, in "Annie Hall," a United Artists release.

13.2 Publicity still. © 1977 United Artists Corporation. Movie Star News.

Place and Time of Story: Brooklyn (including Coney Island), Manhattan, suburban New York, Los Angeles, and Wisconsin; various stages in Alvy's life
Other:

- The film is rated PG.
- There is no sound during the opening credits.
- "Freud" and "analysis" are referred to several times in the film. Sigmund Freud (1856–1939) was an Austrian physician who originated psychoanalysis (or analysis), the process of trying to help patients discover former and subconscious drives that shape later personality and behavior.

13.3 Publicity still: in this case, an out-take or a photograph not included in the finished film. © United Artists Corporation 1977. Larry Edmunds Bookshop.

13.4 Publicity still illustrating split screen effect used in *Annie Hall*. © 1977 United Artists Corporation. Movie Star News.

Outline

1. To camera Alvy tells two jokes, then says, "Annie and I broke up."
2. Brooklyn, World War II: Alvy and his mother at Dr. Flicker's.
3. Coney Island exterior: Alvy's house under roller coaster.
4. Interior, house: Alvy as child trying to eat soup as the house shakes.
5. Coney Island boardwalk: Three servicemen, girl, and boy Alvy.
6. Coney Island, bumper cars: Dad at work, Alvy at play.
7. Brooklyn schoolroom, 1942: Teachers, classmates, Alvy (age 6) kisses a girl, then justifies himself (Figure 13.5).
8. Alvy on Dick Cavett TV program.
9. Alvy's mother talking to Alvy (unseen).
10. New York City street: Alvy and Rob talk about "Jew" and California.
11. Alvy waiting in front of Beekman Theater: his celebrity treatment, and Annie's arrival.
12. Lobby of Beekman Theater: Annie and Alvy argue.
13. Lobby of New Yorker Theater: In line, Annie, Alvy, a film critic, then Marshall McLuhan.
14. Clips from *The Sorrow and the Pity*.
15. Bedroom: Annie and Alvy, their different sexual appetites.
16. Backstage: Alvy meets Allison.
17. Alvy on stage at Adlai Stevenson rally (1956).
18. Allison and Alvy on bed, Alvy "withholding his attention" from her (it's 1964 or so: references to Warren Commission).
19. Country house: Alvy and Annie "cooking" lobster in the kitchen.
20. Annie and Alvy walking near beach.
21. On street, night: Dennis—Annie's first boyfriend.
22. Annie's second boyfriend, an actor. At party, young Annie and actor-boyfriend watched by older Annie and Alvy.
23. Near beach again, sunset: Annie and Alvy, offscreen, continue their conversation.

13.5 Brooklyn public school, 1942: Alvy says he never had a latency period.

24. Alvy at party with his second wife (Robin).
25. Alvy in bedroom watching Knicks game on TV. Alvy tries to seduce his second wife.
26. Bedroom, night: Second wife and Alvy; her sexual frustration and his.
27. Lobby and hallway of inside tennis court: Alvy and Rob talk about New York and California.
28. Tennis court: During doubles match, Annie and Alvy meet for the first time.
29. Lobby, after match: Annie and Alvy talk.
30. In VW convertible Annie gives Alvy a lift.
31. Street outside Annie's place: Parking, then talking on sidewalk.
32. Inside Annie's apartment: A drink and conversation (Alvy mentions that it's 1975).
33. Outside, roof patio: Another drink and more conversation—with subtitles (Figure 13.6).
34. Nightclub: Annie sings "It Had to Be You" to a "restless" audience.
35. On street: Alvy reassures Annie about her singing and gives her an early good-night kiss.
36. Delicatessen: They talk about his background.
37. Annie and Alvy in bed, after lovemaking.
38. Bookstore: Alvy chooses books about death for Annie.
39. Park: Alvy identifies passers-by for Annie.
40. Dock, sunset: Annie and Alvy declare their love for each other.
41. Alvy's apartment: Annie moving in; they argue.
42. Countryside: Annie driving Alvy in her car.
43. Bedroom of country house, night: Talk of college courses, party, sex, marijuana; Annie's double watches Annie and Alvy.
44. Agent's office: "Comedian" asks Alvy to write material for him (Alvy does not yet deliver his own jokes).
45. Auditorium of University of Wisconsin: Part of Alvy's act.
46. Backstage: Annie and Alvy talk briefly as he signs autographs.

13.6 Shortly after Annie has met Alvy, she's thinking one thing while she says something else. © 1977 United Artists Corporation. All rights reserved.

47. Exterior view of Annie's parents' home.
48. The meal in dining room of Annie's family home the next day.
49. Split screen: Annie's family and Alvy's family, their dialogue.
50. Room of Annie's brother, Duane: His confession to Alvy.
51. Downstairs in house: Annie saying good-bye to her parents.
52. Car, night: Duane driving Annie and Alvy to airport.
53. Street, New York, day: Annie is angry that Alvy's been spying on her. They argue.
54. Voice-over transition. Kitchen, Alvy's apartment, a month earlier: Annie tells Alvy about her first session with the analyst.
55. Street, New York: Annie and Alvy argue again and break up. Alvy questions strangers on the street.
56. Cartoon: Queen from *Snow White* (with Annie's voice) and Alvy and Rob (Figure 13.7).
57. Corridor: Reporter from *Rolling Stone* and Alvy, her enthusiasm and interests. "God" comes out of the men's room.
58. Bedroom: After the "Kafkaesque" sexual experience with the reporter, Alvy receives an emergency call from Annie.
59. Annie's apartment: Alvy to rescue; a reconciliation.
60. Bedroom: Annie and Alvy agree not to break up again.
61. Annie's car, road, day (the weekend following previous scene): Annie, Alvy, and Rob on way to Brooklyn.
62. Outside Alvy's old house under the roller coaster: Memory.
63. Inside Alvy's house: Annie, Alvy, and Rob watch Alvy's parents in years past argue; then they watch two scenes from a 1945 welcome-home party.
64. Street, New York: Annie and Alvy, day before Annie's birthday.
65. Inside: Annie's two birthday presents.
66. Nightclub: Annie sings "Seems Like Old Times"—with better results.
67. Annie and Alvy at bar: Tony Lacey's congratulations and invitations.
68. At *The Sorrow and the Pity* again.

13.7 Rob advising Alvy to forget about Annie and find someone else.

69. Split screen and overlapping dialogue: Annie and Alvy at separate analysts discuss same subjects (Figure 13.4).
70. Annie and Alvy with couple with cocaine, a week before the trip to California.
71. Street, Beverly Hills: Rob driving Annie and Alvy around, and the three discussing New York and California.
72. Street views: Restaurants and movie theater.
73. Television control room: Alvy, Rob, and a technician; Rob is orchestrating laughs for his TV show.
74. Hotel room: Alvy with doctor and Annie; Alvy is nervous about making an award on TV, then hungry after he learns he need not do it.
75. Street: Rob, Annie, and Alvy arrive at a large house.
76. Inside: Tony Lacey's party; Alvy and Rob and woman in white; Tony with Annie.
77. Tony gives tour of house to Annie and Alvy.
78. More partying.
79. On plane back to New York: Annie's thoughts and Alvy's and their spoken admissions that their relationship isn't satisfactory.
80. Alvy's apartment (still Christmastime): Annie packing up.
81. Outside theater: After their breakup; strangers talk to Alvy.
82. Country house: Alvy, lobster, and new girl without a sense of humor.
83. Dockside: Alvy alone.
84. Bedroom: On phone, Alvy asking Annie to return.
85. Shot of plane in flight (presumably Alvy on way to California).
86. L.A. airport: Alvy calls Annie from a phone booth.
87. Alvy "driving" car.
88. Outdoor health food café: Alvy proposes marriage to Annie; her rejection, their argument.
89. Parking lot: She drives away; he tries to, cross-cut with those Coney Island bumper cars. Policeman and Alvy.
90. Inside jail: Alvy being released from his cell.
91. Outside: Alvy and Rob walk to car and get ready to drive away.
92. Studio: Alvy watches part of a rehearsal of his play.

13.8 Early in the film's last shot, which lasts about 55 seconds. © 1977 United Artists Corporation. All rights reserved.

93. Shot of Thalia Theater: Alvy runs into Annie and her date.
94. Sometime later, restaurant: Annie and Alvy have lunch and talk about old times.
95. Montage of earlier shots of Annie and Alvy as we hear Annie sing again "Seems Like Old Times."
96. Street corner in background; restaurant (same one as in scene 94): Annie and Alvy say good-bye as we hear Alvy's voice-over tell one last joke (Figure 13.8).

End Credits

Questions and Observations

1. What pulls Annie and Alvy together? What keeps them apart? Why are the latter forces finally stronger than the former? Annie and Alvy meet at a tennis match; she gives him a ride; they have a drink at her place (scenes 28–33 above). When they break up for the last time, she meets him at a sidewalk restaurant in L.A.; he tries to drive away; Rob gets Alvy out of jail; Alvy watches a rehearsal of his new play (scenes 88–92). In what ways have Annie and Alvy changed? Why? What are the consequences?
2. Who is the source of our views of Annie and Alvy? How reliable is that source?
3. How important is it that you know exactly how much of Allen's and Keaton's lives are mirrored in the story of Alvy and Annie? Explain.
4. What is satirized or made fun of in the film? How would you describe the satire: gentle, harsh, or what? Why do you say so? What is *not* satirized?
5. Discuss in some detail, the last shot of the film (see Figure 13.8), especially its mood(s) and composition.
6. Describe the dominant color and lighting of the New York City scenes. Then describe the dominant color and lighting in the California scenes. How do you account for the differences? New York and Los Angeles are compared throughout the film. What pictures emerge of those two cities?
7. The script makes a number of references to "analysis" and Freud. What other knowledge does the script assume the audience has?
8. Earlier films directed by Allen were often criticized as lacking unity, as being a string of amusing, yet often unrelated scenes. How valid is this criticism if applied to *Annie Hall*? Do any of the scenes not advance the story and/or reveal important aspects of character? If so, what functions do they serve?
9. Examine closely the outline of scenes printed above. What scenes hold together as a sequence? What unifies them? From the plot of *Annie Hall*, reconstruct the story of Annie and Alvy: the chronological order of events in their lives. The plot jumps back and forth in time. Is it ever confusing? If so, where and why? What are the advantages and justifications of this nonchronological order? What are the disadvantages?

10. It's been reported that Woody Allen originally wanted to call the film *Anhedonia,* which means the inability to feel pleasure. Which is the better title for the film, *Anhedonia* or *Annie Hall*? Why do you say so?

11. What techniques in the film are unusual for a commercial feature? What purposes do they serve? Do any of the techniques call undue attention to themselves? If so, which ones and how so?

12. At the beginning of the film, Alvy says,

There's an old joke. Uh, two elderly women are at a Catskills mountain resort, and one of 'em says: "Boy, the food at this place is really terrible." The other one says, "Yeah, I know, and such . . . small portions." Well, that's essentially how I feel about life. Full of loneliness and misery and suffering and unhappiness, and it's all over much too quickly. The—the other important joke for me is one that's, uh, usually attributed to Groucho Marx, but I think it appears originally in Freud's wit and its relation to the unconscious [*sic*]. And it goes like this—I'm paraphrasing: Uh . . . "I would never wanna belong to any club that would have someone like me for a member." That's the key joke of my adult life in terms of my relationships with women. . . .

At the conclusion of the film, Alvy says,

After that it got pretty late. And we both hadda go, but it was great seeing Annie again, right? I realized what a terrific person she was and—and how much fun it was just knowing her and I—I thought of that old joke, you know, this—this—this guy goes to a psychiatrist and says, "Doc, uh, my brother's crazy. He thinks he's a chicken." And, uh, the doctor says, "Well, why don't you turn him in?" And the guy says, "I would, but I need the eggs." Well, I guess that's pretty much how how I feel about relationships. You know, they're totally irrational and crazy and absurd and . . . but, uh, I guess we keep goin' through it because, uh, most of us need the eggs.[1]

13. "*Annie Hall* is frequently funny; but not integrally funny. The slight story of a vapid affair is heavily festooned with *mots* and gags that run on without adding up; after a while they seem ad hoc, defensive, timid, merely tactical self-depreciations even when Woody is trying to lure us, as Alvy lures Annie, into his language-field. Alvy's seduction of Annie is less sexual than terminological: he teaches her—trains her—to talk his lingo, the Village patois, and ridicules her Midwestern colloquialisms, like "neat," even though these are clearly part of her charm for him. She learns the ropes too well and, her own woman, finally leaves him floundering in his own wry *Weltschmerz*. His antagonists are smoothies (like the recording mogul she leaves him for) and pseudo-intellectuals (he shows up a boor in a ticket line by magically producing Marshall McLuhan to confute the fellow's phony explications of McLuhanism); the Prince of Darkness is a name-dropper, one who invokes the portentous frivolously. Alvy may not prevail, but he always has the privilege of the last word."[2]

[1] *Four Films of Woody Allen* (New York: Random House, 1982).
[2] M. J. Sobran, Jr. "Boy Meets Shiksa," *National Review* 29 (27 May 1977).

14. "The film is one man's memories, an attempt to come to grips with a life at a point of crisis. The film is about a man obsessed with the past and the need to comprehend it. He makes connections based on his own experiences; a word, a phrase, a minor event can set off another series of mental images. This is basically the way the human mind works, and it's the way *Annie Hall* works. Thus, this seemingly complex narrative is actually one of Allen's most accessible."[3]

15. "Love is the subject here—not sex as in previous films, though sex is never far away, but the possibilities of successful love. The script begins and ends with two avowedly old jokes. (There's an equally old unavowed one in the middle—about parking far from the curb.) These flanking jokes set the tenor of the piece: (1) Life is rotten but who wants less of it? (2) Life is crazy, but it's crazier not to go along with the craziness. Between those borders we get the story of a modern hyperconscious fellow for whom those two commandments have long replaced the original ten but who keeps rescrutinizing them for some hint about making love last."[4]

contrasting screens

flashbacks
subtitles } *physicological?*
split screen
animation
fantasy

Suggested Readings

Contexts

Monaco, James. *American Film Now.* New York: New American Library, 1979, pp. 239–48. On Allen and his films.

Moss, Robert F. "Creators on Creating: Woody Allen." *Saturday Review* 7 (November 1980): 40–44. An interview.

Rich, Frank. "Woody Allen Wipes the Smile Off His Face." *Esquire* 87 (May 1977): 72–76 & 148–49. Based upon an interview with Allen.

Rosenblum, Ralph, and Robert Karen. *When the Shooting Stops . . . the Cutting Begins: A Film Editor's Story.* New York: Viking, 1979. The chapter on the editing of *Annie Hall* was excerpted and reprinted in *New York,* 8 October 1979.

Yacowar, Maurice. *Loser Take All: The Comic Art of Woody Allen.* New York: Frederick Ungar, 1979.

Scripts

Four Films of Woody Allen. New York: Random House, 1982. Cutting continuities with occasional frame enlargements for *Annie Hall, Interiors, Manhattan,* and *Stardust Memories.*

[3] Warren Spector, *CinemaTexas Program Notes* 19, no. 1 (4 September 1980).
[4] Stanley Kauffmann, *Before My Eyes* (New York: Harper & Row, 1980), from a reprint of one of Mr. Kauffmann's reviews in *The New Republic.*

Analyses and Reviews

Asahina, Robert. "Don't Play It Again, Woody." *The New Leader* 60 (6 June 1977): 22–23. Completely negative review of the film.

Dawson, Jan. "*Annie Hall.*" *Monthly Film Bulletin* 44, no. 525 (October 1977): 207–8. Includes credits; summary of story, not plot; and an analysis.

Geduld, Harry M. "Woody Allen and Galatea." *The Humanist,* July/August 1977, pp. 54–55. Analyzes the film as a variation on the myth of Pygmalion and Galatea.

Gilliatt, Penelope. "Woody at His Best Yet." *The New Yorker* 53 (25 April 1977): 136–37.

Kauffmann, Stanley. *The New Republic* 176 (14 May 1977): 22–23; reprinted in Kauffmann, *Before My Eyes* (New York: Harper & Row, 1980).

Siska, William. "The Laughter of Survival." *The Christian Century* 94 (22–29 June 1977): 593–94.

Sobran, M. J. Jr. "Boy Meets Shiksa." *National Review* 29 (27 May 1977): 622–23.

Westerbeck, Colin L. Jr. "Love's Labor's Lost." *Commonweal* 104 (13 May 1977): 306–7.

· 14 ·

Bicycle Thieves

1948

14.1 Original poster. *Cult Movie* (Italy).

Background

Other Titles:
   Ladri di Biciclette (Italian)
   The Bicycle Thief (other English title)
Country of Production: Italy
First Release: 1948
Process: Black and white; 1.33:1 aspect ratio
Approximate Running Time: 90 minutes
Versions: So far as I know, all prints in circulation are complete and identical.

Production: The film was shot on location on the outskirts of Rome; the interiors of the municipal pawnshop were filmed in an abandoned warehouse (Figures 14.2–14.4). Two months were spent in editing the film.

Selected Credits:

- Producer: Produzioni De Sica
- Director: Vittorio De Sica (1902–1974). Matinee idol in Italian films of 1920s and 1930s. During World War II began directing films. Probably best known for three films he made with the writer Cesare Zavattini: *Shoeshine* (1946), *Bicycle Thieves* (1948), and *Umberto D* (1951). Other films directed include *Two Women* (1960) and *The Garden of the Finzi-Continis* (1971).
- Scriptwriter: Cesare Zavattini (Figure 14.5). His script was very loosely based upon the novel of the same title by Luigi Bartolini.
- Dialogue and scene arrangement by Vittorio De Sica, Cesare Zavattini, and five other writers.
- Design: Antonino Traverso
- Cinematographer: Carlo Montuori
- Editor: Eraldo da Roma
- Music: Alessandro Cicognini
- Sound: Not credited

Major Characters and Performers:

- Antonio Ricci (REE chee): Lamberto Maggiorani
- Bruno Ricci: Enzo Staiola

14.2 Shooting on location. Museum of Modern Art/Film Stills Archive.

14.3 Filming an interior shot. Museum of Modern Art/Film Stills Archive.

14.4 Director De Sica with the woman who plays Maria. Museum of Modern Art/Film Stills Archive.

14.5 Writer Cesare Zavattini. Museum of Modern Art/Film Stills Archive.

- Maria Ricci: Lianella Carell
- Baiocco (Ricci's friend)
- Thief in German forage cap
- Old man
- Medium

Place and Time of Story: Rome, about 1946, a time of high unemployment, inflation, and recovery from World War II

Other: Neorealist cinema is defined as follows:

> An influential movement of filmmaking in Italy, usually dated from 1945 to the early 1950s. Neorealistic films tend to feature unextraordinary men and women in their social and economic contexts and often lack a certain psychological sophistication. Such films also tend to use unobtrusive techniques: functional and chronological editing, natural lighting, eye-level medium and long distance camera placement, and on-location settings.
>
> Although Luchino Visconti's *Obsession* (1942) was a harbinger of neorealistic films, Roberto Rossellini's *Rome, Open City* (1945), which shows Catholics and Communists resisting the Nazi occupation, was the first full-fledged neorealistic film. Rossellini's *Paisan* (1946) and *Germany, Year Zero* (1947) are also important examples of neorealism, as is Visconti's *The Earth Trembles* (1947). The neorealistic films probably best known outside Italy are those scripted largely by . . . Cesare Zavattini and directed by Vittorio De Sica: *Shoeshine* (1946), *Bicycle Thieves* (1948), and *Umberto D* (1951).
>
> These and many similar films were appreciated, especially abroad, as honest yet compassionate. In them ordinary characters are beset by problems of post-war Italy—poverty, exploitation, unemployment, loneliness—yet often respond with resilience and dignity.

Neorealistic filmmakers attempted to present events with a minimum of distortion, and their films show how expressively the documentary potential of film may be realized in narratives.[1]

Outline

During the credits in the Italian version a bus arrives near some buildings; many men get off and approach a building; a man waves them back.

I. Friday, day
  1. Ricci learns of job as bill poster, his first in two years.
  2. Outside and near his apartment: He tells his wife Maria about the job.
  3. In their apartment: She takes sheets off bed.
  4. They pawn their sheets.
  5. Ricci reclaims his bike and leaves with Maria.
  6. He reports to his new employer.
  7. Outside: He shows Maria his new cap and tells her about his job.
  8. At Maria's request, Ricci takes her to the building of a fortune-teller. . . .

II. Saturday
  A. Day
    9. Bruno and Ricci prepare to leave for their jobs (Figure 14.6).

14.6 Ricci and Maria, before he leaves for work. Courtesy Cornith Films.

[1] William H. Phillips, "Neo-realistic Cinema," *The Reader's Encyclopedia*, 3d ed. Harper & Row, in preparation.

10. Ricci and Bruno on way to work.
11. Ricci drops Bruno off at his job at a service station. . . .
12. Ricci learns how to put up posters.
13. Ricci putting up a poster. His bicycle is stolen by a man in World War II German cap and two accomplices.
14. The chase.
15. Back at job location: Ricci's dejection (Figure 14.7).
16. At police station, Ricci gets neither help nor sympathy.
   B. Night
17. Dusk: . . . Ricci comes to pick up Bruno. They start walking home.
18. Ricci leaves Bruno at home.
19. At Workers' Party headquarters, Ricci interrupts a political speech. He talks to his friend Baiocco. Maria arrives and, depressed, the two leave for home.
III. Sunday, day
20-23. . . . Ricci, Bruno, Baiocco, and two other men looking for Ricci's bicycle at Piazza Vittorio. Confrontation with man painting bicycle frame cross-cut with Bruno accosted by man.
24. Baiocco's co-worker gives Bruno and Ricci a ride to another market. Rain.
25. At market of Porta Portese, Bruno falls in rain. Ricci sees the thief give an old man money, but the thief escapes.
26. Ricci and Bruno look for the old man. . . .
27. They follow him into the communion of the poor in a church. Eventually, he slips away from them.
28. Outside, Bruno scolds his father; Ricci slaps him . . . (Figure 14.8).
29. Ricci looks for old man by the river, then fears Bruno may be drowning.
30. Ricci tries to get Bruno to talk, then invites him to go eat.
31. Ricci takes Bruno to an expensive restaurant.
32. The two go to the fortune-teller.
33. In street, Ricci spots the thief and chases him.
34. Thief slips into brothel. Uproar. Ricci and thief are pushed out of brothel.
35. In street of thief's neighborhood a crowd gathers. Thief has epileptic seizure (probably). Crowd threatening. Bruno brings a policeman.
36. Ricci, Bruno, and policeman search the thief's apartment.
37. Back on street: Without evidence or witnesses Ricci decides not to try to press charges. Crowd jeers and threatens Ricci. . . .
38. In the middle of a street: Bruno is nearly hit by two cars.
39. Near soccer stadium Ricci sends Bruno to a trolley, but he misses it. Ricci steals a bicycle. Bruno sees him pursued (Figure 14.9). Ricci is caught by bystanders. Seeing Bruno, the owner decides not to press charges.

14.7 Ricci just after his bicycle has been stolen. Courtesy Cornith Films.

14.8 After Ricci slaps Bruno. Courtesy Cornith Films.

14.9 Reaction shot of Bruno as he sees his father being chased on stolen bicycle. Courtesy Cornith Films.

40. Ricci and Bruno walk away. Bruno hands his father his hat. A passing truck nudges Ricci's shoulder. Ricci trying to hold back tears. Bruno takes his father's hand (Figure 14.10). Shot of the two as they recede from camera into the crowd (Figure 14.11). *Fine* (Italian for "End") superimposed, then fade-out.

14.10 Film's next-to-last shot. Courtesy Cornith Films.

14.11 Last shot: Ricci and Bruno fade into crowd before the final fade-out. Courtesy Cornith Films.

Questions and Observations

1. What are Ricci's most appealing characteristics? What are his shortcomings? How do you feel about him? Why?
2. Imagine the film without Bruno. What would be lost? (Be sure to answer this question in detail.) In what ways is Bruno a child? In what actions/reactions is he an adult? In what sense can it be argued that Bruno is the film's most important character?
3. In Ricci's search for his stolen bicycle, who is helpful to him? Who impedes him?
4. Discuss Ricci's changing emotional states in the scenes where he discovers Bruno has not drowned and where the two of them go to the restaurant and eat. Are his changing moods adequately motivated? How well do they enjoy their meal? Why?
5. Reconsider the last scene (described in some detail in the outline), after Bruno and Ricci have been left "free." What feelings does the scene generate? How does it manage to do so?
6. Does the film offer any hope of changing the economic situation that Ricci and his family find themselves in? If so, in what way? What does the film suggest as a solace for life's trials?
7. The film's title is sometimes translated as *The Bicycle Thief.* The Italian title is in the plural. Which is the better title, *The Bicycle Thief* or *Bicycle Thieves*? Why?
8. The major performers are nonactors: Ricci was played by a factory worker; De Sica found the boy who played Bruno in a crowd; and Maria was played by a journalist who had come to interview De Sica. Are the three major performances successful or not? How so? Are their faces, body builds, and gestures appropriate or not? Explain.
9. Where is space within the frame used to suggest emotional distance between characters? Where are characters packed into the frame suggesting entrapment?
10. How noticeable are the film's techniques, for example, its editing, camera work, and music? How appropriate is this style for the story?
11. If you have seen *Open City, Shoeshine, Umberto D,* or any other of the Italian neorealist films, describe what qualities they share with *Bicycle Thieves*.
12. De Sica is quoted as saying, "My idea is to 'deromanticize' the cinema. I would like to teach men to look at day-to-day life and everyday events with the same passion that they read a book."[2]
13. The following observations by Herbert L. Jacobson were published in 1949:

[T]hat broad humanitarian sympathy combined with gentle cynicism . . . Italians alone bear as their trademark. It is an old Italian recipe for living, buried under the garbage of Fascism for a quarter century but

---

[2] Quoted in Georges Sadoul, *Dictionary of Films,* trans. Peter Morris, (Berkeley: University of California Press, 1972), p. 184.

never really lost; the war, which scraped over the country like a rake, served to turn it up again. In a world still spinning from the blows of war there are few formulae [of general pity for suffering humanity without any special solution for its problems] more practical for day-to-day living, or for making films that a confused humanity will recognize as true.[3]

14. "The meaning of *The Bicycle Thief* is problematic indeed. The traditional view construes the work as a political film which combines a presentation of pressing social problems with an implicit denunciation of a particular socioeconomic system. Closer analysis, however, reveals this view to be only one of several plausible interpretations, for the film may also be seen as a pessimistic and fatalistic view of the human condition, as well as a philosophical parable on absurdity, solitude, and loneliness. Antonio Ricci emerges in the opening shot from a crowd at an employment agency; in the moving closing shot, he merges back into the crowd at a soccer match with his small son and disappears. Crowds and masses of people outside Ricci's immediate family are always threatening rather than reassuring forces in the film, hardly the proper iconography for a work depicting proletarian solidarity or class consciousness. When Ricci receives his job, his fellow unemployed are more than eager to take it from him; when he comes to the union hall to seek assistance for his stolen bicycle, vague offers of aid are forthcoming but no real understanding of his personal tragedy emerges from a gathering that understands only collective action; he is threatened by crowds waiting for buses, and the final destruction of his self-respect before the eyes of his son occurs within the hostile crowd that captures him after his attempted theft. This act of a hostile crowd is in direct contrast to the complete lack of assistance Ricci receives from another crowd when he tries to prevent the theft of his own vehicle. Of course, De Sica shows us bureaucrats, police officials, and pious churchgoers who do not understand Ricci's plight either, but the fact that members of his own class are no more sympathetic to him than they are is even more devastating. In De Sica's universe, economic solutions are ultimately ineffective in curing what is a meaningless, absurd, human predicament."[4]

Suggested Readings

Contexts

Armes, Roy. *Patterns of Realism: A Study of Italian Neo-Realist Cinema*. New York: A. S. Barnes, 1971. Includes a chapter on *Bicycle Thieves*.

Bondanella, Peter. *Italian Cinema: From Neorealism to the Present*. New York: Frederick Ungar, 1983. Basically, the book examines post–World War II

---

[3] Herbert L. Jacobson, "De Sica's 'Bicycle Thieves' and Italian Humanism," *Hollywood Quarterly* 4, no. 1 (Fall 1949).

[4] Peter Bondanella, *Italian Cinema: From Neorealism to the Present* (New York: Frederick Ungar, 1983).

Italian cinema as an art, with emphasis on the works of such major directors as Rossellini, De Sica, Fellini, Visconti, Bertolucci, and Antonioni. Based upon research in Italy and foreign as well as English-language scholarship. Written for the general reader.

Darretta, John. *Vittorio De Sica: A Guide to References and Resources*. Boston: G. K. Hall, 1983. Like other volumes in this series, this one includes biographical background, critical survey of director's films, synopses, credits, bibliography, etc.

Ellis, Jack C. *A History of Film*. Englewood Cliffs, N.J.: Prentice-Hall, 1979. See pp. 241–48: "Postwar Realism" in Italy.

Liehm, Mira. *Passion and Defiance: Italian Film from 1942 to the Present*. Berkeley: University of California Press, 1984. Italian film history, including relationship between Italian film and its historical, cultural, and political contexts.

Robinson, David. *The History of World Cinema*. Revised edition. New York: Stein & Day, 1981. Includes section on Italian neorealism.

Samuels, Charles Thomas. *Encountering Directors*. New York: G. P. Putnam, 1972. Includes an interview with De Sica.

Scripts

De Sica, Vittorio. *The Bicycle Thief*. Trans. Simon Hartog. New York: Simon and Schuster, 1968. A cutting continuity script without divisions into shots or scenes plus credits, introduction by the translator, and more than thirty frame enlargements.

Analyses

Bazin, André. *What Is Cinema?* Vol. 2. Trans. Hugh Gray. Berkeley: University of California Press, 1967–1971. See pp. 47–60 on *Bicycle Thief*.

Jacobson, Herbert L. "De Sica's 'Bicycle Thieves' and Italian Humanism." *Hollywood Quarterly* 4, no. 1 (Fall 1949): 28–33.

Solomon, Stanley J., ed. *The Classic Cinema: Essays in Criticism*. New York: Harcourt Brace Jovanovich, 1973. See pp. 199–221: credits, short introductory essay, and three essays, one a reprint from Bazin's *What Is Cinema?*

Stubbs, John C. "Bicycle Thieves." *The Journal of Aesthetic Education* 9, no. 2 (April 1975): 50–61. Reprinted in *Film Study Guides: Nine Classic Films* (Champaign, Ill.: Stipes, 1975). Background essay, credits, sequence outline, study questions, suggestions for additional reading.

· 15 ·

Citizen Kane

15.1 Black-and-white photograph of original color lobby card. Eddie Brandt's Saturday Matinee.

Background

Country of Production: U.S.A.
First Release: May 1941
Process: Black and white; 1.33:1 aspect ratio
Approximate Running Time: 119 minutes
Versions: The original release print has the RKO logo at the beginning. The prints released to television in the 1950s replace this with the "C & C"

company logo and are missing part of the closing credits and all of the accompanying music.

Production: Filmed from July 30 to October 23, 1940, in the RKO Studios in Hollywood.

Selected Credits:

- Producer: Orson Welles (1915–   ). Extensive experience in theater, radio, film, both as director and actor.
- Director: Orson Welles. *Citizen Kane* was the first film he directed. Other films include *The Magnificent Ambersons, The Lady from Shanghai, Macbeth,* and *Touch of Evil.*
- Scriptwriters: Herman J. Mankiewicz (1897–1953) and Orson Welles. Mankiewicz (Figure 15.4), together with producer John Houseman (Welles's partner in the Mercury Theatre), wrote the early drafts of the script. Whether Mankiewicz or Welles contributed more to the screenplay has been the subject of long debate. Mankiewicz was a journalist, then drama reviewer, then screenwriter.
- Design: Though art department head Van Nest Polglase received principal credit (department heads often had this written into their contracts), Perry Ferguson was the working art director on this film. Ferguson's other credits include *Bringing Up Baby, Ball of Fire, The Stranger,* and *Rope.*
- Cinematographer: Gregg Toland (1904–1948). Well known for his experimentation, inventions, and contributions to the art of cinematography. Films he worked on include *Mad Love, Wuthering Heights, The Grapes of Wrath, The Long Voyage Home, The Little Foxes, The Best Years of Our Lives.*
- Editors: Robert Wise (and Mark Robson). Wise was first an editor (of *The Magnificent Ambersons* and others), then director (*The Body Snatcher, The Day the Earth Stood Still, West Side Story* (co-directed), *The Sound of Music, Star Trek—The Motion Picture,* others). Later Robson directed also.

15.2 Orson Welles and Gregg Toland line up an extreme low-angle shot on a set of *Citizen Kane.* Museum of Modern Art/Film Stills Archive.

15.3 On a set of *Citizen Kane:* Orson Welles with actor George Coulouris. The man behind Welles taking a reading with a light meter is the cinematographer Gregg Toland. Museum of Modern Art/Film Stills Archive.

15.4 Writer Herman Mankiewicz, 1926. Museum of Modern Art/Film Stills Archive.

- Music: Bernard Herrmann (1911–1975) (Figure 15.5). Wrote the music for many films directed by Alfred Hitchcock, including *The Trouble with Harry, Vertigo, North by Northwest,* and *Psycho*. He also did the music for *The Day the Earth Stood Still, Taxi Driver,* and many other films. One phonograph record in RCA's Herrmann Classic Film Scores series includes a performance of a brief suite of the *Citizen Kane* music.
- Sound: Bailey Fesler and James G. Stewart

Major Characters and Performers:

- Charles Foster Kane: Orson Welles, actor in *The Third Man, Moby Dick, A Man for All Seasons, Touch of Evil,* many others.
- Jedediah or Jed Leland: Joseph Cotten (1905–   ), formerly an occasional newspaper drama critic, an actor with Mercury Theatre Co., then a performer in films, including *The Magnificent Ambersons, Shadow of a Doubt, The Third Man,* many others.
- Susan Alexander Kane: Dorothy Comingore, billed as "Linda Winters" in her previous films.
- Kane's mother: Agnes Moorehead (1906–1974). *Citizen Kane* was the first of many films she appeared in, including *The Magnificent Ambersons* and *Journey into Fear*.
- Emily Norton Kane: Ruth Warrick

15.5 Orson Welles with composer Bernard Herrmann. Museum of Modern Art/Film Stills Archive.

- James W. Gettys: Ray Collins (1888–1965)
- Mr. Bernstein: Everett Sloane (1909–1965), actor in *Journey into Fear, The Lady from Shanghai, Patterns,* many others.
- Mr. Carter: Erskin Sanford
- Thompson, the reporter: William Alland
- Raymond: Paul Stewart
- Walter Parks Thatcher: George Coulouris
- Signor Matisti: Fortunio Bonanova (1893–1969), Spanish singer in many supporting roles in U.S. films.
- Rawlston: Philip Van Zandt (1904–1958)

Place and Time of Story: Numerous locations, 1868–1940 (see Table 15.1).

Other: In 1937, Welles and John Houseman founded the Mercury Theatre Company, which was known for its innovative productions of classics and Shakespeare, first on stage, later on the radio. On Halloween eve, 1938, the group put on a radio version of H. G. Wells's *The War of the Worlds.* Although the broadcast contained periodic announcements that the program was fictitious, many listeners panicked, and the broadcast created a sensation.[1] Most of the major performers in *Citizen Kane* were Mercury Theatre players.

The parallels between the lives of Charles Foster Kane and William Randolph Hearst (1863–1951) were noted even before the film was released. Although there are numerous differences, the similarities include the facts that both built up a newspaper empire from a single newspaper; both advocated entry into the Spanish-American War; both collected art objects and statues; both built enormous estates, although Hearst built his on a large hill facing the California coast. Both character and person had mistresses, though Hearst's was a talented actress, not a "singer." For a fuller discussion of the similarities and differences, see Charles Higham, *The Films of Orson Welles,* pp. 21–24, reprinted in Ronald Gottesman, ed., *Focus on Citizen Kane,* pp. 137–42.

Outline

I. Xanadu
    A. Night. Outside: "No Trespassing" sign; views of Xanadu in fog.
    B. Day. Inside (Figure 15.8): Kane's death.
II. À theater: A film and its analysis
    A. Newsreel.
        Xanadu and its collections, Kane's funeral, his newspaper career, Kane's holdings, his parents, politics, marriages, Susan's opera ca-

---

[1] For brief descriptions and analyses of the broadcast, see James Naremore, *The Magic World of Orson Welles,* pp. 22–25, and James F. Scott, *Film, The Medium and the Maker,* pp. 141–42. For a detailed discussion of the broadcast and its repercussions, see Howard Koch, *The Panic Broadcast* (1970), which includes the complete text of the radio play, photographs, and reprints of numerous newspaper accounts.

15.6 Publicity still. Not this much of the wedding party is visible in the newsreel section of *Citizen Kane*. Movie Star News.

15.7 Publicity still. The teddy bear beneath the floor lamp shows up among items left in Xanadu after Kane's death; see Figure 15.14. Movie Star News.

15.8 The glass paperweight as seen midway through a zoom shot in the opening minutes of *Citizen Kane*. Courtesy RKO General Pictures.

15.9 Frame from a shot that is 45 frames long, or less than two seconds, of Kane's second family and his second sled, "The Crusader." Courtesy RKO General Pictures.

       reer, Xanadu, his campaign for governor, scandal, twenties depression, public appearances, Kane as invalid in Xanadu, the death announcement.

    B. Compilers discuss the newsreel and "Rosebud." Rawlston gives Thompson his assignment.

III. Atlantic City night club. Rain. Thompson finds Susan drinking and unwilling to talk about Kane.

IV. Thatcher Memorial Library in Philadelphia (next day)

    A. . . . Thompson begins reading portions of Thatcher's unpublished memoirs.

    B. Thatcher's account.

       1. 1871 (Colorado), young Charles turned over to bank that is to manage Colorado Lode and act as his guardian. Charles meets Thatcher.

       2. Charles (presumably the following Christmas) receiving sled as Christmas gift from his guardian (Figure 15.9). Voice-over transition.

       3. Christmastime, Charles nearly 25. Kane wants to take over New York *Inquirer*.

       4. He does so and defends the interests of the underprivileged.

       5. He also promotes Spanish-American War and argues with Thatcher.

       6. Winter 1929: To Thatcher and his bank Kane gives up control of some of his newspapers.

    C. Thompson leaves the library.

V. Bernstein office in New York City

    A. Rainy day. Bernstein tells Thompson about a girl on a ferry, some comments about Kane, some background on Leland.

    B. Bernstein's account.

       1. First day at *Inquirer,* introductions and settling in.

2. Establishing additional new policies and declaring principles (Figure 15.10).
3. *Inquirer*'s rapid, purchased growth.
4. Party: Kane's song (its words are reprinted in the Questions and Observations section below, item 14).
5. His welcome back from abroad; his engagement announcement and hasty departure (Figure 15.11).

    C. Night. Bernstein recommends again that Thompson see Leland.

VI. Hospital (New York City)

    A. Leland talks to Thompson about Kane.

    B. Emily's and Kane's deteriorating marriage (montage).

    C. Leland talks briefly with Thompson about Kane and love.

    D. Leland's account.

1. On street: Kane meets Susan; in her room (Figure 15.12); in the parlor: a concert, sound-over transition.
2. Leland giving speech in support of Kane's candidacy for governor, voice-over transition.
3. Kane's political speech to large audience.
4. After speech: scene with Emily.
5. Confrontation with Gettys.
6. Scandal and lost election; Leland goes into a bar.
7. Kane campaign headquarters: . . . Kane and an intoxicated Leland talk; Leland asks to be transferred to Chicago.
8. Kane marries Susan.
9. Susan's opera debut in Chicago.

15.10 Kane in the dark as he signs "Declaration of Principles" and Leland looks on admiringly. Courtesy RKO General Pictures.

15.11 This is the first frame of this 5½ second shot/scene. In the preceding scene Kane's newspaper employees had given him a welcome-home cup. To one of the carriage drivers Kane gives the cup to put in back of the carriage. When Kane sees his newspaper employees looking out the window at him, he calls to the worker and takes the cup back; with the cup in hand, Kane waves up to his newspaper employees. Courtesy RKO General Pictures.

  10. Chicago *Inquirer* office: Kane finishes Leland's negative review—and fires him.
 E. Leland makes a few more comments about Kane and then is led off by two nurses.
VII. Atlantic City night club
 A. Thompson with Susan again.
 B. Susan's account.
  1. A voice lesson, Kane gets his way, voice-over transition.
  2. Her Chicago opera debut and its reception.
  3. Susan angry about Leland's review; Leland returns pieces of Kane's check and "Declaration of Principles," which Kane tears up.
  4. Her opera career (montage).
  5. Aftermath of her suicide attempt; . . . Kane finally relents.
  6. Xanadu: their life-style, Susan's frustration.
  7. "Picnic": quarrel and slap.
  8. Susan packing to leave; Kane attempts to stop her (Figure 15.13), but she leaves.
 C. Thompson with Susan. Dawn. Thompson: ". . . I feel kind of sorry for Mr. Kane." Susan: "Don't you think I do?" Good-byes.
VIII. Xanadu
 A. Raymond, the butler.
  1. Thompson with Raymond.
  2. Raymond's account: Susan leaving Kane. He tears up her room (finds a hidden liquor bottle), stops when he sees the paperweight, picks it up and whispers, "Rosebud," carries the paperweight out of the room, and walks past the opposing mirrors that reflect self, self, self.
  3. Further talk with Raymond.

15.12 Second of three similar shots in Susan's room: notice the glass paperweight on the left side of her dresser. Courtesy RKO General Pictures.

15.13 Marital confrontation. Courtesy RKO General Pictures.

B. Leaving Xanadu.
   1. Inside: picture-taking, taking inventory, leavetaking, Rosebud and other things (Figure 15.14). Rosebud in flames. Fade-out to darkness.
   2. Outside, night: smoke coming out of chimney, lap dissolve during vertical pan down to "No Trespassing" sign, lap dissolve to gate with "K" on top in foreground left and Xanadu with smoke coming out of chimney in background right (Figure 15.15). "The End" faded in and superimposed over last shot. Fade-out.

   End credits with music (Kane's theme song).

15.14 Sled next to picture of child and woman (young Kane and his mother), teddy bear from parlor in Susan's building (Figure 15.7), doll from Susan's room in Xanadu (Figure 15.13), and other objects. Courtesy RKO General Pictures.

15.15 Last shot, before "The End" is faded in and superimposed over this image. Courtesy RKO General Pictures.

Questions and Observations

1. How do you *feel* about Kane by the end of the film? What is it about the film that makes you react the way you do?
2. What do the architecture, art, and furnishings of Xanadu reveal about Kane?
3. In what ways does Kane change during his life? Why does he change?
4. View again the one scene between young Kane, his father and mother, and Thatcher. What does this scene reveal about each of the four characters? How well does the scene help you understand Kane's later personality and life?
5. How accurate and adequate an assessment of Kane's life does the newsreel provide? Why do you say so?

Table 15.1
"Implied Chronology of *Citizen Kane*" by Joe Hill

mid 1860's:	Kane born	
1868:	deed to mine	NEWSREEL*
1871:	Thatcher takes Kane boy	THATCHER'S
'92:	Kane takes over *Inquirer*	MEMORY
'92–'98:	newspaper exposés	
1898:	Kane urges entry into war with Spain; buys *Chronicle* staff	BERNSTEIN'S
1898–1900:	Kane in Europe	MEMORY
1900:	Kane engaged to (and marries) Emily	
1900–1909:	Kane's gradual estrangement from Emily	LELAND'S MEMORY
'16:	Kane a candidate for governor	
	Susan scandal; loss of election	
	Emily divorces Kane	
	two weeks after divorce, Kane marries Susan	
1918:	Emily and Junior killed in auto crash	NEWSREEL
'19:	Kane opposes entry into World War I	
1919/20:	Susan sings at Chicago Opera	LELAND'S MEMORY
	Leland fired	
1920:	Susan attempts suicide	SUSAN'S MEMORY
1925:	Thatcher denounces Kane as a Communist before Congress	NEWSREEL
	Kane denounced as Fascist also	
'29:	a Kane paper closes	
	Raymond begins working for Kane	RAYMOND STATES
	first shot of Susan doing puzzle at Xanadu	
1930–32:	puzzles/seasons sequence	SUSAN'S MEMORY
'32:	picnic in the Everglades	
	Susan leaves Kane	
	Kane wrecks Susan's room	RAYMOND'S MEMORY
	collapse of Kane empire	NEWSREEL
1935:	Kane assures "no war" in Europe	
	Kane writes Leland; Leland doesn't answer	LELAND STATES
1935–40:	Kane alone at Xanadu	
'40:	Kane dies	NEWSREEL
	Kane's funeral	

*I have omitted those parts of the newsreel that overlap with the memory sequences; the remaining parts (those that don't overlap memories) usually present events of a negative nature—Kane losing things and people, people turning against Kane, Kane making foolish statements, etc. [Hill's note].

From *Film Reader*, vol. 1 (1975). Mr. Hill informs me that this version is a draft, not the completed version he intended. Reprinted with permission of J. F. Hill.

6. What does each narrator's account reveal about the storyteller? Which narrator seems the most reliable? How can you be sure? How reliable is the composite picture of Kane? Why do you say so?

7. The newsreel gives us many of the basic facts about Kane's life. In the rest of the film there is little chance for suspense. For instance, as we watch the events in his political campaign, we know that scandal and defeat approach relentlessly with the turning of the film reel. Even though the film is not suspenseful, how does it hold audience interest?

8. Some viewers believe that after they learn the significance of Rosebud, they understand Kane: he was simply cut off from his family as a young boy and yearned for those lost, innocent days. Others point out that Thompson feels that he has really learned very little about Kane, and even if he knew the significance of Rosebud he would still not know Kane very well. Who is right: the viewers who feel that Kane's character is rather simple after all, or Thompson? Why do you say so?

9. The glass paperweight appears three times in the film: during the opening sequence at Xanadu where Kane holds it, then drops it after he says, "Rosebud" (see Figure 15.8); on Susan's dresser the night Kane meets her (Figure 15.12); and in her room in Xanadu (we see it after Kane has torn up her room in a rage; outline section VIII.A.2). As completely as you can, explain *why* the paperweight seems to be so important in the film.

10. View again each montage in the film (see outline sections VI.B and VII.B.4). Discuss the importance of each montage. What does it reveal? How does it fit into the story? What does a montage achieve that other editing techniques cannot?

11. The story of Kane's life could easily have been told chronologically and with a single perspective (see "Implied Chronology of *Citizen Kane*," Table 15.1). Instead, it is told more or less chronologically (with overlapping coverage of certain events) by several different sources. What is gained by using this structure and means of narration? What is lost?

12. Many of the film's techniques will not be noticed by most people during the first viewing. If you have seen the film more than once, try to explain the use of some of the following techniques:
    a. Editing
    b. Light and shadows
    c. Wide-angle photography
    d. Low-angle shots
    e. Sound, including voice- and sound-over transitions, overlapping dialogue, sound to suggest size and texture of a location
    f. Music

13. What significant details—visual and aural—are likely to be missed in watching the film on a television set or monitor with a small speaker? What do those details contribute to the film?

14. The words to the Kane song:

    There is a man—
    A certain man—
    And for the poor you may be sure
    That he'll do all he can.
    Who is this one—

This fav'rite son—
Just by his action
Has the Traction magnates[2] on the run.
Who loves to smoke—
Enjoys a joke—
Who wouldn't get a bit upset
If he were really broke
With wealth and fame—
He's still the same—
I'll bet you five you're not alive
If you don't know his name.[3]

15. David A. Cook has written:

"The March of Time" was a popular series of skillfully (some would say slickly) produced film news journals released monthly in the United States between 1935 and 1951. Each issue was twenty minutes long, and, generally, focused on a single subject. These films were usually shown as preludes to features, so that *Citizen Kane*'s original audiences might well have watched an authentic "March of Time" newsreel just before seeing the parodic "News on the March" in *Kane*. "The March of Time" series was politically conservative, reflecting the editorial policies of its financial backer, Time-Life, Inc., and of Time-Life's director, Henry R. Luce (1898–1967). Time-Life succeeded the Hearst empire, which was badly crippled by the Depression, to become a major shaper of public opinion during the thirties, forties, and fifties. The identification in *Citizen Kane* of Rawlston's news organization with the Luce press is entirely deliberate, since it extends the Kane/Hearst analogy.[4]

16. Robert L. Carringer has written:

The little glass globe (not Rosebud) is the film's central symbol. . . . The shattering of the globe (not the appearance of Rosebud) is the film's main symbolic "event." . . .

A closer look at this important symbol is highly suggestive. Globular; self-enclosed; self-sustaining; an intact world in miniature, a microcosm. Placid; still; free of disturbing images or presences. Sealed off to intrusion from outside. Free also of human presence—and therefore of suggestions of responsibilities to others. But by the same token, free of human warmth—a cold, frozen world of eternal winter. Suggestive, more than anything else, of Charles Foster Kane. . . .[5]

17. Pauline Kael has written:

Right from the start of movies, it was a convention that the rich were vulgarly acquisitive but were lonely and miserable and incapable of giving or receiving love. As a mass medium, movies have always soothed and consoled the public with the theme that the rich can buy everything

---

[2] Traction magnates are important and influential people in the railroad transportation business.

[3] *The Citizen Kane Book* (Boston: Little, Brown, 1971), pp. 356–58.

[4] David A. Cook, *A History of Narrative Film* (New York: W. W. Norton, 1981).

[5] Robert L. Carringer, "Rosebud, Dead or Alive: Narrative and Symbolic Structure in *Citizen Kane*," *PMLA* 91, no. 2 (March 1976): 187 and 191.

except what counts—love. . . . In popular art, riches and power destroy people, and so the secret of Kane is that he longs for the simple pleasures of his childhood before wealth tore him away from his mother—he longs for what is available to the mass audience.[6]

18. James Naremore has written:

Actually, the entire film works according to an identical principle, so that everything evokes its opposite and all statements about the protagonist are true in some sense. There are, to choose one minor example of the method, two snow-sleds. The first, as everyone knows, is named "Rosebud"; the second is given to Kane as a Christmas present by Thatcher, and is seen only briefly—so briefly that audiences are unaware that it, too, has a name. If you study the film through a movieola or an analyzing projector, you will discover that for a few frames sled number two is presented fully to the camera, its legend clearly visible. It is named "Crusader," and where the original has a flower, this one is embossed with the helmet of a knight.

Welles was probably unconcerned when his symbolism did not show on the screen. "Crusader" was a tiny joke he could throw away in a film that bristles with clever asides. I mention it not only because I am foolishly proud of knowing such esoterica, but also because it is a convenient way to point up the split in Kane's character and in the very conception of the film. In many ways it is appropriate that Thatcher should try to win the boy over with a sled named "Crusader." Kane will repay this gift by growing up to be a crusading, trust-busting newspaperman, out to slay the dragon Wallstreet. . . . On another level, the two sleds can be interpreted as emblems of a sentimental tragedy: Kane has lost the innocence suggested by "Rosebud" and has been transformed into a phoney champion of the people, an overreacher who dies like a medieval knight amid the empty gothic splendor of Xanadu.[7]

19. David Bordwell has written:

The film's complexity arises from the narrators' conflicting *judgments*, their summing-ups of Kane. Each one sees a different side of him at a different stage of his life, yet each takes his estimate of Kane as definitive. To Thatcher, Kane is an arrogant smart aleck who became "nothing more nor less than a Communist." Bernstein's Kane is a man of high principles, with a sharp business sense and a love of the common man. Leland's Kane, only "in love with himself," is a man of no convictions, a betrayer of the masses. Susan sees Kane . . . as a selfish but piteous old man. And Raymond's story of Kane as a lonely hermit betrays the cold detachment of his own nature. Each narrator judges Kane differently, and each judgment leaves out something essential. As T. S. Eliot puts it in *The Confidential Clerk:* "There's always something one's ignorant of/About anyone, however well one knows him;/And that may be something of the greatest importance."

The effect of seeing so many conflicting assessments is to restrain us from forming any opinions of Kane we might take as definitive. As each character tells his story, the reporter's search for an accurate judgment is taken up by the audience as well. Thompson, whose face we never

---

[6] Pauline Kael, "Raising Kane," in *The Citizen Kane Book,* pp. 70 and 73.
[7] James Naremore, *The Magic World of Orson Welles* (New York: Oxford University Press, 1978).

see, is a surrogate for us; his job—voyeuristic and prying, yet ultimately disinterested and detached—is the perfect vehicle for the curiosity without consequences that film uniquely gratifies.[8]

Suggested Readings

Probably more has been written about *Citizen Kane*—at least in the English language—than about any other film ever made. A thorough bibliography on its contexts, scripts, and analyses would make up a sizable book in itself.

Contexts

American Cinematographer 56, no. 4 (April 1975). Includes Welles filmography and five articles about Welles or *Citizen Kane,* including Gregg Toland's "Realism for 'Citizen Kane,' " which was originally published in the February 1941 issue of *American Cinematographer.*

Carringer, Robert L. *"Citizen Kane": The Road through Xanadu.* Berkeley: University of California Press, in press. An illustrated history of the creative evolution of the film, with detailed accounts of Welles's work with his principal collaborators, such as screenwriter Herman Mankiewicz, cinematographer Gregg Toland, art director Perry Ferguson, and composer Bernard Herrmann.

Cowie, Peter. *The Cinema of Orson Welles.* New York: A. S. Barnes, 1965. Reprinted in *A Ribbon of Dreams: The Cinema of Orson Welles* (New York: A. S. Barnes, 1973).

Evans, Mark. *Soundtrack: The Music of the Movies.* New York: Hopkinson and Blake, 1975. See pp. 55–62 on Herrmann's music.

Gottesman, Ronald, ed. *Focus on Orson Welles.* Englewood Cliffs, N.J.: Prentice-Hall, 1976. A collection of essays—"The Man," "The Techniques," and "The Films"—plus a filmography, selective annotated bibliography, and fourteen stills.

Herrmann, Bernard. "Score for a Film." *New York Times,* 25 May 1941, sec. 9, p. 6. Reprinted in Gottesman, *Focus on Citizen Kane,* pp. 69–72 (see Analyses section, below).

———. "Bernard Herrmann, Composer." In Evan William Cameron, ed., *Sound and the Cinema: The Coming of Sound to American Film* (Pleasantville, N.Y.: Redgrave, 1980), pp. 125–30.

Higham, Charles. *The Films of Orson Welles.* Berkeley: University of California Press, 1970. The chapter on *Citizen Kane* includes both analysis and extensive background information.

McBride, Joseph. *Orson Welles.* New York: Viking Press, 1972. Critical study of the films directed by Welles up through *The Immortal Story.*

---

[8] David Bordwell, *"Citizen Kane,"* in Bill Nichols, ed., *Movies and Methods* (Berkeley: University of California Press, 1976), p. 279.

Naremore, James. *The Magic World of Orson Welles*. New York: Oxford University Press, 1978. Some biography but mostly detailed analyses of films Welles directed.

Scripts

The Citizen Kane Book. Boston: Little, Brown, 1971. Includes a long essay by Pauline Kael, "Raising Kane," the shooting script, notes on differences between the shooting script and the finished film, and a detailed cutting continuity script.

Analyses

Beja, Morris. *Film and Literature: An Introduction*. New York: Longman, 1979. Chapter on *Citizen Kane* includes background, "Topics to Think About," and bibliography.

Bordwell, David, and Kristin Thompson. *Film Art: An Introduction*. Reading, Mass.: Addison-Wesley, 1979. On pp. 60–69 and 221–29, the authors discuss the film's narrative form, supply "linear segmentations" for the film's major sequences and the newsreel sequence, and analyze the film's style.

Cameron, Evan William. *"Citizen Kane:* The Influence of Radio Drama." In Cameron, ed., *Sound and the Cinema: The Coming of Sound to American Film* (Pleasantville, N.Y.: Redgrave, 1980), pp. 202–16.

Carringer, Robert L. *"Citizen Kane." The Journal of Aesthetic Education* 9, no. 2 (April 1975): 32–49. Reprinted in *Film Study Guides: Nine Classic Films* (Champaign, Ill.: Stipes, 1975). Background, credits, sequence outline, study questions, and suggestions for additional reading.

Gottesman, Ronald, ed. *Focus on Citizen Kane*. Englewood Cliffs, N. J.: Prentice Hall, 1971. Cast and credits, introductory essays, reviews, essays, commentaries, plot synopsis, content outline, script extract, filmography, selected bibliography, and nine stills.

Reisz, Karel, and Gavin Millar. *The Technique of Film Editing*. New York: Hastings House, 1968. See pp. 115–22: a description and interpretation of the Kane-Emily breakfast montage, including ten frame enlargements and descriptions of each of the thirty-four shots in the montage.

· 16 ·

The General

16.1 Black-and-white photograph of original color lobby card. Eddie Brandt's Saturday Matinee.

Background

Country of Production: U.S.A.
First Release: December 1926, Los Angeles
　　　　　　　January 1927, London
　　　　　　　February 1927, New York
Process: Black and white; 1.33:1 aspect ratio
Approximate Running Time and Projection Speed: The running time of this film is listed in a bewildering variety of times, and I have been unable to discover the original length. The Museum of Modern Art rental print runs 79 minutes at sound speed, 24 frames per second.
Versions:

- Different prints have a few scenes in different order than in the outline below.
- One version of this film excised the intertitle cards and superimposed subtitles over the appropriate shots. That same version includes some sound effects along with a musical sound track.
- Other prints are only about an hour long and have music and narration.

Production: Filmed on location near Cottage Grove, Oregon, where the appropriate narrow-gauge track was still in use. Part of the Oregon National Guard was hired as extras. Shooting began in spring 1926; in September the crew returned to Hollywood to do the studio scenes. In October some final location shots were taken in Oregon. At no time were miniatures used. Before shooting began, Keaton had a broad outline of the scenes. During shooting, details were improvised or worked out. During the filming a forest fire was set off, which added nearly $12,000 to the production costs. Keaton had complete control over the production: script, shooting, and editing.

Selected Credits:

- Producer: Joseph M. Schenck for United Artists
- Directors: Buster Keaton and Clyde Bruckman. In the 1920s, Keaton produced and directed a number of feature films he starred in: *The Three Ages, Our Hospitality, Sherlock Jr., The Navigator, Seven Chances, Go West, Battling Butler,* and *The General.*
- Scriptwriters: Buster Keaton and Clyde Bruckman. The script was based upon a Civil War account by William Pittenger, first published in 1863 and thereafter variously titled. Its original title: *Daring and Suffering: A History of the Great Railroad Adventure.*
- Cinematographers: Dev Jennings and Bert Haines
- Editors: J. Sherman Kell and Harry Barnes

Major Characters and Performers:

- Johnnie Gray: Buster Keaton (1895–1966). Was in vaudeville with his parents (Figure 16.2); later acted in short films, then features, including *Our Hospitality, Sherlock Jr., The Navigator, Sunset Boulevard, Limelight* (with Charlie Chaplin), *A Funny Thing Happened on the Way to the Forum.*
- Annabelle Lee: Marion Mack
- Annabelle's father

16.2 Keaton at age six with his parents in a vaudeville gag. Museum of Modern Art/Film Stills Archive.

- Annabelle's brother
- Captain Anderson
- General Thatcher
- The *General,* Johnnie's train

Place and Time of Story: Georgia and perhaps Tennessee (near Chattanooga), spring 1861
Other:

- The story was based upon a memoir by William Pittenger. *The General* includes a love interest and the second chase, limits the number of trains involved in the chase, and drops the hangings of the Union spies. Unlike the book, the film reflects a Confederate perspective.
- The story was remade as *A Southern Yankee* (M-G-M, 1948) with Red Skelton in the main role.
- In 1956, the same source was used as the basis of Disney's *The Great Locomotive Chase,* an alternative title of Pittenger's Civil War account.

Outline

This outline is based on an Essex Films print; other versions vary in details, but it is difficult to determine which version is most authoritative.
  I. Marietta, Georgia: Johnnie, the *General,* Annabelle, the war
      1. Western and Atlantic Flyer train approaching Marietta, Georgia, spring 1861.

2. Johnnie arrives in town in his *General*. Two young fans. His two loves. Fade-out.
3. Fade-in. Annabelle receives a book.
4. Johnnie on way to see her. She follows him the last part of the way.
5. Johnnie visits Annabelle; tricks two boys; his gift (Figure 16.3).
   . . .
6. Annabelle's brother tells their father that Fort Sumter has been fired upon. Annabelle's brother and father leave to enlist. After Annabelle asks Johnnie if he's going to enlist, he goes, too.
7. Street: Annabelle's father and brother are joined by another man. Johnnie approaches them from behind, then dashes off to the right, presumably to take a short cut.
8. At recruiting office: Johnnie's attempts to sign up. He's rejected— because he's too valuable to South as engineer—but he's not told why. Booted out.
9. Outside: Annabelle's father and brother try to get Johnnie into the enlistment line.
10. Johnnie at the *General*.
11. Annabelle by the front gate of her house, looking down the street.
12. Johnnie at the *General*, starts to leave, rubs his leg where he got kicked, and sits down again.
13. Annabelle's brother and father tell her that Johnnie didn't enlist. She starts to leave.
14. Inside the house: The father discards Johnnie's photograph.
15. At the *General*, Annabelle says she doesn't want to see Johnnie again until he's in a uniform. Johnnie sitting on the side of the *General:* an amusing but dangerous gag. Fade-out.

II. Plan and theft of the *General*
16. Fade-in. A year later, a Union encampment near Chattanooga. Night. General Thatcher and his chief spy, Captain Anderson. An-

16.3 Johnnie's gift to Annabelle.

derson explains his plan to steal a train, burn bridges, and thus cut off enemy supplies. General Thatcher says he'll "have General Parker advance to meet you." Fade-out.

17. Fade-in. Day. Marietta: Annabelle's wounded brother seeing her off to visit their wounded father. She snubs Johnnie. Train leaves. Fade-out.
18. Fade-in. On train: announcement about approaching Big Shanty. Annabelle sitting next to Captain Anderson.
19. At Big Shanty: a dinner stop. Annabelle looking for something in her trunk in the baggage car; Johnnie washing up; Anderson and his ten men steal the *General* (and inadvertently kidnap Annabelle). Johnnie and others run after train.

III. First Chase: Cutting between the Raiders and Johnnie

Raiders	*Johnnie*
20. In baggage car, men tie and gag Annabelle.	
21. Anderson gesturing. Train stops. Men jump out.	
22. Telegraph operator starts to send a message.	
23. Man cutting telegraph wire.	
24. Telegraph operator	
	25. Johnnie runs down track. Gets a hand car out of shed.
26. Men damaging track behind train.	27. Johnnie on way on hand car.
28. Men finish damaging track.	29. Johnnie on hand car.
30. *General* passes a stationary train (in Kingston, we learn later).	31. Johnnie derailed. Takes bicycle.
32. Train has stopped again. Anderson gets package. In background, man climbs telegraph pole.	33. Johnnie unseated.
34. Train under way again. Anderson unwraps package: Southern uniform; he starts to change into it.	35. Johnnie arrives in Kingston, gets another train, the *Texas*—at least the engine and fuel car. . . .
36. On *General*: Anderson and his men.	37. Johnnie realizes he's alone. Stops by a train car with cannon mounted on it.
38. *General* taking on water and wood.	39. *Texas* under way with cannon hooked up behind.
40. Men on *General* see other train coming and leave. . . .	41. Johnnie gets doused.
42. Anderson says he doesn't want to stop and fight because they are outnumbered.	43. Johnnie in cab of *Texas*.
44. On fuel car: Anderson starts to chop into the next boxcar.	45. On top of the *Texas*: Johnnie takes a look (Figure 16.4).
46. Anderson has chopped a hole into next boxcar (baggage) and motions the men out (leaving Annabelle tied up).	47. Johnnie gets on cannon car. Prepares cannon—he thinks. Lights fuse.
48. Anderson and his men start to climb on top of the baggage car.	49. Cannon shot: Disappointing. Johnnie loads up again. A snag develops (Figure 16.5).

16.4 Johnnie getting a better view.

16.5 Lighted cannon aiming at Johnnie.

50. Anderson's men arrive at back of last boxcar.
52. Anderson gestures.
54. Men unhook last boxcar and it falls behind.

56. Man chopping out back of last car.

58. Through hole in back of last boxcar the men drop a railroad tie onto tracks.

60. Men dropping more ties onto tracks.

51. Johnnie hides on cowcatcher of *Texas*. A curve and an impressive shot.
53. Johnnie still on cowcatcher.
55. Johnnie, still on cowcatcher, sees boxcar approaching. Scrambles up before boxcar touches cowcatcher.
57. Johnnie disposes of unwanted boxcar—he thinks, but quickly learns he hasn't.
59. Johnnie burns hand and is distracted. Boxcar in front of him is derailed by the tie on track. Johnnie's reaction (Figure 16.6).
61. Johnnie slows engine and clears tracks—with dexterity (Figure 16.7).

16.6 Johnnie amazed to see boxcar is now *not* in front of him.

16.7 Johnnie, on cowcatcher, clearing track.

62. Man changing track switch. *General* under way again.

63. On top of fuel car: Johnnie gathering wood.

64. Annabelle moved from baggage car to top of fuel car.

65. *Texas* goes off on left track (thanks to the action of scene 62), but Johnnie stops train just before it runs out of track.

66. Men tearing up baggage car.

67. Johnnie backs up *Texas,* changes switch, loses traction, nearly loses train.

68. Burning boxcar left in covered bridge.

69. *Texas* slowly enters bridge and pushes burning boxcar before it.

70. Men on *General*.

71. Johnnie approaching switch; burning boxcar in background.

72. Southern army ordered to retreat.

73. Anderson and his men duck out of sight.

74. Johnnie chops wood, oblivious to Southern army in background.

75. Army retreating.

76. Johnnie still chopping.

77. Anderson's men now pop up.

78. Johnnie still preoccupied.

79. General Parker's Northern army advancing.

80. Johnnie in foreground, still unaware of action behind him.

81. Northern troops marching.

82. Anderson's men wave to them. Anderson takes off Southern uniform.

83. Johnnie *still* working. *Now* sees army and ducks down into cab.

84. *General* goes under a tall railroad bridge.

85. Johnnie in cab of engine.

86. Annabelle still tied up on top of fuel car. *General,* now on top of tall bridge, stops; men shower Johnnie's train with planks.

87. Johnnie looks up.

88. They see that there is only one man in pursuit. Anderson orders his men off train.

89. Johnnie grabs top hat and coat, stops train, scrambles out. In bushes. Rain. Fade-out.

IV. Rescue of Annabelle

90. Night. Johnnie slides up to house, enters window, takes food, and hides under table. Hears Northern plans. Annabelle brought in, then locked in a room. Officers leave.

91. Annabelle's room: She's nervous.

92. In other room: Johnnie gets out from under table.

93. Outside: We see a guard get bonked on the head, then Johnnie over the unconscious man, tugging at his uniform.

94. Annabelle in her room.

95. Outside again: Johnnie bonks another guard.

96. Annabelle's room: the rescue.

97. Outside: They run off into darkness and rain. Lightning. A bear. Separation and reunion. Bear trap. Settling down for the night. Fade-out.

V. Rescue of the *General*

98. Fade-in. "After a nice, quiet, refreshing night's rest." Fade-out. Fade-

16.8 Johnnie stuffing Annabelle into a shoe sack.

in. Morning. Enormous pine cone awakens Johnnie. Shoesack and Annabelle (Figure 16.8).

99. Near *General*. Unhooking train. Loading Annabelle. Knocking out officer in *General*'s cab. (At end of film, we see that it's General Thatcher.) Escaping.

VI. Second Chase: Cross-Cutting between raiders in *Texas* and *Columbia* engines and Johnnie in *General*

Raiders	*Johnnie and Annabelle*
100. Northern reactions and commands. Anderson orders supply train to follow *Texas*.	101. Johnnie pulls down telegraph lines.
102. Telegraph operator in tent reacting.	103. Johnnie chops rope pulling telegraph pole, which stays on the tracks. He begins chopping at baggage car.
104. One train, the *Texas*, with fuel car leaving Northern post. Supply train follows.	105. Johnnie has now made a hole in the baggage car wall. Goes in. Gets Annabelle. With difficulty pulls her out through hole onto top of fuel car.
106. *Texas* in pursuit.	107. Johnnie and Annabelle in cab of *General*. They stop for more wood; loading/unloading it.
108. *Texas* stops. Men remove telegraph pole from tracks.	109. Annabelle's trap. Johnnie skeptical. They see *Texas* approaching and leave.
110. *Texas* runs into Annabelle's trap, and it works; they have to stop.	111. Inside a boxcar, Johnnie chops at a wall.
112. *Texas* under way again, followed closely by the supply train.	113. Johnnie still chopping at boxcar wall.
	114. Annabelle helpless in cab.
	115. Wall of boxcar finally drops out, and we see the *Texas* close behind.

116. Train stops; men clear tracks.

117. Johnnie strewing tracks with contents of baggage car.

118. Men clearing tracks.

119. Annabelle in cab. Northern officer starts to revive, then is knocked out again, by a piece of falling wood (thrown by Johnnie?). Johnnie takes officer's pistol.

120. Men clearing tracks.

121. In cab: Johnnie finds Southern uniform that Anderson had worn earlier.

122. At water tank: dousing Annabelle, then giving water to the *General*. Hasty departure. . . .

123. *Texas* and men on supply train get doused.

124. Johnnie and Annabelle: She rejects a piece of wood with hole in it.

125. Anderson in cab giving orders.

126. Annabelle sweeping cab.

127. *Texas* in pursuit.

128. Annabelle's sweeping. Johnnie's irony, choke, and kiss (Figures 16.9–16.12).

129. *Texas* hooks onto back of baggage car behind *General*. Johnnie immediately unhooks baggage car from *General* and gets shot at.

130. *Texas* disposes of baggage car onto side track—then backs into the supply train.

131. Johnnie shows Annabelle how to operate train; then he gets out and ties chain to switch. As *General* inches forward, it wrecks switch. Runaway *General*.

132. Annabelle helpless.

133. Johnnie chases *General* down hill and up. . . . Reunion. As *General* finally comes to a stop, *Texas* and supply train go off and up side track. Abrupt stop and collision. *General* off and running again.

134. *Texas* and supply train back up. Men discover broken switch.

135. Johnnie stokes boiler, then gets lamp from *General*'s light housing.

136. At Rock River Bridge: They stop in middle.

16.9

16.10

16.11   16.12

16.9–16.12 Four frames from the same shot: Annabelle cleaning up the cab, Johnnie ironically giving her a toothpick-sized piece of wood, Johnnie shaking and choking Annabelle, and Johnnie kissing her.

137. Attempt to repair switch.

138. Johnnie stacking pieces of wood on bridge behind *General*.

139. "The Northern Division nearing the bridge to meet the supply trains."

140. Annabelle sets off fire too soon. Johnnie jumps into water, swims to shore, rejoins *General*.

141. Further futile attempts to fix switch.

142. Johnnie—still in Union uniform—waves to Southern soldier and gets shot at. He changes to Southern uniform.

143. *General* arrives at town, Southern Division headquarters. Johnnie brings news. Preparations and departures. Annabelle reunited with her father.

144. Trainman easily fixes switch.

VII. Showdown
    145. Near burning bridge, Union troops, *Texas*, and supply train converge.
    146. Famous last words by a Northern officer and the *Texas* in a $50,000 gag (Figure 16.13).
    147. Battle begins.
    148. Johnnie co-directs with Southern officer. The problem of the sniper. Presumably Johnnie's cannon shot bursts dam, flooding Northern soldiers.
    149. Supply train hit by cannon shot and derails.
    150. Johnnie gets Confederate flag and a scolding. Fade-out.
VIII. Aftermath
    151. Fade-in. "Heroes of the day." Fade-out. Fade-in. Confederates marching back. Townspeople welcome them.

16.13 No miniature this.

16.14 Last shot of film, at least in most prints.

152. On his *General,* Johnnie captures reviving Northern officer, General Thatcher.
153. Johnnie turns him over to Southern commander. As Annabelle and her father watch, Johnnie is enlisted and promoted to lieutenant.
154. Johnnie and Annabelle at the *General*: interruptions, his invention, the kiss (Figure 16.14).

Fade-out

The End

Questions and Observations

1. What emotions does Keaton's face express? What would happen to our response to him if he were to smile?
2. Where and in what ways does Keaton display physical abilities? What do his physical talents contribute to the film?
3. What functions does the *General* serve? When does Johnnie go to it and why? Why does the photograph of Johnnie and his train (Figure 16.3) get a laugh from the audience?
4. At one point Johnnie chokes Annabelle, then kisses her (scene 128 and Figures 16.9–16.12). What do these actions reveal about his feelings for her? What functions does Annabelle serve in the film?
5. Basically, was the film made to tell a story or to get laughs? Why do you say so?
6. What role does chance play in Johnnie's success? What role does skill play?
7. Does the film approve or disapprove of the military and war? Why do you say so?

8. Generally, how close to the subjects does the camera get? From what angles do subjects tend to be filmed? What lenses are used: normal, wide-angle, telephoto?

9. Describe the editing style: arrangement, pace, transitions. Where and why are fade-outs and fade-ins used?

10. Illustrate the following generalization: often in *The General* the humor results not just from *what* is shown but also from *how* it is depicted.

11. When *The General* came out in 1927, it was not a big commercial hit. Now, decades later, most viewers enjoy and admire it. Why, do you think, is the film a success now?

12. In the conclusion to his chapter on *The General,* Daniel Moews writes:

The [last] scene provides his [Keaton's] last demonstration of ingenious efficiency, of how to do two things at once. Appropriately, it is also one last demonstration of how to remain human and funny even when employed in the highly mechanized and serious professions of railroads and war. Appropriately, too, in the final shot Johnnie, Annabelle, and The General are together again, for if the machine is a machine and the humans are humans, in the affirmatively mechanical world of the film they have also been fantastically and approvingly presented as alike. Girl and train have been equated in their kidnapping and rescue and by the hero's equitably divided love. Hero and train have been equated as Johnnie, a Keaton kinetic hero in an age of admirable machines, acquired some of The General's mechanistic glory through being its expert engineer. Charging down the line with it, he himself became a miniature driving juggernaut, unstoppable and unbeatable. Posed together now—boy, girl, locomotive—they form a romantic and dynamic trio whose shared adventures have united them at the end.[1]

13. "Like *The Navigator, The General* . . . is almost all movement, balletlike, although it has a stronger plot premise in Buster's obsessive pursuit of his chance to help win the war and the girl, and (not necessarily least) to retrieve his beloved locomotive, 'the General.' Every piece of comic action develops the dramatic motivation. Through all the gags and toppers, the graceful, and often beautiful, image of Buster coolly and passionately seeking to salvage what he loves from the confusions of war is built. Obsessively Buster tries to master an errant axe and chop the needed firewood, while a whole army passes unnoticed behind him. A number of trains misbehave and interact in intricate maneuvers; a waterspout douses; cannons fire in the wrong direction. A sword doggedly fights Buster's equally relentless efforts to get it out of its scabbard, only to send its broken blade flying when he succeeds—impaling a sniper before he can shoot Buster. But nothing better illustrates the film's integration of gag and drama (and its union of all things, human and non-, in a single world verging on utter disorder) than one small moment on the train. After rejecting (and tossing out) their last piece of firewood because it had a knot, the girl offers a tiny chip as her choice and then

[1] *Keaton: The Silent Features Close Up* (Berkeley: University of California Press, 1977).

proceeds to sweep out the last remaining pieces on the cab floor. Losing control for one brief moment, Buster turns and shakes her violently—then stops, kisses her quickly and lightly, and continues his work."[2]

14. "The films in which he [Keaton] starred and which he largely directed himself—*Our Hospitality* (1923), *Sherlock Jr.* (1924), *The Navigator* (1924), *Seven Chances* (1925), *The General* (1926)—today seem entirely undated, and their silence has more the appearance of choice than necessity."[3]

Suggested Readings

Contexts

Bishop, Christopher. "The Great Stone Face." *Film Quarterly* 12, no. 1 (Fall 1958): 10–22. Short essay on Keaton and his films plus an interview with him.

Dardis, Tom. *Keaton: The Man Who Wouldn't Lie Down.* New York: Scribner's, 1979. A biography, which includes a chapter on *The General,* but little analysis of the film.

Everson, William K. *American Silent Film.* New York: Oxford University Press, 1978. Chapter on comedy includes discussion of Keaton.

Pittenger, William. *Daring and Suffering: A History of the Great Railroad Adventure.* Alexandria, Va.: Time-Life, 1982. Since its original publication in 1863, this source for the film has been reprinted under the titles *Capturing a Locomotive: A History of Secret Service in the Late War* and *The Great Locomotive Chase: A History of the Andrews Railroad Raid into Georgia in 1862.*

Sklar, Robert. "Chaos, Magic, Physical Genius and the Art of Silent Comedy." In his *Movie-Made America: A Cultural History of American Movies.* New York: Random House, 1975.

Warren, Joseph. *The General: A Farcical Novel with an Historical Background Based on Buster Keaton's Comedy Spectacle Film of the Same Name, Inspired by a Glorious Exploit of the American Civil War, Wherein a Lad Chased a Lass and a Locomotive and a Good Time Was Enjoyed by All.* New York: Grosset & Dunlap, 1927. Proof that novelizations of films are not just a recent phenomenon; includes twelve publicity stills.

Wead, George, and George Lellis. *The Film Career of Buster Keaton.* Pleasantville, N.Y.: Redgrave, 1977. Reference source including a short Keaton biography; critical survey of his work; synopsis, credits, and notes for all the films he directed; extensive annotated bibliography; and so forth.

[2] Alan Casty, *Development of the Film: An Interpretive History* (New York: Harcourt Brace Jovanovich, 1973) pp. 94–95.

[3] David Robinson, *The History of World Cinema* (New York: Stein and Day, 1973), p. 117.

Script

Richard J. Anobile, ed. *Buster Keaton's "The General."* New York: Avon Books, 1975. Cutting continuity script, including credits, all intertitle cards, and over 2,100 frame enlargements from the film, many of them cropped. Usually, it is clear where one shot ends and the next begins.

Analyses

Kerr, Walter. *The Silent Clowns.* New York: Alfred A. Knopf, 1975. Includes a chapter, "Two Epics," on *The Gold Rush* and *The General.*

Mast, Gerald. *The Comic Mind: Comedy and the Movies,* 2d ed. Chicago: University of Chicago Press, 1979. Includes a chapter on Keaton.

Moews, Daniel. *Keaton: The Silent Features Close Up.* Berkeley: University of California Press, 1977. Chapter on *The General* includes detailed plot summary-commentary; only one photo in book, but a bibliography that discusses publications about Keaton in detail, and notes on different versions of film prints.

Rubinstein, E. *Filmguide to "The General."* Bloomington: Indiana University Press, 1973. Credits, outline, short essay on Keaton, production information, detailed analysis, "Summary Critique," filmography, annotated bibliography.

· 17 ·

(Battleship) Potemkin[1]

17.1 Title card with subtitle.

Background[2]

Other Titles:

- *Bronenosets Potemkin* (approximately, pah TYOM kin) (Russian)
- *The Armored Cruiser Potemkin* (original title when film was first shown in U.S. in 1926)

---

[1] Professor Steven P. Hill, Slavic Department, University of Illinois, read an earlier draft of this chapter and made numerous helpful suggestions and corrections. On several occasions my colleague Samuel A. Oppenheim also helped me with this chapter. To both I am grateful.

[2] Much of the information for this section was derived from the extremely useful source book *The Battleship Potemkin,* ed. Herbert Marshall (New York: Avon, 1978).

- *Potemkin* (probably the most frequent title used currently in the U.S.)

Country of Production: U.S.S.R.

First Release: December 1925, Bolshoi Theater, Moscow
December 1926, New York City

Process: Black and white; 1.33:1 aspect ratio

Approximate Running Time and Projection Speed: 56 minutes at sound speed (24 frames per second); 75 minutes at silent speed (18 fps). The widely circulated 1950 sound version reprints selected frames; it also has expanded credits and end titles, and runs 68 minutes long.

Versions: The original negative of the film has been destroyed or lost, and all prints shown in the West are incomplete and often at odds with each other. To fit Soviet ideology, the film has been re-edited and re-released a number of times, probably most notably in 1950, when the music by Nikolai Kryukov was added, as was opening and closing narration and new intertitles. For that version a number of scenes were also re-edited.

Ideally, the film should be projected at about 20 frames per second (less than sound speed), and live music should be cued to the action and played in accompaniment.

Production: Filmed on location in Odessa and aboard *The Twelve Apostles*— sister ship of the *Prince Potemkin of Taurida*—in the bay of Sevastopol. Because of bad weather and a change of plans, filming lasted from August to November 1925.

Edited during November and December 1925.

17.2 Filming on the Odessa Steps. Museum of Modern Art/Film Stills Archive.

17.3 During shooting of *Potemkin*. Courtesy Herbert Marshall Archives, Center for Soviet and East European Studies, Southern Illinois University.

Selected Credits:[3]

- Producer: Jacob Bliokh for First Studio Goskino, Moscow
- Director: Sergei Eisenstein (1898–1948). Had training in architecture, engineering, military, theater design and direction; later important as a film director and film theorist. He knew many languages and read widely. His major films besides *Potemkin* include *October* or *Ten Days That Shook the World* (1928), *Alexander Nevsky* (1938), and *Ivan the Terrible* (Part I, 1945; Part II, 1946 but not released until 1958).
- Scriptwriters: Eisenstein and Nina Agajanova-Shutko worked on the earlier, much longer screenplay about the events of 1905. Eisenstein is credited for the finished script of *Potemkin*.
- Design: Vasili Rakhals

[3] Transliterations from the Russian alphabet into the English may be rendered in different ways. Thus, different English spellings of the names listed here may be encountered elsewhere.

17.4 Director Sergei Eisenstein, 1925/26. Courtesy Herbert Marshall Archives, Center for Soviet and East European Studies, Southern Illinois University.

17.5 Cinematographer Edward Tissé. Courtesy Phototeque.

- Cinematographer: Edward Tissé (1897–1961). Worked with Eisenstein on all his major films and is credited in part for their achievement.
- Editor: Sergei Eisenstein
- Music: Scores were composed for the first showings of *Potemkin*, but Eisenstein was dissatisfied with them and went to Berlin in 1926 to work with Edmund Meisel, who wrote an original score in 1926–1927. By different accounts, Meisel's score was so powerful that some jurisdictions in Germany banned the music while allowing the film to be shown. In the 1970s, Arthur Kleiner, long-time accompanist for silent films at the Museum of Modern Art, rescored the surviving "parts" of Meisel's printed score for a showing on PBS television. For the twenty-fifth anniversary of the film's release, in 1950, Nikolai Kryukov wrote a score, which is widely available now.

Major Characters and Performers:

- Vakulinchuk: Alexander Antonov
- Sailor Matiushenko: Levchenko
- Captain Golikov: Vladimir Barsky
- Senior Officer (or Lieutenant) Gilyarovsky: Gregory Alexandrov (also was assistant to Eisenstein)

17.6 Eisenstein at an editing table. Courtesy Herbert Marshall Archives, Center for Soviet and East European Studies, Southern Illinois University.

- Ship's Surgeon Smirnov
- Priest
- Other characters: citizens of Odessa, sailors of the Soviet Black Sea Fleet, and members of the Proletkult Theatre

Place and Time of Story: Black Sea and one of its ports, Odessa, June 1905
Other: For centuries Russia was ruled by absolute monarchs called czars (phonetic spelling: tsars). During the reign of the last czar—Nicholas II, who ruled from 1894 until the revolution of 1917—unrest increased. The year 1905 was particularly unstable; Russia lost a war to Japan and suffered a series of internal disturbances: strikes, demonstrations, riots, and mutinies. Collectively, these events are known as the 1905 Revolution, embracing a period of unrest commencing in January and ending with the unsuccessful efforts of the Bolsheviks to seize power by armed force in December. The mutiny on the *Prince Potemkin* was an aspect of the 1905 Revolution (one whose significance has subsequently been portrayed somewhat out of proportion to its importance by the film itself).[4]

---

[4] For additional background on the 1905 Revolution, see Sidney Samuel Harcave, *First Blood: The Russian Revolution of 1905;* Howard D. Mehlinger, *Count Witte and the Tsarist Government in the 1905 Revolution;* and Leon Trotsky, *1905.*

Originally, Eisenstein and scenarist Nina Agajanova planned an eight-part work on the political events of 1905. Shooting began in August, but bad weather interrupted it. Since Soviet authorities wanted some film by December to use as part of the twentieth-anniversary celebrations of the 1905 uprisings, Eisenstein decided to shorten the project and concentrate on the story of the *Potemkin*.

Outline

I. Situation on the Battleship *Potemkin*[5]
   1. Waves hitting breakwater.
   2. On deck of the *Potemkin*, Vakulinchuk and another sailor say that sailors on the *Potemkin* must stand with workers in the revolution.
   3. Below deck in crew's quarters, men sleeping. Boatswain, looking for suspicious characters, whips a sleeping man.
   4. In crew's quarters: Vakulinchuk's speech calling for rebellion (Figure 17.7).
   5. June 14, 1905,[6] morning. Deck: Officers watching men on deck (Figure 17.8). Some men look at hanging meat and complain to each other about it. Ship's surgeon, Dr. Smirnov, pronounces the meat, which is full of live maggots, fit to eat. . . .
   6. Galley: Cook chopping the meat. Sailors try to stop him.
   7. On deck: cleaning, polishing, repairing.

17.7 Crew member Vakulinchuk calling for rebellion because of the conditions on the Battleship *Potemkin*. Courtesy Cornith Films.

17.8 Officer in foreground; Vakulinchuk in background. Courtesy Cornith Films.

[5] In his writings a decade after the film was completed, Eisenstein himself divided the film into five parts (Men and Maggots, Drama on the Quarterdeck, Appeal from the Dead, The Odessa Steps, and Meeting the Squadron), but his headings and divisions are somewhat different than those I have selected for this outline.

[6] In many prints this date is not supplied.

8–12. Galley: Rotten meat cooking in the soup cross-cut with mess hall, where the men are setting tables.

13. On deck: Sailors angry about the situation. Some eat bread and salt and drink water from mugs.

14. In mess: Lieutenant (or "Senior Officer") Gilyarovsky arrives and looks around. . . .

15. Men buying canned food at canteen; Lieutenant Gilyarovsky pauses, then passes by.

16. Deck: Lieutenant Gilyarovsky reports to other officer that the men refused to eat the soup.

17. Mess: Those two officers; second one checks the bowls on suspended tables.

18. Deck: Second officer talks with the cook.

19. Below deck: Men washing and drying dishes. Sailor throws down a plate in anger. Fade-out.

II. Rebellion

20. Deck: Bugle call to assemble on deck. Men line up. Captain's first appearance. He orders that all who did not eat the soup be hanged. Guards with rifles called to deck. Most sailors break rank and group by turret; those who stay back are covered with a tarpaulin but—because of Vakulinchuk's calling out at the last moment—do not get shot. Fighting on the deck.

21–50. Much cross-cutting of scenes: Sailors going to get rifles, fighting on deck, Lieutenant Gilyarovsky with rifle pursuing Vakulinchuk, priest's intervention (Figure 17.9), Lieutenant Gilyarovsky and Vakulinchuk scuffling, fighting in officer's quarters (Figure 17.10), sailors tossing officers and ship's surgeon overboard, sailors in command, Lieutenant Gilyarovsky shooting Vakulinchuk, his shipmates retrieving his body. Fade-out.

51. On deck: They carry his body up stairs. Iris-out on Vakulinchuk's bloodied head.

III. Aftermath on ship and shore

52. Launch carrying Vakulinchuk's body.

53. Launch arrives at port of Odessa.

54. In port: Vakulinchuk's body in tent on jetty.

55. Dusk: Shots around harbor.

56. Dawn, Vakulinchuk's tent on jetty: People pay their respects.

57. (Figure 17.11) Streets: Masses of people walking, presumably toward jetty. . . .

58. Jetty: Crowds and speeches. One man, a scoffer, says, "Down with the Jews," and the crowd roughs him up.[7] . . . People waving arms and shouting.

---

[7] In some prints, such as the 1950 version, what the anti-Semite says is omitted, as are some of the shots of him. Historically, czarists used anti-Semitism to divide their critics.

17.9 Priest in foreground; ship's smoke in background. Courtesy Cornith Films.

17.10 Officer's quarters: officer firing pistol; picture of Czar Nicholas II on the wall. Courtesy Cornith Films.

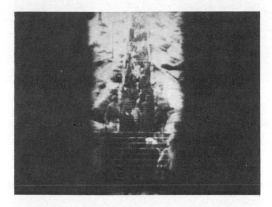

17.11 Masked image in the middle of lap dissolve from empty steps to a shot of people coming down steps. Courtesy Cornith Films.

17.12 Top of famous Odessa Steps: statue of Duc de Richelieu on the left; below are twelve flights of steps, each made up of twenty steps. Courtesy Cornith Films.

59–63. *Potemkin:* Rousing oratory by delegates from shore and raising of red flag cross-cut with people on steps on shore watching the *Potemkin.*

64–74. Small boats take food to the *Potemkin* cross-cut with people watching from steps on the shore.

IV. Repression and reactions

    75. "Suddenly": Marching feet and firing rifles (Figure 17.12). Panic and massacre: Many people killed, then young boy and his mother; small group—except for their leader, a lady with a pince-nez who had appealed to soldiers—and a young woman with baby carriage. Baby carriage descends steps, then overturns; woman with pince-nez gets

slashed in eye by one of the mounted Cossacks at base of steps.[8] (This scene is about six minutes long.)

76–79. *Potemkin* fires its large guns cross-cut with Odessa Theater, headquarters of czarist generals, getting hit.[9] Stone lion seems to rise up (Figures 17.13–17.15).

80. On *Potemkin,* evening: One sailor urges that they land on shore and says the army will join them. Another says it's impossible—other ships of the fleet are moving against them. They decide to confront the twelve ships of the fleet. Lap dissolve to an empty deck. Fadeout.

V. Confrontation and Unification

81–99. Night, *Potemkin:* Some run ship (without officers) cross-cut with other sailors resting.

17.13–17.15 Editing brings stone to life. Courtesy Cornith Films.

[8] In some prints, including the 1950 version, the last four or five shots of this scene are omitted, and it is not implied that the woman with the pince-nez gets injured.

[9] Some prints lack the two intertitles that tell exactly what the *Potemkin* is firing at.

17.16 Last shot of film: prow of *Potemkin* with its czarist imperial crest advancing toward camera. Courtesy Cornith Films.

100–164.[10] Day: Much cross-cutting, mainly between different parts of the ship. Spotting of the fleet and call to stations. Preparations and speeding up.[11] Signal: Join us. Other ships do not fire, and their crews cheer the mutineers and let them pass through. Sailors cheering on decks. Last shot: Prow of the *Potemkin* advancing toward camera, and audience (Figure 17.16).

The End

Questions and Observations

1. How do facial features, clothing, and gestures all help characterize the officers and sailors of the Battleship *Potemkin*? (For a starter, see Figures 17.7 and 17.8.)
2. In the massacre scene on the Odessa Steps, in what ways is the firing squad presented? In what ways are the victims depicted? What effects do the different presentations have?
3. Where does the film's running time exceed the story time? To what effects?
4. What feelings does the film attempt to evoke from the viewer? How successful is it in doing so? Why do you say so?
5. What are the film's political messages and implications? How prominent

[10] There are approximately 65 scenes in this last sequence. Here as elsewhere in this film, it is often difficult to tell what part of the ship we are seeing and therefore difficult to know the exact number of scenes.

[11] In some prints two intertitles explain that the *Potemkin* was escorted by Destroyer 267, which had joined the uprising. Other prints omit those two intertitles, and the sudden appearance of the destroyer is puzzling.

are they? How convincing and memorable are they? Is it possible to enjoy or admire the film if you disagree with its political outlook? Why or why not?

6. Review the discussion of fictional and documentary films in the first chapter and Figure 1.1. Is *Potemkin* a fictional film? Why do you say so? Is *Potemkin* a documentary? Why or why not? Is the film a combination of fictional and documentary? Explain your answer.

7. Define your terms and defend one of the following three observations about *Potemkin:*
   a. The film is propaganda.
   b. The film is a work of art.
   c. The film is both propaganda and a work of art.

8. The film dramatizes specific incidents in 1905 Russia. Does the film have a universal appeal or not? Why or why not?

9. "Some of the effects he [Eisenstein] tries for are just muddled, as in the famous sequence in which the stone lions are seen to rise from slumber and roar. The intent of this has not been made clear in the film, though many people feel that it refers to the revolutionary awaking [*sic*] of the masses from their slumbers after the Odessa massacre. However, since it comes after the Potemkin has destroyed the military headquarters in town, it could just as well refer to the awakening might of the czar, or the idea that in the face of the revolution all the czar can do is roar futilely."[12]

10. "Look intently into the structure of the work.

   "In its five acts, tied with the general thematic line of revolutionary brotherhood, there is otherwise little that is similar externally. But in one respect they are absolutely *alike:* each part is distinctly broken into two almost equal halves. This can be seen with particular clarity from the second act on:

   II. Scene with the tarpaulin $\longrightarrow$ mutiny
   III. Mourning for Vakulinchuk $\longrightarrow$ angry demonstration
   IV. Lyrical fraternization $\longrightarrow$ shooting
   V. Anxiously awaiting the
       fleet $\longrightarrow$ triumph

   "Moreover, at the 'transition' point of each part, the halt has its own peculiar kind of *caesura.*

   "In one part (III), this is a few shots of clenched fists, through which the theme of mourning the dead leaps into the theme of fury.

   "In another part (IV), this is a sub-title—'SUDDENLY'—cutting off the scene of fraternization, and projecting it into the scene of the shooting."[13]

11. "The most important single hero figure in the Soviet cinema has been

---

[12] Valentin Almendarez, *CinemaTexas Program Notes* 6, no. 13 (5 February 1974), 5.
[13] Sergei Eisenstein, "The Structure of the Film," in *Film Form: Essays in Film Theory,* ed. and trans. Jay Leyda (New York: Harcourt, Brace & World, 1949).

the worker, for it was after all the worker who was in the vanguard of the successful revolutionary movement. The worker is portrayed . . . as . . . upright, . . . calm and courageous in adversity, compassionate and self-sacrificing. Physically the worker is strong, clean-limbed and muscular. . . . He is cheerful. . . . He is rarely seen alone, and is certainly never lonely, but is usually depicted . . . as a member of a group. . . . In the unity expressed between the individual and the community lie both their economic solidarity and their political strength. When the workers act together . . . , then they are assured of eventual victory, even if they suffer a temporary defeat."[14]

12. "Eisenstein's variation from the truth, or failure to tell the whole truth (as he knew it), are not necessarily sinister or reprehensible. He was making a feature film, not a work of history. He had been commissioned to produce a work commemorating the 1905 Revolution, but it was intended for general distribution, and was meant to be an entertainment as well as a revolutionary sermon. To achieve this, and to make a film that would appeal to unsophisticated Russian audiences, Eisenstein had to change and simplify the confused story of the mutiny."[15]

Suggested Readings

Contexts

Hough, Richard. *The Potemkin Mutiny*. New York: Pantheon Books, 1960; reprint Westport, Conn.: Greenwood Press, 1975. Historical account in narrative form of the mutiny and its consequences.

Leyda, Jay. *Kino: A History of the Russian and Soviet Film*. 3d ed. Princeton, N.J.: Princeton University Press, 1983. Focus on "artistic development of the Soviet cinema."

Leyda, Jay, and Zina Voynow. *Eisenstein at Work*. New York: Pantheon Books and Museum of Modern Art, 1982. See pp. 153–55 for a detailed chronology of Eisenstein's life and work.

Marshall, Herbert, ed. *The Battleship Potemkin*. New York: Avon Books, 1978. Source book on film's production, reception in the U.S.S.R. and abroad, and the film's influence on other works of art, "Novels, Poetry, Ballet, Opera, and Painting."

Nettl, J. P. *The Soviet Achievement*. New York: Harcourt Brace & World, 1967. A short history of the Soviet Union up to 1964. Includes 144 illustrations, 19 in color, and an index.

Pratt, George C. *Spellbound in Darkness: A History of the Silent Film*. Greenwich, Conn.: New York Graphic Society, 1973. "A compilation of orig-

[14] Richard Taylor, *Film Propaganda: Soviet Russia and Nazi Germany* (London: Croom Helm, 1979), pp. 72–73.

[15] D. J. Wenden, "*Battleship Potemkin*—Film and Reality," in K. R. M. Short, ed., *Feature Films as History* (Knoxville: University of Tennessee Press, 1981).

inal readings from contemporary sources" for films from the period 1896–1929.

Seton, Marie. *Sergei M. Eisenstein: A Biography.* London: Bodley Head, 1952.

Wenden, D. J. "Battleship Potemkin—Film and Reality." In K. R. M. Short, ed., *Feature Films as History* (Knoxville: University of Tennessee Press, 1981). Comparison of historical accounts and film's depiction of them plus a bibliography in three parts: "General Works," "The Making of the Film," and "Accounts of the Mutiny and of Events in Odessa."

Scripts

Bronenosets "Potemkin": Sbornik (The Battleship "Potemkin": A Collection). Compiled by N. I. Kleĭman and K. B. Levina. Moscow: Iskusstvo, 1969. In Russian, but even without knowledge of that language, some interesting information can be gleaned from the book, which includes reproductions of posters advertising the film, production information and stills, and on pp. 106–81 a cutting continuity script with hundreds of frame enlargements. This is a difficult book to locate. Its Library of Congress card number is 76–480997.

Eisenstein, Sergei. *Eisenstein: Three Films.* Trans. Diana Matias. Ed. Jay Leyda. New York: Harper & Row, 1974. Includes shooting scripts for *Potemkin* and *October,* plus a scenario for *Alexander Nevsky.*

Mayer, David. *Sergei M. Eisenstein's Potemkin: A Shot-by-Shot Presentation.* New York: Grossman, 1972. A detailed cutting continuity script derived from the Museum of Modern Art version of the film, divided into shots; numerous frame enlargements.

Potemkin: A Film by Sergei Eisenstein. Trans. Gillon R. Aitken. New York: Simon and Schuster, 1968. Cutting continuity script, compiled in 1934, by a Soviet film scholar, without division into shots; 39 stills.

Analyses

Beja, Morris. *Film and Literature: An Introduction.* New York: Longman, 1979. See pp. 100–106: "Background," "Topics to Think About," and "Further Readings."

Cook, David A. *A History of Narrative Film.* New York: W. W. Norton, 1981. See pp. 149–71 for an essay on the production and structure of the film, plus nearly 200 frame enlargements from it.

Fulton, A. R. *Motion Pictures: The Development of an Art.* Revised edition. Norman: University of Oklahoma Press, 1980. See pp. 114–30 for an analysis of the film.

Kauffmann, Stanley. *Living Images: Film Comment and Criticism.* New York: Harper & Row, 1975. See pp. 290–98 for an essay of analysis, reprinted from *Horizon* 15 (Spring 1973): 110–17.

· 18 ·

The Seven Samurai

Other Titles: *Shichinin no Samurai* (Japanese)
The Magnificent Seven, title in U.S. until another film of the same title and subject was released in 1960 (Figure 18.1).
Country of Production: Japan

18.1 *The Magnificent Seven,* U.S. remake of *The Seven Samurai.* Movie Star News.

261

First Release: 1954

Process: Black and white; 1.33:1 aspect ratio

Approximate Running Time: 208 minutes

Versions: According to film scholar Donald Richie, the film was 200 minutes long when released in major Japanese cities in 1954. Shortened versions were soon made, including 160- and 141-minute ones, and for some years the complete version was unavailable anywhere. Sometime in the 1970s, the complete 208-minute version was reconstructed. Today in the United States one may rent or lease either the 141-minute version or the complete 208-minute one. In 1982, the 208-minute version was re-released commercially with a new four-track stereo sound track.

Production: The 130 shooting days were extended over a ten-month period (the average Japanese film of the time was shot in thirty days). Three months were spent on location at the foot of Mount Fuji. At the time of its making, it was the most expensive feature film ever made in Japan.

Selected Credits[1]

- Producer: Shojiro Motoki for Toho
- Director: Akira Kurosawa (1910–   ) (Figure 18.2). Director of *Rashomon, Ikiru, The Throne of Blood, The Lower Depths, Yojimbo, Dersu Uzala,* and others.
- Scriptwriters: Shinobu Hashimoto, Hideo Oguni, and Akira Kurosawa
- Design: So Matsuyama
- Cinematographer: Askazu Nakai
- Lighting: Shigero Mori
- Editors: Kurosawa and others? (not listed in available sources for credits, nor in the Japanese credits on the film itself)
- Music: Fumio Hayasaka
- Sound: Fumio Yanoguchi

Major Characters and Performers:[2]

- Kambei (CAM BAY): Takashi Shimura (1905–1982), actor in *Rashomon, Ikiru,* many others.
- Kikuchiyo (key KOO chee oh): Toshiro Mifune (1920–   ), actor in *Rashomon, The Throne of Blood, Yojimbo, Red Beard, Hell in the Pacific,* many others.
- Gorobei (go ROW bay)
- Kyuzo (CUE zoe), swordsman
- Heihachi (hay AH gee), samurai "of the wood chopping school"
- Shichiroji (she tee low gee), Kambei's old friend
- Katsushiro (kuh THOO she low), young, inexperienced samurai

- Gisaku (gee SAY koo), village patriarch
- Rikichi (lee KEY she), moody farmer who wants to fight the brigands

---

[1] Spellings of transliterated Japanese names may vary elsewhere.

[2] Because of the differences between Japanese and English, it is difficult to render accurate pronunciations of Japanese names. At best, my attempts will help you approximate their correct pronunciation.

18.2 Director Kurosawa during filming of *The Seven Samurai*. Museum of Modern Art/Film Stills Archive.

- Mosuke (mos ske), farmer prominent in the story
- Yohei (YO hay), sad-faced farmer
- Manzo (MON zoe), farmer worried about presence of samurai in village
- Shino (SHE no), Manzo's daughter

- Brigand chief

Place and Time of Story: Japan, late sixteenth century, a time of civil war and lawlessness

Other: The samurai's topknot was a special badge of honor. When the priest shaves Kambei's off early in the film, the people are amazed that a samurai would allow his topknot to be shaved. Perhaps the crowd infers that the samurai is going to join the priesthood.

Since the subtitles to this film are often difficult to read, you may want to read the opening sections of the script before you see the film for the first time.

Although the Japanese film industry is old and large, its films were rarely shown in Western countries before the 1950s. In the early 1950s several Japanese films won prizes at international film festivals and began to be shown in the West, at least in large cities.

Excerpts from a Chronology in *Currents in Japanese Cinema: Essays by Tadao Sato* (1982):

1945
Defeat [of the Japanese in World War II]. . . . Motion picture com-

panies are placed under the Occupation forces, which prohibit films with themes of revenge or antidemocratic principles. . . .
1950
. . . Kurosawa directs *Rashomon,* an innovative period drama with sexual and psychological themes and avant-garde techniques. . . .
1951
. . . *Rashomon* wins the Grand Prix at the Venice Film Festival, the first time a Japanese film becomes known internationally. . . . Japan's first feature-length color movie. . . .
1952
. . . The Occupation [of foreign troops] ends, and the theme of revenge is immediately restored to period drama, as well as plenty of sword-fighting scenes. . . .
1953
. . . Mizoguchi's *Ugetsu* and Ozu's *Tokyo Story.* . . .
1954
. . . Kurosawa makes *Seven Samurai.* . . .

Outline

This outline is for the complete, 208-minute version.

I. The Problem
   1. . . . Brigands arrive at ridge overlooking the farmers' village and decide to return after the barley is ready for harvest (Figure 18.3).
   2. The villagers meet (Figure 18.4); most of them are in despair; they decide to go see the village patriarch, Gisaku.
   3. At the meeting with Gisaku, he says they'll hire samurai to defend their village.
II. Recruiting
   4. In a town, four of the farmers—Rikichi, Manzo, Yohei, and Mosuke. Rikichi is rebuffed by a proud samuari.
   5. . . . Three men—in the script they are called laborers—taunt the four farmers.
   6. Night. In an inn, the four are taunted again by the laborers. A cowardly samurai is humiliated.
   7. Day. Since their recruiting efforts are going badly, Manzo and Rikichi are fighting about whether to give in to the brigands or not.
   8. . . . The four farmers see Kambei, a samurai, cut off his topknot and get his head shaved by a priest. Our first views of Katsushiro and Kikuchiyo. Kambei kills a thief holding a child hostage and rescues the child. Katsushiro and the four farmers are impressed.
   9. On a road, the four farmers follow Kambei. Kikuchiyo approaches Kambei but says nothing. Katsushiro asks to be Kambei's disciple.
   10. Katsushiro still asking Kambei to take him on as a student. Kikuchiyo again seems to want to talk with Kambei but says nothing to him. Now in the town, Rikichi goes down on his knees at Kambei's feet and says "please."

18.3 At beginning of film: brigand leader and his unruly horse.

18.4 Village meeting.

11. The farmers have asked Kambei to defend their village. He's thinking it over. Kambei learns that the farmers are sacrificing by eating millet while they give rice to him.
12. . . . Village: Two of the farmers who went to the town, Mosuke and Manzo, tell the village patriarch that they'll need seven samurai; Gisuku gives his approval.
13. In town: An attempt to recruit another samurai fails because he's uninterested given the meager conditions of employment.
14. Village: Manzo and Mosuke in front of the graveyard: Manzo worried about what will happen to the farmers and their families after the samurai come to the village.
15. Town: Gorobei senses something is amiss and avoids getting hit on the head. (He passes Kambei's test.)
16. Gorobei agrees to serve with Kambei because he is fascinated by his character.
17. The farmers' rice has been stolen. Katsushiro gives Rikichi and Yohei some money. Kambei arrives with Shichiroji, his former colleague in arms, and he also agrees to join with Kambei.
18. Gorobei, looking for samurai, hears about a wood-chopping samurai and talks with him (Heihachi).
19. Kambei and Katsushiro see Kyuzo win two duels with a man.
20. Kambei tells Gorobei about Kyuzo, and Gorobei tells about recruiting Heihachi.
21. Kambei reluctant to take along Katsushiro because he is young. Kyuzo arrives but is unseen by all except Heihachi. Others convince Kambei to take Katsushiro after all. Kyuzo joins them. Kikuchiyo—intoxicated—fails samurai test and gets whacked on the head; he makes a big scene.
22. Next morning, Rikichi, Yohei, and the six samurai set off for the village.
23. At the village: Manzo chases his daughter, Shino, in order to cut off her hair.

24. Mosuke is angry that Manzo is thinking only of himself, and he criticizes him.
25. On road, Kikuchiyo following the six samurai and two farmers.
26. By waterfall, as others eat, Kikuchiyo catches a fish with his hands and cooks it.
27. On road again: Kikuchiyo now ahead of others.

III. Preparations in the village
28. Near village: Samurai arrive and see villagers scatter.
29. In village: No welcome; Rickichi upset; all but Kikuchiyo leave to go see the village patriarch.
30. At Gisaku's residence, inside a mill, they talk to him, then hear an alarm. Everyone assumes that the brigands are coming.
31. Villagers and samurai run to the village square, where they learn that Kikuchiyo sounded the alarm.
32. In Rikichi's house: Samurai will sleep there. Rikichi upset when the subject of a wife comes up.
33. Kambei, Gorobei, and Katsushiro study layout and defense of the village.
34. Shichiroji with his contingent of men moving logs.
35. Kambei, Gorobei, and Katsushiro still studying layout of the village and discussing ways to defend it.
36. Kyuzo training farmers in use of spears.
37. Kambei, Gorobei, and Katsushiro planning further defenses.
38. Heihachi talking to his group of farmers. . . .
39. Kikuchiyo training some men with spears; he makes fun of Yohei and discovers that some farmers have samurai spears.
40. Kambei, Gorobei, and Katsushiro in a forest; Katsushiro decides to stay behind. He enjoys the beauty of the place—and meets Shino.

18.5 Kikuchiyo talks about plight of farmers.

18.6 A few shots later, a reaction shot of Kambei in the foreground with tears in his eyes.

41. Kambei explaining defenses to four other samurai. Kikuchiyo wearing armor shows up with farmers who are carrying armor of vanquished samurai. The samurai are offended. Kikuchiyo's impassioned speech about farmers—and samurai who make farmers as they are (Figures 18.5 and 18.6). Village patriarch arrives with Rikichi and is told everything is all right.
42. Katsushiro sees Kikuchiyo sulking outside (Figure 18.7) and soon learns he's in a foul mood.
43. Night. Rikichi sleeping in stable; Kikuchiyo joins him.
44. Day. Raining. Kyuzo leaves to practice his swordsmanship. Heihachi making a banner to symbolize the farmers and samurai. Katsushiro slips out.
45. In rain, Kyuzo practicing (Figure 18.8). He sees Katsushiro bring Shino some food and meet with her. Shino says she'll take the food to a grandmother.
46. Samurai eating. Katsushiro says he's not hungry; Kyuzo says he isn't either. Kambei asks what's going on.
47. Samurai with a very old woman (the grandmother referred to in scene 45) who wants to die. (Presumably they have brought her rice.) Kyuzo and Katsushiro slip out separately. . . .
48. Samurai share their rice with the village children.
49. Mill: Samurai talk with village patriarch about defenses and evacuation of three houses, one of them Mosuke's, and the mill.
50. Outside: Samurai giving instructions to villagers. Mosuke leads a small rebellion, because villagers don't want to abandon any houses. Kambei quickly quashes the uprising. Kambei's speech on unity.

Five-minute intermission, with music.

51. Harvesting. Kikuchiyo pleased with all the women. Heihachi asks Rikichi why he's unmarried, and Rikichi goes off in a huff. . . .

18.7 Kikuchiyo outside in wind; Katsushiro approaching him cautiously.

18.8 Kyuzo practicing in rain.

52. In dense, cut bamboo cane: Samurai, who have presumably tried to catch up with Rikichi, talk about how upset he was.

53. Night. Raining. Heihachi fails to get Rikichi to talk about what's troubling him.

54. Just before Katsushiro talks about Shino in his sleep, Kambei and Gorobei get up (to go check defense points).

55. Kikuchiyo sleeping on guard duty. Kambei's gentle lesson and reprimand.

56. Day. Kikuchiyo is unimpressed with Yohei's horse.

57. Farmers digging a ditch.

58. Flooding it. . . .

59. Farmers thrashing grain.

60. Kikuchiyo rides Yohei's horse—at least for a while.

IV. Confrontations

61. In forest: Shino and Katsushiro; she's nervous and aroused. They hear horses, then see them and leave.

62. Shichiroji, then Katsushiro, report that three brigands have been spotted. . . . Villagers panic.

63. . . . Three brigand scouts spot Kikuchiyo. Kikuchiyo, Kyuzo, and Katsushiro go to catch them (Figure 18.9).

64. In woods by brigands' horses: As Katsushiro watches nervously, Kyuzo kills two brigands, and Kikuchiyo captures the other.

65. In the village, the farmers want to kill the captured brigand. Samurai try to defend him as a captured prisoner, then let an old woman (of scene 47) kill him to avenge her son's death.

66. Samurai plan raid on brigand fort.

67. On the way: Kikuchiyo, Heihachi, Kyuzo, and Rikichi. Kikuchiyo's unruly mount (Yohei's horse). . . .

68. The four approach the fort, then set it afire. Inside, a woman (we learn later it's Rikichi's wife) sees the smoke and fire but does not scream out a warning. The samurai kill a number of the brigands. Rikichi tries to retrieve his wife. Heihachi tries to retrieve Rikichi but gets shot.

69. Village graveyard: Heihachi has been buried. Kikuchiyo gets banner symbolizing farmers and samurai and climbs a roof with it. Brigands' arrival.

70. Fence keeps the brigands out.

71. Katsushiro brings news to Kambei, who's with Gorobei and his group of men.

72. Gorobei and his men run to a different section of the village. Gorobei shoots a brigand with an arrow. Other brigands leave, presumably to test other defense points.

73. Katsushiro brings news to Kambei.

74. Gorobei and his men come to Kambei and get new instructions.

75. Kikuchiyo and his men at a bridge. Gisaku's son and his wife want to go to the village patriarch in the mill. Kikuchiyo allows them to do so (she's carrying a child in her arms).

76. Gorobei, Kyuzo, and their men wait. They see Shichiroji leading his men in a cheer and do so with their men, too.

18.9 All seven samurai in the same frame (left to right): Kyuzo, Kikuchiyo, Shichiroji, Heihachi, Kambei, Katsushiro, and Gorobei. For all seven to be in the frame is unusual; we never see all seven together and in full face; this is the last time all seven are together.

18.10 Kikuchiyo holding baby and saying that the same thing happened to him as a child. Burning mill in background.

77. Kikuchiyo and his men moving logs; they stop and yell, too. Brigands shoot at Kikuchiyo, then burn three houses. Kambei and Katsushiro arrive, then the villagers, who are quite upset. Mosuke gets the villagers back to their posts. The mill is burning, too. Kikuchiyo goes off toward it to get the young couple and child.

78. In stream: Speared mother with baby. Kikuchiyo and Kambei try to help her. She gives her baby to Kikuchiyo, who is moved by the baby's plight (Figure 18.10). . . .

79. Night. Kikuchiyo and his men fend off an attack by a small group of brigands.

80. Shichiroji and his men have a battle, too. Gunshot. Manzo hit— only grazed.

81. Another group fighting in a flooded field. Rikichi, fighting fiercely, kills a brigand.

82. Kambei crosses off six symbols representing brigands and says where the next attack will probably be. . . .

83. Katsushiro bringing dummy dressed in samurai uniform; he crosses paths momentarily with Shino.

84. Katsushiro holds out dummy, which gets shot twice. Kyuzo leaves to capture a gun from the brigands.

85. Near dawn: Kyuzo returns with a gun (and says he killed two). Katsushiro's admiration.

86. Day: Brigands attack; one let through the outer defense.

87. That brigand is killed in the village.

88. Outpost: . . . Brigands charge again; two get in.

89. In village: One of the two brigands is killed.

90. At the outer defense station: Second brigand fights his way out; man on a spooked horse gets through the defense.

91. In village, the brigand on the kicking horse is disposed of.
92. Kambei says that the brigands are getting wise (to the samurai strategy of attrition).
93. Kambei crosses off six more circles representing brigands.
94. Katsushiro praising Kyuzo to Kikuchiyo. After Katsushiro leaves, Kikuchiyo does, too.
95. Briefly, Kikuchiyo with Yohei, who is being suited up in armor.
96. Kikuchiyo running in woods.
97. Kikuchiyo near brigands' horses; he sees two deserting brigands get shot. After brigand chief and others leave, Kikuchiyo takes clothing from one of the shot brigands.
98. Later Kikuchiyo with a brigand with a rifle; Kikuchiyo kills him, takes his rifle, and gets chased.
99. From village outpost: Samurai see Kikuchiyo chased by brigands. Kambei scolds Kikuchiyo for leaving his post. . . .
100. Another brigand attack. One horseman let in.
101. In village, that brigand is killed by the women.
102. Defense post: Two brigands get by.
103. In village, those two do much damage.
104. At another defense post, Kikuchiyo and others repulse another attack.
105. In village, two brigands continue to inflict heavy damages: Yohei and others killed. The two are finally subdued. Two gun shots are heard.
106. Outer post: Gorobei has been shot.
107. Village: Kikuchiyo exhausted.
108. Night. Graveyard. Kikuchiyo subdued.
109. Kambei crosses off seven more circles representing brigands. Katsushiro drowsy, then sleeping. Kambei and Kyuzo talking strategy. Kambei expects the decisive battle to be in the morning.
110. Katsushiro brings word to Shichiroji that the showdown will be in the morning. . . .
111. Katsushiro returns to Kambei and Kyuzo.
112. Katsushiro sees Shino. She's hysterical and aroused.
113. Manzo looking for Shino among sleeping villagers.
114. Farmers bring sake and special food to Kambei and Kyuzo.
115. Manzo still seeking Shino.
116. Kambei takes sake to Kikuchiyo at grave site; he guzzles it.
117. Manzo sees Katsushiro, then Shino and puts one and one together. Manzo beats Shino. Kambei, returning from the graveyard, restrains him. Others gather to see what's going on. Kambei figures out Katsushiro is the man. Manzo remains angry and unforgiving. It begins raining (Figure 18.11).
118. Day. Kambei sees that the villagers are tense and teases Katsushiro. Loud laughter.
119. Shichiroji with his men at post. He gives them a pep talk.
120. Outer post: Only 13 brigands left. . . . Final attack.
121. In village, much fighting.
122. Inside a house: Brigand chief with rifle.
123. Outside: More fighting. Kyuzo shot, then Kikuchiyo, but he man-

18.11 Near end of scene: Shino and Katsushiro after the news gets out that they have been intimate. In background Kambei looks back at Katsushiro.

18.12 Kikuchiyo dead in the rain.

18.13 End of the final battle for the three surviving samurai (left to right): Katsushiro, Kambei, and Shichiroji.

18.14 Last shot, near the beginning of the final fade-out: four samurai graves.

ages to kill brigand chief before collapsing (Figure 18.12). Battle over. Three samurai survive (Figure 18.13). Fade-out.

V. Aftermath

124. Fade-in. Planting rice; three samurai watch. At graveyard: Three samurai look up to four samurai graves. Shino snubs Katsushiro. He follows after her a short distance. Kambei says, "Again, we're defeated. The winners are those farmers. Not us." (Translation is from a film print, not script.) Kambei and Shichiroji look up to the four graves. Seven Samurai theme music, then the final fade-out (Figure 18.14).

Fade-in. "The End." Fade-out.

Questions and Observations

1. Which samurai do you admire? Why? Which samurai evokes the strongest feelings from you? Why? What qualities as a leader does Kambei have? In what ways are Kyuzo and Kikuchiyo similar? In what ways different?

2. Study the passage about Kikuchiyo in Chapter 7 (pages 129–130). When you agree with its generalizations, illustrate them. Where you disagree with the passage, refute.

3. What is your attitude toward the farmers? Why? Comment upon Rikichi's importance to the story, then upon Shino's importance.

4. What is your attitude toward the bandits? Can you feel any sympathy for them? Why or why not?

5. How do the actions of the samurai, farmers, and brigands all illustrate the value of working together? Who tends not to think of the group but of himself? What are the consquences?

6. By what means are the four samurai killed in battle? From the evidence of the film, what seems to be the fate of samurai in sixteenth-century Japan?

7. In Figures 18.6, 18.7, 18.10, 18.11, and 18.13, the objects in the foreground and background are in clear focus and are related to each other in significant ways. Point out several additional shots or scenes that use deep focus compositions. For each image you choose, be sure to explain in what ways the foreground and background components are related to each other.

8. Describe the camera angles and distances used in photographing the samurai. Describe the angles and distances used to photograph the brigands. How do you account for the differences?

9. What techniques of photography, editing, and sound are employed in the battle scenes? What do those techniques add to the experience of seeing the film?

10. Review the film's first shot and its last shot (Figure 18.14). Explain their importance for the film.

11. Describe the different melodies used in the film. Where are they used? What does the music contribute to the film?

12. Some viewers start to get up during the fade-out after the final battle. Should they sit a little longer and watch the final scene, labelled "Aftermath" in the outline above? Why or why not?

13. Compare and contrast the subjects, treatments, and effects of *The Seven Samurai* with U.S. Western films, especially *The Magnificent Seven* (a remake of *The Seven Samurai;* see Figure 18.1) and *The Wild Bunch* (an enormously popular film with the Japanese).

14. What qualities of *The Seven Samurai* make it hold the attention of its audiences for nearly three and a half hours? List and explain each quality.

15. ". . . Kurosawa—here perhaps more than in any other single film—insisted that the motion-picture be composed entirely of *motion*. The film opens with fast pans of the bandits riding over hills, and ends with the

chaos of the battle itself, motion so swift we can almost not see it at all. There is no shot that does not have motion, either in the object photographed, or in the movement of the camera itself. The motion may be small (the quivering nostrils in the long-held image of the village elder) or it may be great (the huge, sweeping frescoes of the charges) but it is always there."[3]

16. Critic John Simon has written:

We realize the profound verity the film has painstakingly built up to: Warrior castes, whether noble or ignoble, are declining, slowly exterminating one another. There remain the timid and weak but canny peasants, who, for a fraction of their humble earnings, can buy the lives of noble champions and death for the outlaws. And when the samurai, too, have died of bandits, inanition, or uselessness, the world will become peaceable, industrious, uneventful.[4]

17. "The older admirer, the counterfeit samurai Kikuchiyo (Toshiro Mifune) . . . finds himself attracted to Kambei as much out of curiosity as respect. Unlike the obedient Katsushiro, he does not articulate his submission to a superior, but watches, prods, criticizes, improvises and makes tragic mistakes while providing the major source of amusement in the film with his clowning—emphasized by his own personal bongo-drum, piccolo and bassoon theme music. Kurosawa uses this comic figure, however, to present an undisguised truth: that farmers are the sly and sniveling creatures they are largely because they have been abused and intimidated into it by the warrior class. Mifune's defensive tirade . . . brings into the open the issue that the ending of the story underscores. When the bandits are destroyed, there is no longer any need for samurai, and the three survivors are ignored as the peasants resume their peaceful life work of planting. To people who have been exploited for centuries by warrior-landlords, these mercenaries are no more than a temporary necessary evil employed in order to combat their own kind. . . .

On a more universal level, the heroic efforts of the samurai . . . remain unsung. Kurosawa's existentialists must accept the fact that there is no reward for their good deeds, and that human nature will not change because of their self-sacrifice. Yet he has them decide that the little bit of good they can do, so that ordinary people can live in peace and with a modicum of comfort, is worth doing to the utmost, even to the point of death."[5]

[3] Donald Richie, *The Films of Akira Kurosawa*, 2d ed. (Berkeley: University of California Press, 1970). This same passage is reprinted as part of the introduction to the Simon and Schuster script; see Suggested Readings below.

[4] John Simon, *Private Screenings* (New York: Macmillan, 1967), p. 32.

[5] Audie Bock, *Japanese Film Directors* (Tokyo: Kodansha International, 1978), p. 177.

Suggested Readings

Contexts

Draeger, Donn F., and Robert W. Smith. "Japan." *Asian Fighting Arts*. Tokyo: Kodansha International, 1969. See p. 81 ff.

Erens, Patricia. *Akira Kurosawa: A Guide to References and Resources*. Boston: G. K. Hall, 1979. Essay on Kurosawa's life; chapter on his films; synopsis, credits, and notes for each of his films; annotated bibliography, indexes, etc.

Higham, Charles. "Kurosawa's Humanism." *Kenyon Review* 27, no. 4 (Autumn 1965): 737–42.

Kaminsky, Stuart M. "Comparative Forms: The Samurai Film and the Western." *American Film Genres*. Dayton, Ohio: Pflaum Publishing, 1974.

Mellen, Joan. *Voices from the Japanese Cinema*. New York: Liveright. 1975. See pp. 37-58 for an introduction to Kurosawa and an interview with him.

Richie, Donald. *The Japanese Movie*. Revised edition. Tokyo: Kodansha International, 1982. A pictorial and social history.

Sato, Tadao. *Currents in Japanese Cinema*. Trans. Gregory Barrett. Tokyo: Kodansha International, 1982. In this first book in English by a Japanese film critic, Sato discusses a wide variety of Japanese films, organized mostly by subjects. Includes 48 pages of black-and-white photos, a chronology of Japanese cinema, and an index.

Varley, H. Paul. *Japanese Culture: A Short History*. New York: Praeger, 1973.

Wolf, Barbara. "On Akira Kurosawa." *Yale Review* 64, no. 2 (1974): 218–26.

Scripts

L'Avant-Scène du Cinéma, no. 113 (April 1971), pp. 1–69. Cutting continuity script divided into scenes, based on a 203-minute version; brackets indicate material omitted in the 160-minute version.

The Seven Samurai: A Film by Akira Kurosawa. Trans. Donald Richie. New York: Simon and Schuster, 1970. Shot continuity based on 160-minute version plus 234 stills and an introduction; a note indicates what shots were cut from the 160-minute version to make the 141-minute one.

Analyses and Reviews

Anderson, Joseph L. "When the Twain Meet: Hollywood's Remake of *The Seven Samurai.*" *Film Quarterly* 15, no. 3 (Spring 1962): 55–58. A comparison of *The Seven Samurai* and *The Magnificent Seven*.

Bock, Audie. *Japanese Film Directors*. Tokyo: Kodansha International, 1978.

Glazer, Nathan. "Seven Samurai." *East-West Review* 1 (June 1964): 38–43.

Leyda, Jay. "Modesty and Pretension in Two New Films." *Film Culture* 2, no. 10 (1956): 3–7, 27. On *The Seven Samurai* and *Moby Dick*.

Nolley, Kenneth S. "The Western as *Jidai-Geki*." *Western American Literature* 11, no. 3 (November 1976): 231–38. Like Anderson's article (see above), a comparison of *The Seven Samurai* and *The Magnificent Seven*.

Richardson, Tony. *"The Seven Samurai." Sight and Sound* 24, no. 4 (1955): 195–96.

Richie, Donald. *The Films of Akira Kurosawa*, rev. ed. Berkeley: University of California Press, 1984. Filmography and bibliography. Most of the essay on *The Seven Samurai* is reprinted as the introduction in the Simon and Schuster version of the script (see above).

· 19 ·

2001: A Space Odyssey

19.1 Black-and-white photograph of original color advertisement for *2001*.
© 1968 Metro-Goldwyn-Mayer Inc. Memory Shop West.

Background

Country of Production: Great Britain
First Release: 3 April 1968; New York City (first public showing)
Process:

- Metrocolor and Technicolor.
- Filmed in Super Panavision (65 mm nonanamorphic).
- First shown in Cinerama theaters: single projector; 70 mm prints; large, deeply curved screen; 2.2:1 aspect ratio from central seats; multitrack magnetic sound.
- Released in 35 mm anamorphic Panavision prints in December 1968.
- Later, 16 mm anamorphic prints were made up for nontheatrical showings.
- Now video versions are available for sale or rent.

Approximate Running Time: 141 minutes. Following the New York release of the film, director Kubrick cut the film from 160 minutes to its present running time.
Versions: The running time of most prints is 141 minutes, but about half of the picture is cut off on the sides in television and video showings and in scanned prints sometimes used in nontheatrical showings. Compare Figures 19.2 and 19.3.
Production:[1]

- December 1965: Filming began, Shepperton Studio, near London.
- January 1966: Production moved to M-G-M Boreham Wood Studio.
- March 1968: Film edited.
- Late March and early April: Film previewed, released, then cut by 19 minutes.
- Finished film was $4.5 million over original $6 million budget.

19.2 Theatrical Showings. 2.2:1 aspect ratio. From the M-G-M release *2001: A Space Odyssey* © 1968 Metro-Goldwyn-Mayer Inc.

[1] Most of the following information was taken from the production calendar in Carolyn Geduld's *Filmguide to 2001: A Space Odyssey* (Bloomington: Indiana University Press, 1973), pp. 21–28.

19.3 Showings on television sets or monitors. 1.33:1 aspect ratio. In these "scanned prints" only about half of the original image is visible—not necessarily the center portion. From the M-G-M release *2001: A Space Odyssey* © 1968 Metro-Goldwyn-Mayer Inc.

- July 1968: Novel published after extensive collaboration between Arthur C. Clarke and Kubrick. Unlike most novel/film combinations, the book supplies many more explanations than the film.
- July 1969: Armstrong and Aldrin become the first men to walk on the moon.

Selected Credits:

- Producer: Stanley Kubrick for M-G-M. (Kubrick is the producer of all his films since 1963.)
- Director: Stanley Kubrick (1928–   ) (Figure 19.4). Still photographer for *Look* magazine, director of features: *Killer's Kiss* (1955), *The Killing* (1956), *Paths of Glory* (1957), *Lolita* (1961), *Dr. Strangelove or: How I Learned to Stop Worrying and Love the Bomb*[2] (1963), *A Clockwork Orange* (1971), *Barry Lyndon* (1975), and *The Shining* (1980).
- Scriptwriters: Stanley Kubrick and Arthur C. Clarke (Figure 19.5). Script based loosely upon Clarke's short story "The Sentinel" (1950).
- Design: Tony Masters, Harry Lange, Ernie Archer
- Special Photographic Effects Designer and Director: Stanley Kubrick
- Special Photographic Effects Supervisors: Wally Veevers, Douglas Trumbull, Con Pederson, and Tom Howard
- Cinematographer: Geoffrey Unsworth (1914–1978). Director of photography for *Cabaret, Murder on the Orient Express, Tess,* many others. *Superman,* one of his last films, is dedicated to his memory.
- Editor: Ray Lovejoy

[2] The title on film prints, the Library of Congress copyright application, and Columbia Pictures Production Notes all punctuate the title as shown above, but numerous publications punctuate it in various other ways.

19.4 Director Stanley Kubrick on a set with actors and crew. Movie Star News.

19.5 Writer Arthur C. Clarke on a set of *2001*. © 1968 Metro-Goldwyn-Mayer Inc. Movie Star News.

- Music: Richard Strauss: *Thus Spake Zarathustra*
  Johann Strauss: *The Blue Danube*
  Aram Khatchaturian: *Gayne Ballet Suite*
  György Ligeti: *Atmospheres, Lux Aeterna,* and *Requiem*
- Sound: Winston Ryder

Major Characters and Performers:

- Dave Bowman: Keir Dullea (*David and Lisa, The Fox, De Sade,* others)
- Frank Poole: Gary Lockwood (*Splendor in the Grass,* others)
- Dr. Heywood Floyd: William Sylvester (according to Halliwell's *The Film-goer's Companion,* "American leading man, in British films since 1949")
- HAL's voice: Douglas Rain (a Canadian stage actor who replaced Martin Balsam, whose voice was judged as too expressive)

Place and Time of Story: Earth, space station between earth and moon, moon, space on way to Jupiter, and "Jupiter and Beyond the Infinite"; "The Dawn of Man" (about 4 million B.C.), around 2001, and at the end of the story, who can say?

Other:

- Numerous allusions to and parodies of *2001* attest to its popularity and influence. Examples are innumerable, e.g., the parody in *Mad* magazine (March 1969), many allusions in "Electric Company" shows on PBS, the short film "K-9000: A Space Oddity," and the allusions in the feature film *Dark Star.* For other examples of the film's influence, see the book *The Making of Kubrick's 2001* (cited in Suggested Readings below).
- Arthur C. Clarke wrote in an epilogue to the 1982 reprinting of the novel: "The crew of *Apollo 8,* who at Christmas 1968 became the first men ever to set eyes upon the lunar Farside, told me that they had been tempted to radio back the discovery of a large, black monolith: alas, discretion prevailed . . ." (ellipses are Clarke's).
- *2001* was first shown just before the current U.S. rating system came into effect, so the film is unrated. In Britain when the film first came out, it was rated A, meaning suitable for adults only.
- Late in the film, a recording by Dr. Floyd explains something about a monolith. The last part of what he says is reprinted in the outline below, in scene 36. Most viewers seem to pay little attention to what he says. You'll be glad if you do.
- Several commentators have pointed out that of the film's 141 minutes, only 43 minutes are with dialogue.
- In November 1982, Arthur C. Clarke published *2010: Odyssey Two,* a sequel about a joint U.S.-Soviet expedition, including Dr. Heywood Floyd, to recover *Discovery One* and find out what happened to its crew and computer.

Outline

I. "The Dawn of Man"
   1. Man-apes (as they are called in the novel) and tapirs eating same kind of plants. Leopard attacks a defenseless man-ape. Fade-out (F.O.)
   2. Fade-in (F.I.) Rival groups of man-apes want same territory with water hole. Much jumping and noise making, and rivals retreat. F.O.
   3. F.I. Leopard with dead zebra.
   4. Night. Small group of man-apes listening. F.O.
   5. F.I. Day. Man-apes discover monolith (Figure 19.6).
   6. A man-ape looking at bones; shot of monolith in alignment with sun and moon; man-ape discovers use of bone as weapon—to kill tapirs.
   7. Man-apes eating tapir meat.
   8. Rival groups fighting again. Bone used to kill intraspecies and rival tribe withdraws. (Figures 19.7 and 19.8).
II. Dr. Floyd's Mission to Clavius
   9. Spaceship with Dr. Floyd as only passenger docking with spinning space wheel station.
   10. Inside, Dr. Floyd's arrival and clearance (and film's first dialogue).
   11. His phone call to his daughter on Earth.
   12. In conversation with Soviet scientists he's reticent about his mission to Clavius, a U.S. base on the moon.
   13. Dr. Floyd's spaceship on way to moon.
   14. Landing on moon.
   15. Conference room: In his speech Dr. Floyd explains that his mission is to gather facts and opinions and to make recommendations about how the news of the discovery on the moon is to be announced.
   16. In moon "bus," Dr. Floyd and two others talk about the discovered object being deliberately buried four million years ago.

19.6 Man-apes' reactions to monolith. From the M-G-M release *2001: A Space Odyssey* © 1968 Metro-Goldwyn-Mayer Inc.

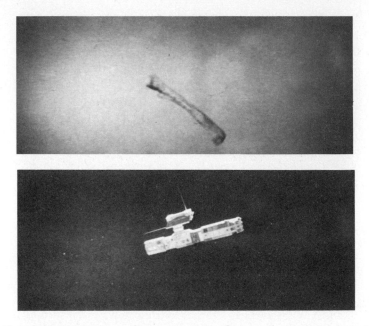

19.7 and 19.8 Match cut from consecutive frames of a bone seen in slow motion to an orbiting spacecraft. From the M-G-M release *2001: A Space Odyssey* © 1968 Metro-Goldwyn-Mayer Inc.

    17. Landing at base.
    18. At excavation site (Figure 19.9), picture taking and a piercing noise.
III. "Jupiter Mission
    18 Months Later"
    19. Spaceship *Discovery One* in transit.
    20. Frank exercising.
    21. Later, Frank eating. Dave joins him. News program transmission (and exposition about the mission).
    22. Transmission of birthday message from Frank's parents; Dave asleep.
    23. Frank's chess game with HAL.
    24. Frank asleep, Dave sketching. His talk with HAL about the mission. HAL reports impending malfunction of a part.
    25. Frank and Dave taking instrument readings.
    26. Frank and Dave get transmissions from Mission Control that it is all right to change unit.
    27. Dave goes outside to replace unit.
    28. Testing unit; no flaw.
    29. Mission Control advises that onboard computer is in error. Frank and Dave question HAL.
    30. In a pod Dave and Frank agree that they may have to partially disconnect HAL, who, unknown to them, is reading their lips.

19.9 At the site of the monolith on the moon. From the M-G-M release *2001: A Space Odyssey* © 1968 Metro-Goldwyn-Mayer Inc.

Intermission in some theatrical showings.

31. Frank outside. (Presumably), pod cuts his air line, and he goes tumbling off into space. . . .
32. Dave in pursuit in another pod.
33. Dave retrieves Frank's body.
34. HAL kills the three hibernating astronauts.
35. Lockout and forced entry. . . .
36. Inside HAL: Partial disconnection. Prerecorded message of Dr. Floyd: ". . . Now that you are in Jupiter space and the entire crew is revived, it [the secret briefing known only by HAL] can be told to you. Eighteen months ago, the first evidence of intelligent life off the Earth was discovered. It was buried forty feet below the lunar surface, near the crater Tycho. Except for a single, very powerful radio emission aimed at Jupiter, the four-million-year-old black monolith has remained completely inert, its origin and purpose still a total mystery." (End of film's dialogue.)

IV. "Jupiter
and Beyond the Infinite"
37. *Discovery One* and monolith in space near Jupiter and its moons. Dave in pod leaves spaceship.
38. Dave in pod in Star Gate (so called in the novel).
39. Dave and pod in room with eighteenth-century decor.
40. Dave, now aged, looks around rooms.
41. He sees older man, his older self.
42. That older self eats, breaks glass, sees an even older self in bed.
43. That older self sees monolith (Figure 19.10). Metamorphosis: old man to embryo.
44. In space, embryo approaching earth. Last shot: embryo facing toward camera (Figure 19.11). F.O.

End Credits

19.10 Dave's oldest self in bed pointing to a monolith. From the M-G-M release *2001: A Space Odyssey* © 1968 Metro-Goldwyn-Mayer Inc.

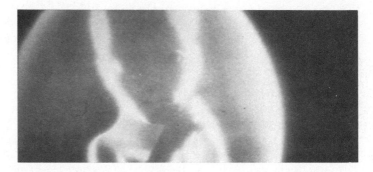

19.11 Film's last shot. From the M-G-M release *2001: A Space Odyssey* © 1968 Metro-Goldwyn-Mayer Inc.

Questions and Observations

1. What does the opening sequence, "The Dawn of Man," suggest about survival and development of early life on Earth?
2. What emotions do the astronauts and scientists have? Discuss, for example, the eating scenes, Dr. Floyd's speech at Clavius, and Dave's reaction to HAL's lockout. What significance, if any, do you ascribe to the fact that stress pills are available onboard the spaceship *Discovery One*?
3. What feelings does HAL seem to have? Is HAL only a product of human engineering, or is he/it an independent, conscious entity? Is HAL a "he" or an "it"? Why does HAL kill?
4. What stages does Bowman go through in the room with the eighteenth-century decor (see outline scenes 39–43)? What is the monolith's function?
5. Discuss the meaning of the film's last shot (Figure 19.11). Is it significant or not that the embryo looks at the audience? Why do you say so?

6. List where the monoliths appear in the story. What do they *do*? What can we infer about the makers of the monoliths?

7. Is it appropriate that most shots in *2001* are of long duration and the movement of objects within the frame is often slow and graceful? Why do you say so? Kubrick decided to cut the film by 19 minutes after its first New York showings. Should he have cut it further or not? Where? Why or why not?

8. Where does the action slow down or stop, while the setting is emphasized? How prominent are the settings in the film?

9. Compare and contrast the editing, plot, and meanings of *2001* with those of *Star Wars* or *The Empire Strikes Back* or *The Return of the Jedi*. Which is the better film? What do you have in mind when you say "better"?

10. Morris Beja asks the following: "Have the extraterrestrial beings 'created' the human race—programmed it, as the humans themselves program computers like HAL? If so, are those extraterrestrial beings God, or gods?"[3]

11. "Bowman comes to rest in a room which the monoliths have created for him, a room in which he will be comfortable, a room which is perhaps a projection of his own mind. The room is singularly cold. The arrangement of furniture [is] formal, the lighting cool, the color scheme subdued. There is not a stimulating shape or shade in the whole place. A sexual romp there would leave chilblains.

    "Bowman fits very quickly into the room. His original astonishment rapidly gives way to a kind of time serving ennui. His formal dinner is eaten without visible relish, the broken crystal glass viewed with only residual concern. In the timelessness of the room Bowman stares, lies down and dies. Then he is reborn out of the ape rubble decaying on the bed. He is reborn without anyone resorting to physical sex. He is now a Star Child, a product of philogenesis: mind birth. The sullied flesh has melted and been refined into something quite different than the astronaut who was, after all, just a fancy model of the killer ape.

    "The end of the film is incredibly like the beginning of the comic strip *Superman*, where the baby in the capsule hurtles toward the earth from the doomed planet Krypton. But one cannot imagine the Star Child growing up to be a Clark Kent, oozing sexuality and athletic ability, and dissipating it by jumping over tall buildings. This *ubermensch* [*sic*] has nothing to do with either the pleasures or pains which flesh is heir to. He is intelligence raised to its infinite power, the Messiah without the humanity of being born of woman. He is the new Odysseus grown wise without the wisdom of the couch."[4]

12. Thomas Allen Nelson has written,

    Why . . . does HAL make such a simple and uncharacteristic mistake

---

[3]Morris Beja, *Film and Literature* (New York: Longman, 1979).

[4] Jack Fisher, "Too Bad, Lois Lane: The End of Sex in *2001*," *Film Journal* 2, no. 1 (September 1972): 65.

about a well-functioning AE-35 unit? Could it be an expression of insecurity about his role in the Jupiter mission and a desire to cut off communication with Earth? After all, only Mission Control, the 9000 twin, and the hibernators know the truth: that HAL's infallibility as a machine and benevolence as a deity are compromised by his part in one of Floyd's earth-inspired conspiracies. Once programmed to be "human," HAL loses the machine purity which, no doubt, his twin still possesses; he becomes imbued with a consciousness of his own autonomy and denies his function as a tool. Therefore, his unconscious mind—where, like a hibernator, the truth sleeps—associates Bowman's drawings with his own fallibility and initiates a plot to break contact with Earth and the threat of his "perfect" twin. Later, when Floyd's screen image and voice are brought into the Logic Memory Center, Kubrick not only "explains" the mission but HAL's behavior, as that play of light and sound represents the last flickerings of his unconscious mind and the secret that drove him to madness. Bowman, on the other hand, succeeds at the expense of HAL's failure: symbolically, once Poole, Bowman's Earth twin, is murdered by his "rational" and mechanical alter ego, Bowman undergoes a traumatic awakening even more dramatic than Moon-Watcher's discovery of the bone. He forces himself back into *Discovery*'s fossilized womb, destroys HAL, and frees technological man from the tyranny of his own tools.[5]

Suggested Readings

Contexts

Agel, Jerome, ed. *The Making of Kubrick's 2001*. New York: New American Library, 1970. No table of contents or index, but 96 pages of photos, mostly of production but also of the last pages of the unpublished M-G-M continuity script; a reprinting of Clarke's story "The Sentinel"; interviews with various scientists; numerous reviews; a list of companies that supplied technical information and ideas; a reprinting of the 1968 *Playboy* interview with Kubrick; plus miscellaneous pieces.

American Cinematographer 49, no. 6 (June 1968). Special issue on *2001,* including articles on the photography and special effects.

Ciment, Michel. *Kubrick*. trans. Gilbert Adair. New York: Holt, Rinehart and Winston, 1982. Discussions of films directed by Kubrick, up through *The Shining,* with numerous stills, some in color. Interviews with Kubrick and his colleagues, filmography, and bibliography.

Clarke, Arthur C. "The Sentinel." In William Kittredge and Steven M. Krauzer, eds., *Stories into Film* (New York: Harper & Row, 1979), and Jerome Agel, ed., *The Making of Kubrick's 2001* (see above), pp. 15–23. A 1950 short story that was the source of *2001*.

———. *2001: A Space Odyssey*. New York: New American Library, 1968. Novel ("based on a screenplay by Stanley Kubrick and Arthur C.

---

[5] Thomas Allen Nelson, *Kubrick: Inside a Film Artist's Maze* (Bloomington: Indiana University Press, 1982).

Clarke") that appeared a few months after the film did; this edition includes 22 black-and-white stills.

————. *The Lost Worlds of 2001*. New York: New American Library, 1972. Reprints "The Sentinel," accounts of different versions of *2001,* and an account of the interplay between Clarke and Kubrick.

Coyle, Wallace. *Stanley Kubrick: A Guide to References and Resources*. Boston: G. K. Hall, 1980. Includes biographical background; critical survey of films directed by Kubrick; synopses, credits, and notes for 14 films; bibliography; "Writings and Other Film Related Activity"; archival sources; film distributors; literary works adapted for the cinema by Kubrick; author index; and film title index.

Geduld, Carolyn. *Filmguide to 2001: A Space Odyssey*. Bloomington: Indiana University Press, 1973. Credits, outline (but not in outline form), essay on Kubrick and his films, calendar on the production, analysis (pp. 29–72), summary critique, filmography for Kubrick, bibliography, and rental information.

Kagan, Norman. *The Cinema of Stanley Kubrick*. New York: Holt, Rinehart and Winston, 1972. Analyses of films directed by Kubrick, through *Clockwork Orange*.

"*Playboy* Interview: Stanley Kubrick." *Playboy,* September 1968, p. 85 ff. Reprinted in Agel, *The Making of Kubrick's 2001* (see above).

Scripts and Outlines

"2001: *L'Odyssée de l'espace*." *L'Avant-Scène du Cinéma,* nos. 231/232 (1/15 July 1979), pp. 19–53. Cutting continuity divided into 612 shots excluding end credits, plus numerous black-and-white stills; also included in this issue is a cutting continuity for the 1956 version of *Invasion of the Body Snatchers (L'Invasion des profanateurs de sépultures* in French translation).

Synopses of the film can be found in Coyle and Geduld (see above) and *Monthly Film Bulletin* (see below), but so far as I am aware, no outlines have been published.

Analyses and Reviews[6]

Alpert, Hollis, and Andrew Sarris, eds. *Film 68/69*. New York: Simon and Schuster, 1969. See pp. 53–63 for reprints of reviews by Penelope Gilliatt, Hollis Alpert, and Joseph Morgenstern.

---

[6] Wallace Coyle points out that the critical writings about the film are essentially of four different kinds: popular reviews of the film when it first came out, technical analyses of the 205 special effects shots, thematic studies, and examinations of *2001* as science fiction film. See Coyle, *Stanley Kubrick: A Guide to References and Resources*.

Beja, Morris. *Film and Literature: An Introduction*. New York: Longman, 1979. See pp. 283–93 for background on the story, novel, and film; "Topics to Think About"; and bibliography.

Daniels, Don. "A Skeleton Key to *2001*." *Sight and Sound* 40, no. 1 (Winter 1970/71): 28–33.

Feldmann, Hans. "Kubrick and His Discontents." *Film Quarterly* 30, no. 1 (Fall 1976): 12–19. Analyses and comparisons of *2001, Clockwork Orange,* and *Barry Lyndon*.

Fisher, Jack. "Too Bad, Lois Lane: The End of Sex in *2001*." *Film Journal* 2, no. 1 (September 1972): 65.

Johnson, William, ed. *Focus on the Science Fiction Film*. Englewood Cliffs, N.J.: Prentice-Hall, 1972. See pp. 126–47 for reprints of three articles on *2001*.

Monthly Film Bulletin 35, no. 413 (June 1968): 88–89. Credits, synopsis, short analysis.

Westerbeck, Colin L. Jr. "Looking Backward at the Film *2001*." In Nobile, Philip, ed., *Favorite Movies: Critics' Choice* (New York: Macmillan, 1973).

· 20 ·

The World of Apu[1]

Background

Other Title: *Apur Sansar* (Bengali) (literal translation: Apu's Family)

Country of Production: India (Northeast section, state of West Bengal) and parts of present-day Bangladesh, a country with widespread poverty and short life expectancies.

First Release: 1959

Process: Black and white; I haven't been able to discover for certain, but I believe the film was intended for 1.33:1 aspect ratio showings, though it was sometimes shown theatrically in the United States, at least, in 1.85:1 by cropping the image on the top and bottom.

Approximate Running Time: 103 or 106 minutes

Versions: Some sources list the running time as 106 minutes, some at 103. So far as I have been able to determine, however, there is only one version of this film.

Selected Credits:[2]

- Producer: Satyajit (SAW teeᷦyah JIT) Ray (RYE) (1921–   ). Commercial artist, a founder of Calcutta Film Society, then a director. Before Ray directed his first film, he trained himself, in part, by the method described in the following quotation: "When a film adaptation of a well-known work was about to appear, he would study the book and write a complete film script. Watching the produced film, he compared it inwardly with his own version, noting opportunities he might have missed and matters on which he would have improved on the produced film. By this technique he gained knowledge of his medium—and mounting confidence in himself."[3]
- Director: Satyajit Ray (*Devi* or *The Goddess, Two Daughters, Days and Nights in the Forest, Distant Thunder,* and others). Subject of a 28-minute docu-

---

[1] For translations and information about Bengali culture, I am indebted to Mohammad Khaled, who was generous with his time and patient with my many questions.

[2] Spellings of Bengali names in English may vary in other publications.

[3] Erik Barnouw and S. Krishnaswamy, *Indian Film,* 2d ed. (New York: Oxford University Press, 1980), p. 222.

mentary film, called *Satyajit Ray,* which includes some excerpts from films he directed.

- Scriptwriter: Satyajit Ray, based upon the Bengali novel *Aparajito* (in Bengali meaning Undefeated) by Bibhuti Bandapaddhay.
- Design: Bangsi Chandragupta
- Cinematographer: Subrata Mitra
- Editor: Dulal Dutta
- Music: Composed and played on the sitar by Ravi Shankar (Figure 20.1), plus some solo flute music
- Sound: Durgadas Mitra

Major Characters and Performers:

- Apu (oh POO) Roy: Soumitra Chatterji
- Aparna (ah POOR nah): Sharmila Tagore (14 years old at the time the film was made)
- Pulu (poo LOO): Shapan Mukerji
- Kajal (a common boy's name in Bengali; the name means "mascara"): S. Aloke Chakravarty

20.1 Ravi Shankar, some years after *The World of Apu,* with sitar. Eddie Brandt's Saturday Matinee.

Place and Time of Story: India; 1943 plus at least six years
Other:

- The movie that Apu and Aparna see (scene 37 in the outline below and Figures 20.2 and 20.3) is typical of Indian movies of the 1940s, whereas the films directed by Ray are not.
- The Indian film industry is the largest in the world, but its films are usually for home consumption, and few are shown abroad.
- *The World of Apu* is the third in a trilogy of films that include Apu. In the first film, *Pather Panchali* (1955), "A would-be writer [who is also a Brahmin priest] . . . and his wife . . . live poorly in a Bengal village and try to raise their children, Apu . . . and his sister Durga . . . , and support an aged relative. . . . The father leaves for the city and the mother is left to raise the children on her own. She becomes shrewish and eventually drives out the old relative into the country-side where she dies. Durga also dies [and their house is wrecked by a monsoon] before the father returns. The family pack their belongings and sadly leave for Benares."[4]
- In the second film, *Aparajito* (1956), the ten-year-old Apu arrives in Benares with his mother and father, "who earns a living by reading scriptures on the banks of the Ganges. The father dies. [Figure 20.5] The mother first works for a rich landlord, then goes to a village to keep house for an old uncle . . . who is a priest and begins to train Apu for the priesthood. But Apu [wins a scholarship and] persuades his mother to send him to school. As an adolescent . . . , Apu goes to university in Calcutta where he works to support himself. Life in the city draws him farther away from his mother

20.2 Detail from a frame enlargement from *The World of Apu*.

20.3 Detail from a frame enlargement from *The World of Apu*.

[4] Georges Sadoul, *Dictionary of Films* (Berkeley: University of California Press, 1972).

20.4 Apu in *Pather Panchali*, the first film in the Apu trilogy. Museum of Modern Art/Film Stills Archive.

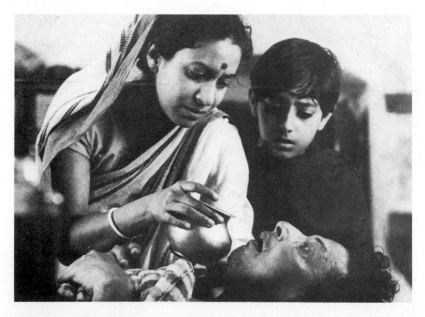

20.5 Apu and his parents in *Aparajito*, the second film in the Apu trilogy. Museum of Modern Art/Film Stills Archive.

and village life. While he is studying, his mother falls ill, dying before he can reach home. He returns to Calcutta."[5]

- A number of times in the film, Apu and Pulu pay respect to older characters by touching both of their feet, then putting the hand to the forehead. The Bengali phrase for this custom translates as "to take the dust."
- The Bengali language, which shares little in common with Hindi, is spoken in West Bengal—a predominantly Hindu state of India—and in Bangladesh, a predominantly Muslim country.

A Brief Chronology

pre-1947: Time of strikes, riots, demonstrations against British rule.

1947: Indian independence from Britain and formation of Pakistan (West Pakistan and, 900 miles away, East Pakistan) out of predominantly Muslim areas of India.

1955: *Pather Panchali (Song of the Road)*
1957: *Aparajito (The Unvanquished)*
⎱ first two films directed by Ray and first two in the Apu trilogy

1958: *Paras Pathar (The Philosopher's Stone)* and *Jalsaghar (The Music Room)*
⎱ two more films directed by Ray

1959: *Apur Sansar (The World of Apu)*. Action takes place in present-day West Bengal, India (capital, Calcutta), and present-day Bangladesh, a nation formed in 1971 from East Pakistan.

Apu in Calcutta then Pulu visits

Outline

I. Apu and Pulu in Calcutta
 1. Apu with professor. Apu for lack of funds is leaving the university. Professor encourages him to keep writing. In background is heard the chant of student strikers. Fade-out (F.O.).
 2. Fade-in (F.I.) Opening credits. F.O.
 3. F.I. Apu's room: Apu sleeping, rising, cleaning up (evidently he fell asleep while writing and spilled ink; light is still on in background), exercising in rain.
 4. Lap dissolve (L.D.). Apu's room: Landlord seeking rent.
 5. L.D. Apu selecting some of his books to pawn. Removes a fern leaf from one of the books.
 6. Outside, Apu going out. His neighbor—like Apu, his last name is Roy—gives Apu a letter from a publisher that has accepted Apu's story, "A Man of the Soil." The letter is dated "11/8/43," meaning August 11, 1943. They talk briefly about love.
 7. L.D. Street: Apu arriving at a school.
 8. Apu seeking a job at the school: He's overqualified.

---

[5] Ibid.

9. L.D. Apu at a factory, with a man in office.
10. Apu in hallway, then doorway: Apu views workers, then turns away.
11. L.D. On trolley car, Apu rereads his letter.
12. L.D. On railroad tracks, then near his building, near the end of the day, going home.
13. In his room: His book bag now empty, throwing coins (in handkerchief) onto bed, closing shutters on a young woman across the way, playing his flute. Pulu's visit.
14. At café, the two eat and talk about jobs. (Apu is unemployed because he refused to be a strikebreaker.) Pulu tells Apu about the coming wedding of a cousin in the country and says the two are going to it.
15. L.D. Night. Street. Apu, tipsy, reciting poetry. Apu says he won't after all accept the office job that Pulu can help him get. Apu tells Pulu about the novel he is writing:

It's about a boy, poor but sensitive. His father is a priest. The father dies and the boy goes to the city, not to become a priest but to study. His education, his hardships, broaden his mind and sharpen his wits. We feel that he has in him the seeds of greatness, but—he doesn't make it. No. But that's not important. What's important is that—although things are always difficult for him—he doesn't turn his back on life—he doesn't try to escape reality. He has learned that the whole point of life is in living it, in facing reality.
PULU: Sounds more like autobiography than a novel.[6]

The two argue good-naturedly about Apu's knowledge of love. F.O.

II. Pulu Brings Apu to Aparna
16. F.I. River: The two on a boat. Apu playing flute, then reciting poem by Tagore. Pulu reading Apu's manuscript; he likes it.
17. L.D. Arrival at Pulu's relatives. Introductions (Figure 20.6). F.O.
18. F.I. Music for a wedding. Aparna being prepared.
19. By river: Marching band and escorted groom. Nearby Apu sleeps.
20. Further preparations of Aparna.
21. Groom's arrival; he's insane.
22. Aparna's mother angry at her husband for arranging such a match.
23. Outside the door, Aparna's father tells Pulu that the family is ruined.
24. L.D. Apu still sleeping near the river. Pulu's request, seconded by other men.
25. L.D. With a baby heard crying offscreen, Apu approaches the house. He sees the man intended to be the groom being led away.
26. Outside the house, Apu implies his agreement to the marriage.
27. L.D. Hindu wedding ceremony. F.O.
28. F.I. That night. Bridal bedroom. Apu's background. His apprehension. Aparna's willingness to be wife of a poor man. His decision to take her back to Calcutta. F.O.

[6] Translation from subtitles on a 16 mm print.

20.6 Apu meeting Aparna's family.

20.7 Aparna, shortly after her arrival at Apu's room in Calcutta, with a tear in her eye.

III. Apu and Aparna in Calcutta
  29. F.I. Calcutta. Their arrival at his building.
  30. His room: Apu leaves briefly. Aparna cries, hears a baby, then looks out of the window and sees it (Figure 20.7). Apu returns.
  31. Apu presents Aparna to neighbors downstairs. F.O.
  32. F.I. Morning. New curtain. Aparna gets up. Apu finds a hairpin, and a message on his cigarette package. She works; he gazes. He decides to get a servant; she dissuades him (Figure 20.8). F.O.
  33. F.I. Aparna surprises him as he arrives home.
  34. L.D. He eats; she fans.
  35. Match cut: He fans; she eats.
  36. L.D. He's teaching her English.

20.8 Apu upset that Aparna, who is from a wealthy family, has to do so much manual work now that she is married to him.

20.9 and 20.10 At movie: what Apu and Aparna see.

37. L.D. At the movies (Figures 20.9 and 20.10).
38. L.D. and match cut (Figure 20.11). In horse-drawn cab on way home. She's pregnant and going to stay with her family for two months before the delivery. F.O.
39. F.I. At train station. Good-byes. F.O.

IV. Apu Alone Again

40. F.I. Apu at the office. His talk with a co-worker. Apu reads part of a letter from Aparna.
41. L.D. On trolley, Apu reads another part of the letter.
42. L.D. Apu walking to and on railroad tracks, gets to finish reading Aparna's letter. He moves a baby away from the tracks. Outside his building, he greets his neighbor, Mr. Roy.
43. At home, Aparna's brother waiting. He tells Apu of Aparna's death. Apu slugs him.
44. In his room, Apu's anguish.
45. Two lap dissolves: Much later, Apu is still in his room, grieving and withdrawn. Neighbor lady brings him food. After she leaves, he gets up. The clock is heard getting louder—then stops. A train whistle.
46. L.D. Train tracks. Apu nearly commits suicide.
47. L.D. His letter to Pulu:

Dear Pulu,

By this time you probably heard everything. You are going to London. I wish you all success. I'm also leaving. I don't know where. I don't know why, but I want to escape.

I am taking the manuscript with me. If someday I can finish it, I will send you a copy. If you feel it is appropriate, you can publish it.

Yours
Apu[7]

V. Separate Ways of Apu and Kajal

48. L.D. Apu on train.

[7] This letter, which Mohammad Khaled translated for me, is untranslated in all English-subtitled prints I have seen.

49. His child and the grieving grandmother.
50. Apu by the seashore.
51. L.D. Apu in forest, touches fern leaf.
52. L.D. On hill, Apu throws away the manuscript of his novel (Figure 20.12). F.O.
53. F.I. (Figure 20.13) Kajal hunting. In background, Pulu returning with suitcase in hand. Kajal kills a bird.
54. L.D. His use of it. Kajal bites a man and gets scolded.
55. Aparna's father tells Pulu that Apu has not been there for five years. Pulu learns of Apu's whereabouts.
56. L.D. Near a mine, Apu walking.
57. L.D. Apu at stream. Pulu's arrival. Brief conversation.
58. L.D. Apu learns Kajal's name. Pulu asks Apu to return. Apu asks Pulu to put Kajal into an orphanage or boarding school (Figure 20.14). Pulu declines and later leaves. Apu calls after him. F.O.

20.11 Lap dissolve and match cut from previous shot (Figure 20.10) to carriage window; Apu and Aparna are now on the way home after the movie.

20.12 After Apu has thrown away the manuscript of his novel.

20.13 First view of Kajal.

20.14 Apu withdrawn and grieving; dead tree in background.

20.15 Apu's first paternal/protective act: he saves Kajal from getting hit by his grandfather.

20.16 Last shot in film.

VI. Apu and Kajal

59. F.I. Aparna's parents' home: Apu's return. He has come to take Kajal to friends in his home village.

60. In a room (Apu's and Aparna's bridal bedroom of scene 28) Kajal sleeps (on what was the wedding bed). In background is heard the same song heard in background on Apu's and Aparna's wedding night. Apu sees Kajal, sits for a moment and thinks, then wakes Kajal, who runs away from Apu.

61. Outside, Kajal throws a stone at Apu. Grandfather is going to hit the boy with his cane, but Apu stops him (Figure 20.15). Kajal walks away. F.O.

62. F.I. Kajal rejects Apu's gift.

63. L.D. Apu asking Kajal to be friends. No response. F.O.

64. F.I. Apu about to leave without Kajal. Grandfather annoyed with Apu. "You can't do anything," he says (not "I knew you'd turn out a failure," as in subtitle).

65. Apu walking away from the house, Kajal watching. Kajal says he wants to be taken to his father. Apu says he will take Kajal to him. Kajal runs to Apu, who carries him on his shoulders and smiles (Figure 20.16). F.O.

The End

Questions and Observations

1. Review the film's first two scenes (outline scenes 1 and 3). What do they reveal about Apu's situation and character? What details are especially significant? Why do you say so?

2. Review the description of Apu's novel (outline, scene 15). What does the plot of Apu's novel tell us about him? Compare and contrast Apu and the protagonist of his novel.

called perfect fictions of love in cinema?
what depicts (this in the film)

3. What are several different reasons why Apu agrees to marry Aparna?
4. What experiences shape Kajal's personality?
5. Describe Aparna's character. What significant details reveal what she is like?
6. Review the outline, noting where Pulu appears, then explain his impor tance to the story.
7. What does the film show about the life-styles of a large Indian city? What does it reveal of life in a remote village? Be sure to discuss both the sights and sounds of the two major locations.
8. What knowledge of India helps the viewer better understand and appreciate this film?
9. Review the outline, noting where lap dissolves, fade-out/fade-ins, and cuts are used between scenes. In general, what does each of the three kinds of transitions signify?
10. From what camera angles and distances does Apu tend to be filmed? When does the camera move in close to him? To what effect? From what distance is Aparna filmed as she cries in Apu's room? To what effect?
11. Compare and contrast the appearance, gestures, and personality of Apu before and after Aparna's death.
12. Where and how is offscreen sound used to comment upon the action taking place in the frame?
13. Review the brief plot summaries for the first two parts of the Apu trilogy in the background section above. In what ways does knowledge or experience of the first two films in the trilogy shed light upon *The World of Apu*? In what sense is *Apu* an independent film, not requiring knowledge of the first two parts?
14. John Burgess observed:

> The restraint of Ray's camera is remarkable: close-ups are handled religiously, their length governed by a sensitive discrimination. The first close-up of Aparna is after her entry into Apu's wretched student room in Calcutta. . . . She turns to peer through a rent in the curtain at a laughing child, and the camera moves away as she wipes her tears and adjusts herself in the new environment. Thus our first real contact with Aparna, apparently trivial, establishes a near emphatic sympathy with her and negates the ratiocinative criticism that the accident of their marriage is a real obstacle to sympathy. The intimacy of the couple is conveyed with fine economy in two masterly sequences: on rising, and in the evening out together. Full close-ups are reserved for major moments such as the separation before Aparna's confinement and the agony of Apu at her death. It sometimes seems that the uncanny camera has a conscience which requires it to withdraw quietly in sensitive moments, as when Apu plays his flute for the first time. As he retires into himself so the camera withdraws, only incidentally making room for Paulu's [*sic*] entry into the frame. Close-ups explore intimate moments but never prolong them beyond their dramatic potential.[8]

[8] John Burgess, "Films of the Quarter: *The World of Apu*," *Film Journal* (Australia), no. 16 (August 1960): 83–85.

15. Review the plot summaries for the first two parts of the Apu trilogy and the outline for *The World of Apu*; then consider the following two quotations:

The Apu trilogy formed an epic that moved from the village to the city, from the distant past to the recent past, from a structured rural life to an anarchic metropolitan milieu, with all its uncertainties for the future. This epic movement may have been especially meaningful to Satyajit Ray because it held parallels to the experience of the Ray clan, which had its roots in rural Bengal and had known many reversals of fortune, finally becoming a Calcutta family deep in the conflicts and problems of the modern world. It also represented the history of modern India.[9]

Throughout the trilogy loss is usually accompanied by gain, and each death leads, either immediately or indirectly, to progress. Durga's [Apu's sister's] death provides the family's final incentive to leave the village for the city; Sarbojaya's [Apu's mother's] releases Apu to follow his own path untrammelled; Aparna's, the most painful of all, leads him eventually (the effect is far more delayed) to a complete maturity and fully adult depth, out of which grows his ability to accept the child with joy. Our dual sense of Apu's emotional rebirth and the boy's release into a new and fuller life with the father whose lack has so disturbed his early childhood provides the whole trilogy with its emotional climax and culmination. The boy is very like the young Apu. Life has come full circle, but it has also advanced: the life into which Apu will be able to initiate his son is richer in potentialities for development than that into which Apu himself was born. It is not just a matter of physical environment, the city opposed to the village: the crucial presence in the child's environment will be Apu himself, with his hard-won maturity and affirmation. . . . [But] Ray is by no means a simple-minded believer in progress, and the sense of advance at the end of the trilogy will be modified for us, if we glance back over all that has led up to it, by, again, a sense of corresponding loss. If the life Apu has won through to is incomparably richer in potentialities than that into which he was born, it is also fraught with far greater problems and uncertainties.[10]

Suggested Readings

Some Contexts

Barnouw, Erik, and S. Krishnaswamy. *Indian Film,* 2d ed. New York: Oxford University Press, 1980. See pp. 220–45.

Blue, James. Interview with Satyajit Ray. *Film Comment* 4, no. 4 (Summer 1968): 4–17.

[9] Erik Barnouw and S. Krishnaswamy, *Indian Film,* 2d ed. (New York: Oxford University Press, 1980), p. 234.

[10] Robin Wood, *The Apu Trilogy* (New York: Praeger, 1971), pp. 16–17.

Isaksson, Folke. "Conversation with Satyajit Ray." *Sight and Sound* 39, no. 3 (Summer 1970): 114 ff.

Satyajit Ray: An Anthology of Statements on Ray and by Ray. New Delhi: Directorate of Film Festivals, Ministry of Information and Broadcasting, 1981. Most of the book is devoted to the films Ray directed up to 1981. A short summary, credits, a few photographs, and reviews or extracts from reviews are supplied for each film. Also included are an essay, "The Beginnings—in India and the West"; excerpts from interviews with Ray (Ray on Ray); an essay on Ray as a graphic artist; a filmography; and a bibliography.

Seton, Marie. *Portrait of a Director: Satyajit Ray.* Bloomington: Indiana University Press, 1971. Biography and analyses; inside cover of book has a useful map of Bengali area.

Published Scripts and Outlines

None, but a cutting continuity script in French for the first film in the Apu Trilogy, *Pather Panchali,* was published in *L'Avant-Scène du Cinéma,* no. 241 (February 1980).

Published Analyses

Burgess, John. "Films of the Quarter: *The World of Apu.*" *Film Journal* (Mount Albert, Australia), no. 16 (August 1960): 83–85.

Das Gupta, Chidananda. *The Cinema of Satyajit Ray.* Ghaziabad, India: Vikas Publishing House, 1980. See pp. 20–25 on the source novel and film trilogy.

Rhode, Eric. "Satyajit Ray: A Study." *Sight and Sound* 30, no. 3 (Summer 1961): 133–36. Reprinted in Julius Bellone, ed., *Renaissance of the Film* (New York: Macmillan, 1970).

Taylor, John Russell. "Satyajit Ray." *Directors and Directions: Cinema for the Seventies.* New York: Hill & Wang, 1975. Reprinted with slight alterations and short addendum in Richard Roud, ed., *Cinema: A Critical Dictionary* (New York: Viking, 1980).

Wood, Robin. *The Apu Trilogy.* New York: Praeger, 1971. Detailed analyses, black-and-white stills, credits, Ray filmography, and bibliography.

Glossary

Many film terms used in published writings and glossaries—such as "scene" and "sequence" and the numerous terms for scripts—lack precision or universal acceptance, or both. In the following glossary, I have tried to define terms as they are used in this book and—as much as possible—as used widely in other publications.

As in the English language as a whole, many terms are related to visuals, few to sound, perhaps because relatively little critical attention has been paid to the sound component of the film experience.

Throughout the glossary, words in boldface indicate words defined elsewhere in the glossary.

I have tried to supply definitions and (frequently) examples of some of the most useful terms for beginning students in film analysis. For more complete and authoritative dictionaries of film terms, see the University Film Association, Monograph No. 2: *Glossary of Film Terms,* compiled by John Mercer; *The Focal Encyclopedia of Film and Television Techniques,* general editor, Raymond Spottiswoode; and Virgina Oakey's *Dictionary of Film and Television Terms* (1983).

analysis: Detailed **description** of various viewer responses to a film or films. Normally, more detailed than a **review** and based on a closer examination of the film. See Table 1.1.

analyzer projector: A kind of movie **projector** that allows the viewer to run the film at different speeds, still-frame any image, and view parts over and over. Some models have a **frame** counter. Used by film students, athletic departments, and others to study closely a film or parts of it. See Figure 10.1.

anamorphic lens: A lens that squeezes an image onto film in the camera, making everything look tall and thin. On a **projector** the anamorphic lens unsqueezes the image, returning it to its original shape. Many theatrical films since the 1950s have been filmed and projected with an anamorphic lens. See Figure 11.4.

aperture plate: A small metal plate with a rectangular opening in it, used in cameras to determine the shape and area of light reaching the film; also, a small plate used in projectors to determine the shape and area of the light reaching the screen from the projector. Changing the aperture plate in a projector is one way to change the shape of the projected image.

aspect ratio: The ratio or proportion of the width to the height of the image on a TV or movie screen or on the individual **frame**s of the film itself. The most common aspect ratio for nontheatrical film showings is 1.33:1; it is also the aspect ratio of TV screens. The aspect ratio has nothing to do with the *size* of the image; rather it indicates the *shape* (width in proportion to height) of film images. For illustrations of three widely used aspect ratios, see Figure 11.1.

auteur **theory:** Not a theory in the usual sense of the term, but a method of analyzing films and filmmakers. *Auteur* (French for "author") critics usually examine the recurrent meanings and techniques of directors who have left a strong imprint on films they have directed. *Auteur* critics assume that the major creative decisions of a film are the responsibility of one person, normally the director. Begun in France in the 1950s, *auteur* criticism has since then been widely influential in U.S. publications and teachings.

camera or **motion picture camera:** A machine for recording images on a strip of moving motion picture film by use of a lens, shutter, lightproof container, unexposed film, and a mechanism to move the film in a regular manner. Most films projected with a sound track are filmed at 24 **frame**s per second (in Europe, 25 fps).

character: A fictional creation similar to a **person,** found in novels, short stories, plays, and **fictional film**s. Life is full of persons, and persons appear in **documentary film**s. (See Figure 1.1.) "Character" should also be distinguished from "performer," the person who re-creates or enacts a character.

close-up: Camera shot in which the subject fills up most of the **frame** and which shows little of the surroundings. When the subject is a **person** or **character,** the close-up reveals most of the head. Close-ups are used to direct viewer attention to texture, or to a particular detail, or to the expressions on the performers' faces. See Figure 5.16.

composition: The arrangement of people and objects within the confines of the **frame.** Like **editing,** composition is an extremely expressive aspect of filmmaking. Also called *mise en scène.*

criticism: Description of human responses to, and often comparison of various forms of, human expression. Film critics examine the film experience, then attempt to analyze it, and often compare it to other film experiences and art works. Critics point out both positive and negative features, though many people incorrectly believe that critics point out only negative aspects. I have used the term "criticism" to refer to both **review** and **analysis.**

cross-cutting: **Editing** that alternates between actions taking place at two or more locations, often during the same time, as in cross-cutting between a damsel menaced by a villain and the hero on the way to rescue her. Probably the most famous example of cross-cutting occurs in *Intolerance* (1916), which throughout the film cross-cuts between four different locations with four different time periods. Another film that uses extensive cross-cutting is *Ragtime*. This kind of editing is sometimes called "parallel editing."

cut: The most common transition between **shot**s; made by joining the end of one shot to the beginning of the following shot. When projected, the transition from one shot to the next appears as instantaneous. See Figure 5.26 and Table 5.1.

cutting continuity (script): A written **description** of the finished film. Often contains specific technical information, such as **shot** and **scene** divisions, descriptions of settings and actions, dialogue, camera angles and distances, sometimes even the duration of shots and transitions. Extremely useful for the close examination of a film, especially a foreign-language film, since the dialogue is usually translated more completely and more accurately than in the film itself. Sometimes called a shot analysis. See **script, screenplay,** and **shooting script.**

deep focus: Photography in which objects near the camera and those in the distant background and those in between are all in sharp focus. Achieved in photography by use of **wide-angle lens**es or small camera aperture, or both. For an example, see Figure 5.18. Opposite of **shallow focus.**

depth of field: The distances in front of the **camera** in which all objects are in sharp focus. In general, the smaller the camera aperture and the shorter the lens (the more it tends toward **wide-angle**), the greater the depth of field. *Citizen Kane* (Chapter 15) was much admired for its great depth of field, whereas most earlier films had shallow depth of field, and if the subject in the foreground was in focus, the background was not, and vice versa.

description: Word pictures, or words that represent or re-create with a minimum of **evaluation** and **inference.** For example, in this book the outlines in Part Five are descriptions of the films' actions. A film **review** and **analysis** include descriptions, which help convey the film experience, stimulate the memory, and support **evaluation** and **inference.**

dissolve: See **lap dissolve.**

documentary film: Film that seems to have as its primary aim the presentation or re-creation of past events, historical or natural. Famous examples are *Nanook of the North,* an early documentary film that shows various aspects of an Eskimo family's difficult existence, and *Let's Spend the Night Together,* a 1983 documentary about the Rolling Stones. See Figure 1.1.

Dolby sound: Name for a system that reduces noise on optical and magnetic sound tracks. It has been in increasing use by commercial movie theaters in recent years.

dollying: Motion picture photography made by moving the **camera** around on something on wheels, such as a dolly (a wheeled platform like the one seen in Figure 5.24), a wheeled platform that moves on tracks (as in Figure 5.25), a wheelchair, or roller skates. See also **tracking.**

editing: The process of selecting and arranging the processed segments of photographed film. Editors determine which **shot**s to include, what is the most effective **take** (version) of each shot, the arrangement and duration of shots, and transitions between them. Editing is a time-consuming but extremely important aspect of filmmaking.

editor/viewer: A machine for viewing film without projecting an image through the air onto a reflective surface. Usually has **slow motion,** still-framing, fast forward, and fast reverse. Usually, easier to use than a **projector** and easier on the film. Invaluable in editing film since many editor/viewers allow the viewer to compare different versions quickly. Also valuable in the close examination and documentation of a film. See Figure 10.2.

effects: See **sound effects.**

evaluation: Implied or explicit expressions of approval or disapproval. In this book, "evaluation" is used as a synonym for "judgment." Explicit evaluations are usually evident enough, but many words carry with them implied approval or disapproval. Consider, for example, the differences between "politician" and "statesman," or "mother" and "breeder." In a **description,** a writer should try to minimize evaluations. In a **review** or **analysis,** on the other hand, evaluations are desirable, more so if explained and illustrated.

experimental film: A film that has as its primary aim the presentation of images and (usually) sounds for their own sake or as reflectors of feelings or mental states. Differentiated (often sharply) from **fictional films,** which show a fictional story, and **documentary films,** which present a version of past events. Perhaps the most famous experimental film is *Un Chien Andalou,* directed by Luis Buñuel in 1928. See Figure 1.1.

extreme close-up: A camera shot in which the subject or, frequently, part of the subject completely fills up the **frame** and thus looks very large to the viewer. If the subject is a **character** or **person,**

then only part of the body is visible. Unlike the **extreme long shot,** which shows much of the surroundings, the extreme close-up excludes the surroundings and directs attention to a small object or part of an object. See Figure 5.17.

extreme long shot: A camera shot in which the subject appears to be far away from the camera. If a **character** or **person** is the subject, the entire body will be visible (if not obstructed by some intervening object), and much of the surroundings will be visible. Usually, used only in outdoors. See Figure 5.12.

eye-level angle: A camera angle that creates the effect of the audience being on the same level as the subject. In contrast to **low angle** and **high angle** shots, in eye-level angle the film viewer seems to look directly at the subject. See Figure 5.22.

fade-in: Optical effect in which the image changes by degrees from darkness (usually black) to an illuminated image. Often used at the beginning of a shot. Frequently used at the beginning of a film and sometimes at the beginning of a **sequence.**

fade-out: Optical effect in which the image changes by degrees from illumination to darkness. Often used at the end of a **shot.** Frequently used at the conclusion of a **sequence,** and at the end of a film as a kind of gradual farewell.

fade-out, fade-in: One of the transitions between **shot**s (often used between **scene**s or **sequence**s). The concluding shot fades out (usually to black); then, after a pause, the next shot fades in, that is, the image goes from darkness to illumination. Less abrupt connection between shots than a **cut.** See Table 5.1.

fast cutting: **Editing** characterized by many brief **shot**s; sometimes some of the shots are less than a second long. One of the major ways a rapid **pace** is established. U.S. commercial films of recent years are characterized by much fast cutting, whereas the average shot in pre-1950s U.S. films ran much longer.

fast motion: Motion in which the action depicted on the screen is faster than its real-life counterpart, as when the cowboys in 1920s films seem to ride horses faster than any yet seen by people. Achieved whenever the **projector** runs significantly more rapidly than the **camera** filmed, for example when the projector runs at 24 **frame**s per second and the camera filmed at 14 fps.

fictional film: A film that tells an imaginary rather than a factual story (as distinguished from a **documentary film**—which presents facts in a story or nonstory form—and an **experimental film;** see Figure 1.1). Fictional films depict experiences, usually human experiences, as **plot**s that show **character**s in selected and significant actions. Used in this book as a synonym for narrative film.

film theory: Considerations of the ways people think, write, and talk about film and the formulation of general principles about the nature and potential of the medium. Such considerations often include the properties of the medium, its techniques, its forms, and its purposes and value.

form cut: See **match cut.**

frame: A separate, individual photograph on a strip of film (see Figure 5.26). When projected at U.S. sound speed, there are 24 frames per second (in Europe, sound film is projected at 25 fps).

frame enlargement: A photograph of an individual **frame** from a motion picture, blown up or enlarged to reveal its details. This book contains over eighty frame enlargements. Not to be confused with **publicity still,** which usually refers to a photograph taken with a still camera during the making of a film for promotional purposes.

freeze frame: A projected yet unmoving image, which looks like a still photograph, achieved by having the film laboratory reprint the same **frame** or two over and over. Sometimes used at the end of a film. Some **videodisc** and **videotape** players have this option, and TV sports programs frequently use videotape to freeze frame a particular action.

high angle: View of subject from above it, taken by the **camera** pointing downward during the filming. See Figure 5.21.

high-key lighting: Lighting with middle and light tones. High-key lighting avoids dark shadows by using sufficient frontal lighting on the subject (see Figure 5.10). Often used to support a light and happy mood, as in many musicals. Opposite of **low-key lighting.**

inference: Statement about something not known with certainty on the basis of what is observed. For example, in the 1941 version of *The Maltese Falcon,* as Sam Spade throws down his glass and storms from Gutman's room, most viewers immediately infer that Spade is angry. This inference turns out to be incorrect, however, for we viewers immediately see that Spade had been pretending. Inferences are commonplace yet potentially misleading, since they are sometimes false or unverifiable. As much as possible, they should be avoided in **description**s.

intertitle: Title card that appears *during* a film; it is called "intertitle" because the title appears between ("inter") some of the film's action. Used in pre-1930s films to supply dialogue, information, or descriptions of actions not shown. Used very infrequently since then. Not to be confused with **subtitle.**

iris: An optical effect of two kinds. In *iris-in,* the image is initially dark, then a widening opening, usually a circle or oval, reveals more and more of the next image, usually until it is fully revealed. In *iris-out,* the revealed image is closed out as a constricting opening closes down on it, usually fully obliterating it. Both iris-in and iris-out can be used to draw attention to certain details within the image (as in *Potemkin*), though both are used less frequently today than in the pre-1930s. The iris is also one way filmmakers can change the shape and size of the projected image.

judgment: See **evaluation**.

jump cut: A transition or connection between **shot**s which is disruptive to the viewer. For example, one shot shows a person reaching out to turn on a car ignition; the following shot switches abruptly to the hand letting go of the key in the ignition. Used to shorten the depiction of an action and/or to disorient the viewer. See Table 5.1.

lap dissolve: A frequently used transition between **shot**s in which the first shot begins to **fade out** as the next shot **fades in,** briefly or slowly overlapping the first shot before replacing it. In pre-1930s films, sometimes used within a **scene**; since then, often used between **scene**s or **sequence**s to suggest a change of location or a later time, or both. Also frequently known as a "dissolve." See Table 5.1.

long shot: Refers not to the duration of a shot but to the seeming distance of the camera from the subject. In the long shot, the subject is small in relationship to its surroundings: it may be seen in its entirety, and much of its surroundings is visible. See Figure 5.13.

low angle: View of subject as seen from below. In some contexts, the low angle bestows a sense of dominance or power to the subject. See Figure 5.23.

low-key lighting: Lighting with predominant dark tones; by using little or no frontal lighting, parts of the image are immersed in dark shadows (see Figure 5.3). Often used to contribute to a dramatic or mysterious effect, as in many U.S. detective films of the 1940s and 1950s and in many horror films. *The Third Man* (see the frame enlargements in Chapter 2) often uses low-key lighting. Opposite of **high-key lighting.**

masking: Technique used to block out part of the image so that the projected film's shape is altered temporarily. Used more often in early silent films than in sound films. See Figure 17.11.

match cut: Transition between two **shot**s in which an object or movement in a shot closely resembles an object or movement in the next shot. Also known as a "form cut." See Table 5.1 and Figures 19.7 and 19.8.

meanings: The stated and, much more often, implied significance of a story (fictional or documentary). Not to be equated with **topic** (subject matter) or **thesis** (main idea of expository writing).

medium close-up: Camera shot in which the subject fills most of the **frame,** though not as much as in a **close-up.** When the subject is a **person** or **character,** the medium close-up usually reveals the head and shoulders. As with the close-up, medium close-up shots are used to direct viewer attention to a part of something or to show facial expressions in some detail. See Figure 5.15.

medium shot: Camera shot in which subject and surroundings are both seen in some detail. When the subject is a **character** or **person,** he or she is usually seen from the knees or waist up. See Figure 5.14.

mise en scène: See **composition.**

mixing: The process of selecting sound tracks of one or more of the following: music, dialogue, **sound effects;** adjusting their volumes; and combining them into a composite sound track. See Figures 5.28 and 5.29.

montage: (1) A series of **shot**s, usually combined by **lap dissolve**s, used to present a condensation of events. In *The Godfather,* for example, the gang warfare set off after Michael kills the rival gang leader and the police captain is presented via a montage, as is Calloway's presentation of evidence about Lime's criminal activity in *The Third Man.* (2) A kind of **editing,** especially **fast cutting** and frequent jarring juxtapositions, practiced in the 1920s by Soviet filmmakers (as in *Potemkin*) and advocated by Soviet film theorists (like the director Sergei Eisenstein).

narrative film: See **fictional film.**

normal lens: Of all camera lenses, this one provides the least amount of distortion of images and movements. The normal lens comes closest to approximating the perceptions of the human eye, though it creates some distortion in **close-up**s and **extreme close-up**s. Compare normal lens with the **wide-angle lens** and **telephoto lens** in Figures 5.18–5.20.

objective camera: Camera placement that makes the viewer feel like an observer of the action, rather than part of the action, as is the case with **subjective camera.**

pace: The viewer's sense of how rapidly or slowly a story progresses. If many actions are shown one after another and the film uses **fast cutting,** as in most of *Raiders of the Lost Ark,* the pace is rapid. If a film uses **slow cutting** and has little fast physical action, as in *2001: A Space Odyssey,* the pace is slow. Most films vary the pace from **scene** to scene and even within scenes. For an illustration of pacing/editing, see S. Scott Smith's essay on the editing in a scene from *Jaws* in Chapter 8.

panning: Effect achieved when a camera on a stationary base pivots horizontally. Used frequently, for example, to show the vastness of a location, such as a sea, plain, or mountain range. The term derives from the word "panoramic," because with this movement the camera can give a wide view of an extensive area. Occasionally, a 360-degree (circular) panning shot is used to show the surroundings on all sides of the camera.

parallel editing: See **cross-cutting.**

person: A living human being. Not to be equated with a **character** in a fictional story, though many writers carelessly do so. See Figure 4.1.

plot: The arrangement and presentation of actions in order to tell a fictional story. The actions are not necessarily chronological and are usually discontinuous; that is, certain minor actions are omitted. See Figure 4.4.

point-of-view shot: See **subjective camera.**

projector or **motion picture projector:** A machine used to move the **frame**s of a film in a continuous and regular manner past an intermittent light source which projects the images through a lens(es) to a reflective surface. Most projectors also re-create sounds from an optical or magnetic sound track. Compare with an **editor/viewer,** an alternative machine for viewing motion picture films.

publicity still: A photograph taken, usually during production, to help publicize a film. Used in various forms of advertising the film. Often taken on location with a still camera, though occasionally a **frame enlargement** from the film itself is used. For a sample publicity still, see Figure 2.17.

pull focus: See **rack focus.**

rack focus: Shifting of the focus of the image during a **shot.** For example, the background may be in soft focus and the foreground in sharp focus. By refocusing during the shot, the background may be brought into sharp focus as the foreground goes out of focus. Often done quickly and unobtrusively (for example during some movement on screen) to shift viewer attention from foreground to background details or vice versa. Also known as "pull focus."

reaction shot: A frequently used **shot** that shows how a **character** or **person** is reacting to some action or object. Often in **medium shot** or **close-up.** Reaction shots are illustrated by Figures 2.5 and 14.9.

review: Short (usually) **description** of a viewer's responses to a film, published or broadcast to help people decide whether or not to see a film. Newspapers, magazines, TV, and radio often give film reviews. Contrast "review" with **analysis,** and see Table 1.1.

satire: Method of depicting a subject in an amusing yet disapproving way. For example, *Stripes* is an often amusing satire of army life; *Dr. Strangelove* is a satire of military, political, and scientific thinking and behavior during a time of crisis.

scene: A **shot** or, much more often, a series of related shots that gives the impression of an action taking place during one continuous time and in one location. Most fictional films are made up of numerous scenes, as are many **documentary film**s. See also **shot** and **sequence.**

screenplay: Variously defined in film publications. In this book, the earliest version of a script, a script written before filming begins. Usually the finished film varies considerably from the original screenplay. See **script, shooting script,** and **cutting continuity.**

script: Variously defined in writings about film. In this book, the general term for all written **description**s of a film: planned **(screenplay),** in production **(shooting script** or "continuity"), or finished **(cutting continuity).**

sequence: A series or related **scene**s, perceived as a major section of the film.

shallow focus: Photography with sharp focus in only a short range of distances between the camera and the background, for example, between 10 and 15 feet from the camera. Achieved in photography by using long or **telephoto lens**es or large apertures, or both. Sometimes used to de-emphasize the background and focus attention on the subject in the foreground or vice versa. For an example, see Figure 5.20. Opposite of **deep focus.**

shooting script: The version of the script used by the director and other filmmakers during filming. Because of frequent changes during filming and **editing,** the shooting script often varies considerably from the finished film, as is the case with the published shooting script for *The Third Man*. See **script, screenplay,** and **cutting continuity.**

shot: An uninterrupted strip of processed motion picture film made up of at least one **frame,** though nearly always of many. When projected, the shot normally shows a continuous action or, if no action, some immobile subject during an uninterrupted passage of time. During **editing,** the editor may shorten the shot. See Figure 5.26 and (for a description of some consecutive shots) Table 8.1.

shot analysis: See **cutting continuity script.**

slow cutting: Edited film characterized by frequent lengthy **shot**s. One of the ways a slow or leisurely **pace** is established in a film. Example: *2001* has slow cutting; *Raiders of the Lost Ark,* **fast cutting,** as do many contemporary movies.

slow motion: Motion in which the action depicted on the screen is slower than its real-life counterpart, as when the runners in *Chariots of Fire* are seen running in a labored yet graceful manner. Achieved whenever the **camera** films at a much more rapid speed than the **projector** runs—for example, when footage shot at 48 frames per second is projected at 24 fps.

sound effects: Various sounds normally added to the dialogue and music sound tracks as the completed sound track is made up or mixed. Sometimes called just "effects." Examples of sound effects are a door slamming, a car backfiring, a dog barking in the distance, distant thunder. For illustrations of how the various sound tracks are mixed, see Figures 5.28 and 5.29.

subjective camera: Camera placement at the approximate location of a **character** or **person,** which gives a view similar to what that character or person would see. It's as if the character or person had the camera strapped on. Often called a point-of-view or p.o.v. shot. Sometimes, adapting a term from literature, it is called first-person camera. Rarely used for a sustained period of time in a film, although in *Lady in the Lake* (1947), it was used throughout the film. Opposite of **objective camera.**

subtitle: Words superimposed on the bottom of individual **frame**s. Most often used to give translations of foreign-language films, but sometimes used to give dates, times, locations. Not to be confused with **intertitle.** (*Sub* means "under," as in "submarine"; *inter* means "between," as in "intercollegiate.") For an example of the use of subtitles, see Figure 13.6.

superimposition: Two or more images printed on top of each other. Can be achieved in camera or in the film laboratory. At the beginning of many films, the credits are superimposed on the opening action. As another example, during a **lap dissolve,** one image is momentarily superimposed on another. Sometimes, as in the classic German film *The Last Laugh,* several shots may be superimposed to suggest emotional or physical instability.

symbol: An object that represents some **meanings.** In *Citizen Kane,* for example, the glass paperweight Kane drops at the beginning of the film (Figure 15.8) and his two sleds suggest certain meanings and are not just objects serving practical functions.

take: A version of a **shot.** Different takes of each shot are usually made in shooting theatrical films, though often not TV movies. One of the jobs of the **editor** is to select the most effective take of each of the shots used in the finished film.

telephoto lens: A lens that makes images appear closer and larger than is the case with a **normal lens.** With its long barrel, it resembles a telescope. For other properties of the telephoto lens, see Figure 5.20. Not to be confused with a **zoom lens,** which is capable of varying from telephoto range to normal, sometimes even wide-angle while the camera is running.

theme: See **meanings.**

thesis: The central and unifying idea of expository writing, such as essays or books of analysis. Often stated near the beginning of the writing. Not to be confused with "theme" (the meanings of a story) or **topic** (subject matter).

tilting: Effect achieved when a camera on a stationary base pivots vertically, down to up or up to down. Often used as a way of slowly revealing information, as when we first see a character's shoes, then the camera tilts to reveal the wearer.

topic: Subject matter. For example, the topic of *E.T.* is various responses to and the consequences of a visit by an extraterrestrial. Not to be confused with "theme" or **thesis.**

tracking: A shot during which the camera is moved about. Sometimes the camera is on a wheeled cart set on tracks (as in Figure 5.25); sometimes it is hand-held and the camera operator moves or is moved about. In some publications "tracking" and **dollying** are used interchangeably.

videodisc: A disc on which is stored visual and audio information for playback on a videodisc player and viewing through a TV set or monitor. Similar to a phonograph record, but with the addition of the visual component. At present there are two, incompatible systems available for home use: one uses contact between a stylus and the disc (the CED grooved capacitance disc); the other uses a laser to decode information (the LV laser disc system). See Figure 10.3 and Table 10.2.

videotape: Tape used to record (with a video camera or by hooking up to a TV set) and play back visual and audio signals through a TV set or monitor. Long used by TV stations to store and broadcast programs. Now used in a different format in homes to play back and/or record audio and visual materials. See Table 10.2

voice-over: The comments of an unseen narrator, sometimes a **character** in the film, sometimes not. Often used in **documentary films** and commercials but not rare in theatrical fictional films either. For instance, *Dr. Strangelove* begins with a voice-over narration, and it is used frequently in *Annie Hall*.

wide-angle lens: Lens used on camera most often to record a broad angle of view, that is, more of the sides of the image than is possible with a **normal lens.** For other properties of the wide-angle lens, see Figure 5.18.

wide-screen film: Any film with an **aspect ratio** greater than 1.33:1 (a shape wider than that of a TV screen). Most current films shown in U.S. commercial theaters have a wide-screen aspect ratio of 1.85:1; in Europe and Japan, 1.66:1. Wide-screen film formats have been tried out since nearly the beginning of cinema, but have been used in most theaters only since the 1950s, when they were used in the belief that TV could not compete with large, wide pictures. See Figure 11.2.

wipe: Transition or connection between **shot**s, often between **scene**s, in which it appears that one shot is pushed off the screen by the next shot. Many kinds of wipes are possible; perhaps the most common, however, is simply a vertical line (sharp or blurred) that moves across the **frame** from one side to the other, wiping away the first shot and replacing it with the next. See Table 5.1.

zoom lens: A camera lens with variable focal lengths; thus, it can be adjusted during a **shot** to become a **telephoto** or **normal** or **wide-angle.** Zooming in or zooming out from the subject approximates **tracking,** though the trained eye will notice differences. In zooming, the camera appears to move in or away from a flat surface, whereas in tracking, viewers get more of a sense of contour and depth. Beginning film students often incorrectly equate the term "zoom lens" with "telephoto lens."

Selected, Annotated Bibliography

As in all other aspects of this book, I have attempted to prepare the following material with the beginning film student in mind. This selective bibliography concentrates on film analysis, theory, history, and reference sources. Excluded are sources on national cinemas, film movements, genres, scripts, reviews and analyses of specific films, directors, and economic and industrial considerations. The focus, once again, has been on the fictional film, though many of the sources listed below also cover experimental and documentary cinema. The bibliographies that follow the eight films featured in Part Five, the citations for passages quoted throughout the book, plus the following bibliography will, I hope, provide a useful and representative beginning. The reference section of the following bibliography (section II) provides numerous additional sources. This bibliography was prepared with the help of student assistants Joy Goodwin and Kay Wray and the considerable assistance of reference librarian Paula J. Crawford. To all three I am grateful for their research and recommendations.

The bibliography is organized as follows:

Film Studies

Reviews and Analyses

Bordwell, David, and Kristin Thompson. *Film Art: An Introduction.* Reading, Mass.: Addison-Wesley, 1979. Five Parts: film production, film form, film style, critical analysis of films, and film history. Annotated bibliographies throughout, numerous frame enlargements and stills, index.

Carringer, Robert L., et al. "Special Issue: Film IV: Eight Study Guides." *Journal of Aesthetic Education* 9, no. 2 (April 1975). Essay about director, cast and production credits, a sequence outline, study questions, and suggested readings for five Griffith Biograph short films, *Stagecoach, Citizen*

Kane, Bicycle Thieves, The Seventh Seal, North by Northwest, 8 1/2, and *Blow-Up.* Reprinted in *Film Study Guides: Nine Classic Films* (Champaign, Ill.: Stipes, 1975). Includes the eight study guides described above plus a ninth guide, on *Dr. Strangelove.*

Film Review Annual, 1981. Ed. Jerome S. Ozer. Englewood, N.J.: Film Review Publications, 1982. Reprints of 1,547 reviews of more than 200 feature films released in the U.S. during the year. Includes full credits, 10 different indexes, listings of major film awards. A continuation of *Film Review Digest,* 1975+, which reprinted excerpts from reviews.

Filmfacts, 1958–1977; irregular 1969–1977. Contains credits, synopsis of films, and reprints of reviews, sometimes in their entirety.

French, Brandon. *On the Verge of Revolt: Women in American Films of the Fifties.* New York: Ungar, 1978. Detailed analyses of twelve critical and popular films of the 1950s, including *Sunset Boulevard, The Quiet Man, Shane, From Here to Eternity, Marty,* and *Some Like It Hot.* The dust jacket claims that the book gives us "new insight into film history, into the women's movement, and into the cultural contradictions of a period more significant than many have believed." Illustrations, bibliography, index.

Huss, Roy, and Norman Silverstein. *The Film Experience: Elements of Motion Picture Art.* New York: Dell, 1968. Introductory book on film principles and techniques. Photos, diagrams, bibliography, index.

Kael, Pauline. *I Lost It at the Movies.* Boston: Little, Brown, 1965.
———. *Kiss Kiss Bang Bang.* Boston: Little, Brown, 1968.
———. *Going Steady.* Boston: Little, Brown, 1970.
———. *Deeper into Movies.* Boston: Little, Brown, 1973.
———. *Reeling.* Boston: Little, Brown, 1976.
———. *When the Lights Go Down.* New York: Holt, Rinehart and Winston, 1980.
———. *Taking It All In.* New York: Holt, Rinehart and Winston, 1984.
Each title is a collection of her essays, reviews, analyses.

Kauffmann, Stanley. *A World on Film: Criticism and Comment.* New York: Harper & Row, 1966.
———. *Figures of Light: Film Criticism and Comment.* New York: Harper & Row, 1971.
———. *Living Images: Film Comment and Criticism.* New York: Harper & Row, 1975.
———. *Before My Eyes: Film Criticism and Comment.* New York: Harper & Row, 1980.
Each title is a collection of his essays, reviews, analyses.

Kay, Karyn, and Gerald Peary, *Women and the Cinema: A Critical Anthology.* New York: E. P. Dutton, 1977. A collection of 45 essays grouped under seven headings, selected filmographies, bibliographies, stills, index.

Kerr, Walter. *The Silent Clowns.* New York: Alfred A. Knopf, 1975. On American silent movie comedy. Includes discussions of Chaplin, Keaton, Lloyd, Langdon, Laurel and Hardy, Sennett, Arbuckle, Normand, Fields. More than 400 photographs. Index.

Sarris, Andrew. *Confessions of a Cultist: On the Cinema, 1955–1969.* New York: Simon and Schuster, 1970.

————. *The Primal Screen*. New York: Simon and Schuster, 1973. Reprints of essays from various journals and magazines.

————. *Politics and Cinema*. New York: Columbia University Press, 1978. Essays and reviews.

Schatz, Thomas. *Hollywood Genres: Formulas, Filmmaking, and the Studio System*. New York: Random House, 1981. "The central thesis of this book is that a genre approach provides the most effective means for understanding, analyzing, and appreciating the Hollywood cinema." Discusses the studio system, nature of genre, and the genres of western, gangster, hard-boiled detective, screwball comedy, musical, and family melodrama. Stills, bibliography, and index.

Scott, James F. *Film: The Medium and the Maker*. New York: Holt, Rinehart and Winston, 1975. Discussion of creative options filmmaking technology makes available to filmmakers, with many illustrations of the consequences in well-known films. Short annotated bibliography, stills, index.

Simon, John. *Private Screenings*. New York: Macmillan, 1967. Mostly reprints of Simon's reviews from 1963–1966 plus four other essays (for example, on film criticism and criticism in general, and on French director Godard). Index.

————. *Movies into Film: Film Criticism 1967–1970*. New York: Dell, 1971. Reprints of Simon's film reviews grouped under twelve headings, such as Adaptations, Politics and Society, and The Youth Film, plus essays under the headings The Festival and Awards Game, and Critical Matters. Index.

————. *Reverse Angle: A Decade of American Films*. New York: Clarkson N. Potter, 1982. Reprints of Simon's reviews of films of the 1970s plus four introductory essays (mostly on the nature of film criticism) and seven concluding essays on such topics as Rex Reed, Charles Thomas Samuels, Pauline Kael, and Andrew Sarris's book *Politics and Cinema*. Index.

————. *Something to Declare: Twelve Years of Films from Abroad*. New York: Clarkson N. Potter, 1983. Reprints of Simon's reviews of foreign films during a twelve year period. Index.

Slide, Anthony, ed. *Selected Film Criticism*. 6 vols.: 1896–1911, 1912–1920, 1921–1930, 1931–1940, 1941–1950, 1951–1960. Metuchen, N.J.: Scarecrow, 1982, 1983, and in press (vol. 6). Reprints original reviews of feature-length and short films. The reviews, taken from various periodicals, are reprinted in their entirety.

Wood, Michael. *America in the Movies*. New York: Dell, 1975. Examines Hollywood movies from the end of the 1930s to the beginning of the 1960s as reassuring fantasies; includes the topics of loneliness, the dangerous woman, success, self-confidence, innocence, extravagance, etc.

Theory

Andrew, J. Dudley. *The Major Film Theories: An Introduction*. New York: Oxford University Press, 1976. An introduction to the work of some of the most important film theorists, including Arnheim, Eisenstein, Balázs, Bazin, Mitry, and Metz. Bibliography, index, occasional stills.

Arnheim, Rudolf. *Film as Art*. Berkeley: University of California Press, 1957. The book's thesis: the expressiveness and art of the film result from exploiting the very limitations of the medium. No stills. No index.

Balázs, Bela. *Theory of the Film: Character and Growth of a New Art*. Trans. Edith Bone. New York: Dover, 1970. A reprint of the original 1952 edition. Some sample chapters: in praise of theory, visual culture, the close-up, the face of man, editing, expressive technique of the camera, sound, the script. Short index.

Bazin, André. *What Is Cinema?* 2 vols. Trans. Hugh Gray. Berkeley: University of California Press, 1967 and 1971. Selections from and translations of Bazin's numerous analyses and theoretical essays.

Bluestone, George. *Novels into Film: The Metamorphosis of Fiction into Cinema*. Baltimore: Johns Hopkins University Press, 1957. Chapter on "The Limits of the Novel and the Limits of the Film" plus detailed chapters on *The Informer, Wuthering Heights, Pride and Prejudice, The Grapes of Wrath, The Ox-Bow Incident,* and *Madame Bovary*. Bibliography and index.

Eberwein, Robert T. *A Viewer's Guide to Film Theory and Criticism*. Metuchen, N.J.: Scarecrow, 1979. Explanations of major ideas of 20 film theorists and critics, including Münsterberg, Eisenstein, Pudovkin, Bazin, Balázs, Kracauer, Kael, Sarris, Haskell, Rosen, Burch, Metz, and Wollen. Bibliography. Indexes.

Eidsvik, Charles. *Cineliteracy: Film among the Arts*. New York: Random House, 1978. The book is divided into three parts: "How Movies Work," "The Cinema in Cultural Perspective," and "Explorations" (includes values in art and film, films and fiction, film and theater, and a section on the independent cinema). Bibliography, stills, index. For advanced students.

Harrington, John, ed. *Film and/as Literature*. Englewood Cliffs, N.J.: Prentice-Hall, 1977. Articles by various authors on "Adaptation," "Film and Theater," "Film and Novel," "Film and Poetry," "Authorship and Auteurship," "Message, Medium and Literary Art," and "Film's Literary Resources." No index. Some of the essays are for advanced students.

Kerbel, Michael. "Edited for Television. I: Scanning." *Film Comment* 13, no. 3 (May/June 1977): 28–30. By using as examples a television showing of *The Graduate* and other films, the author illustrates how a standard aspect ratio version of a wide-screen film can distort the experience and meaning of the film.

Manvell, Roger. *Theater and Film: A Comparative Study of the Two Forms of Dramatic Art, and of the Problems of Adaptation of Stage Plays into Films*. Rutherford, N.J.: Fairleigh Dickinson University Press, 1979. Part I: "Stage Play and Screenplay: Forms and Principles," Part II: "Examples of Adaptation from Stage to Screen," plus appendixes on two famous critics of theater/film, "Films Recording the Work of Distinguished Theatrical Companies," "Select List of Dramatists Whose Plays Have Been Filmed," bibliography, and index.

Mast, Gerald, and Marshall Cohen, eds. *Film Theory and Criticism: Introductory Readings*. 2d ed. New York: Oxford University Press, 1979. Essays grouped under seven headings: film and reality; film image and film language; the film medium; film, theater, and literature; kinds of film; the film artist; and film and society. Bibliography. No index.

Nichols, Bill, ed. *Movies and Methods: An Anthology*. Berkeley: University of California Press, 1976. Essays are grouped under three headings: Contextual Criticism, Formal Criticism, and Theory. Glossary and index.

Tudor, Andrew. *Theories of Film*. New York: Viking, 1973. Description and interpretation of film theory of Bazin, Eisenstein, Grierson, Kracauer, plus a chapter on *auteur* theory and genre. Some illustrations. Bibliography. No index.

History

Allen, Robert C. "Film History: The Narrow Discourse." *Film: Historical-Theoretical Speculations* in the 1977 [Purdue University] Film Studies Annual: Part Two. Pleasantville, N.Y.: Redgrave, 1977, pp. 9–17. Argues that most film histories are too concerned with aesthetic history and rely too heavily on secondary sources.

Altman, Charles F. "Towards a Historiography of American Film." *Film Journal* 16, no. 2 (Spring 1977): 1–25. Reprinted in Richard Dyer MacCann and Jack C. Ellis, eds., *Cinema Examined: Selections from Cinema Journal* (New York: Dutton, 1980), pp. 105–29. On thirteen approaches to writing U.S. film history: technology, techniques, personality, film and the other arts, chronicle, social, studio, *auteur,* genre, ritual, legal, industrial, and sociological.

Brownlow, Kevin. *The Parade's Gone By . . .* Berkeley: University of California Press, 1968. An account of various aspects of the American silent film and its makers. Analysis, interviews, quotations, reminiscences, numerous high-quality photographs, index.

Cripps, Thomas. *Slow Fade to Black: The Negro in American Film, 1900–1942.* New York: Oxford University Press, 1977. A historical look at the changing attitudes toward blacks in Hollywood and the country, from stereotypical parts to Dooley Wilson in *Casablanca.*

Ellis, Jack C. *A History of Film*. Englewood Cliffs, N.J.: Prentice-Hall, 1979. "[T]he organizing thesis is that certain countries at particular times have contributed most interestingly and importantly to the evolution of the art form." The book includes extra chapters on U.S. film. An introduction on the special characteristics of film history and 22 chapters, each one concluding with lists of films and books of the period; 84 black-and-white stills and an index.

Everson, William K. *American Silent Film*. New York: Oxford University Press, 1978. A history of U.S. silent film from 1893–1929. Many photographs. A chronology; appendix on silent-film books, films, archives, and other reference tools; and an index.

Fell, John L. *A History of Films*. New York: Holt, Rinehart and Winston, 1979. This one-volume history of world cinema concentrates on feature-length narrative films, though among its 21 chapters are chapters on documentary, animation, and experimental cinema. Each chapter includes black-and-white stills and concludes with a summary and a bibliography. Most chapters include lists of major films by major directors. Three indexes.

Harpole, Charles, gen. ed. *History of American Cinema*. The first volumes in the series, vols. 4 and 8, are expected in 1986. Based on extensive original research, the volumes are arranged chronologically, and the approach for the series will "incorporate consideration of aesthetic, socio-economic-industrial, and technological factors in a synthetic historical effort."

Haskell, Molly. *From Reverence to Rape: The Treatment of Women in the Movies*. New York: Holt, Rinehart and Winston, 1974. The portrayal of women in films, especially in the period of the 1920s to the 1960s. Black-and-white stills and an index.

Jacobs, Lewis. *The Rise of the American Film: A Critical History, with an Essay Experimental Cinema in America 1921–1947*. New York: Teachers College Press, 1968. Originally published in 1939, this early history covers U.S. and some foreign films to 1939. Stills, bibliographies, indexes.

Mast, Gerald. "Film History and Film Histories." *Quarterly Review of Film Studies* 1, no. 3 (August 1976): 297–314. Some considerations about writing film history and an examination of some of the English-language film history books written up to 1976.

Short, K. R. M., ed. *Feature Films as History*. Knoxville: University of Tennessee Press, 1981. A collection of articles by film historians dealing with pre-1947 films, showing how films reflect social, economic, and intellectual trends both in the U.S. and Europe. Index.

Other

Barnouw, Erik. *Documentary: A History of the Non-Fiction Film*. New York: Oxford University Press, 1974. A history of the documentary film from the late nineteenth century until the early 1970s. Many stills, bibliography, index.

Barsam, Richard Meran. *Non-Fiction Film: A Critical History*. New York: Dutton, 1973. A critical history with descriptions of numerous films and their contexts. Many illustrations, bibliography, and index.

————, ed. *Nonfiction Film Theory and Criticism*. New York: Dutton, 1976. Contains 26 essays/articles by filmmakers and critics. Bibliography. No photographs; no index.

Blackaby, Linda, et al. *In Focus: A Guide to Using Films*. New York: New York Zoetrope, 1980. On program goals, film selection, program planning, space and time, publicity, discussion formats, projections, evaluations, follow-ups, resources, etc.

Braudy, Leo, and Morris Dickstein, eds. *Great Film Directors: A Critical Anthology*. New York: Oxford University Press, 1978. More than 80 essays, about 23 directors and their films. Also a short introductory essay on the life and work of each of the directors. No photographs. No index.

"Cinema/Sound." Special Issue of *Yale French Studies*, no. 60 (1980). Introductory essay; 15 essays under the headings of Theory, History, Music, and Case Studies; plus a bibliography on sound in film with more than 300 entries.

Corliss, Richard. *Talking Pictures: Screenwriters in the American Cinema 1927–1973*. New York: Penguin, 1974. The book surveys films of 38 screenwriters, including Ben Hecht, Preston Sturges, Dalton Trumbo, Jules Feiffer, Billy Wilder, Samson Raphaelson, Robert Riskin, Herman J. Mankiewicz, Charles Lederer, Frank S. Nugent, and Buck Henry.

———, ed. *The Hollywood Screenwriters: A Film Comment Book*. New York: Avon Books, 1972. A collection of articles and interviews with various U.S. screenwriters plus a symposium of 12 screenwriters, and 50 filmographies. No illustrations; no index.

Crittenden, Roger. *The Thames and Hudson Manual of Film Editing*. London: Thames and Hudson, 1981. A handbook on the function and process of editing. Shooting with editing in mind, language of editing, sound editing, postproduction. Also a chapter on video. Contains 67 illustrations, glossary, index.

Dwoskin, Stephen. *Film Is: The International Free Cinema*. Woodstock, N.Y.: Overlook Press, 1975. About independently made films that are filmmakers' creative expression. Discusses more than 700 such films, from the 1920s to early 1970s, U.S. and foreign. Stills and indexes.

Hodgdon, Dana H., and Stuart M. Kaminsky. *Basic Filmmaking*. New York: Arco, 1981. Discusses basic technology, scriptwriting and preproduction, production, postproduction, and special topics, such as special effects and color. Many drawings and photographs. Glossary and index.

Jacobs, Lewis, ed. *The Documentary Tradition: From Nanook to Woodstock*. New York: W. W. Norton, 1971. Essays by different authors on the nature of documentary film and on different major documentary films, from 1920 to 1970. "[N]ot included . . . documentaries commonly classified as industrials, educationals, art and architecture, training films, and other types of sponsored films primarily aimed at instructing, improving public relations, or increasing sales. I [editor Jacobs] have selected only those films which seem to me to best illuminate the artistic and social concerns of their times and which had the most influence in advancing the genre."

Kittredge, William, and Steven M. Krauzer, eds. *Stories into Film*. New York: Harper & Row, 1979. Source stories for the following films: *Freaks, It Happened One Night, Stagecoach, The Wild One, Rear Window, The Hustler, The Man Who Shot Liberty Valance, Blow-Up,* and *2001: A Space Odyssey,* plus general introduction, head notes for each of the nine stories, two bibliographies on film and literature (40 pp.), and nine filmographies. No photographs.

LaVine, W. Robert. *In a Glamorous Fashion: The Fabulous Years of Hollywood Costume Design*. New York: Scribner's, 1980. A history of costume design in films, from the 1920s to the late 1970s, plus a close look at 10 of Hollywood's most famous designers. Lists Academy Award winners from 1948 to 1979. Many illustrations. Bibliography and index.

Leese, Elizabeth. *Costume Design in the Movies*. New York: Ungar, 1977. A documented record of the contributions costume designers have made to the film industry. Designers are alphabetically listed with a short biography and film credits. More than 200 photos and sketches. Index.

Le Grice, Malcolm. *Abstract Film and Beyond*. Cambridge, Mass.: MIT Press, 1977. A critical introduction to abstract film. Discussion of Richter,

Ruttmann, Ray, Duchamp, Vertov, Whitneys, Brakhage, Warhol, and others. Frame enlargements, bibliography, index. For advanced students.

Manvell, Roger, and John Huntley. *The Technique of Film Music*. Revised and enlarged edition. New York: Hastings House, 1975. Covers music and the silent film, music in early sound films, functions of music, the music director, the composer's view, ways to use music in films as illustrated by analyses of the music in four films. Outline of film music 1895–1972, bibliography, and index.

Marks, Martin. "Film Music: The Material, Literature and Present State of Research." *Notes: The Quarterly Journal of the Music Library Association* 36 (December 1979). Reprinted in *Journal of the University Film and Video Association* 34, no. 1 (Winter 1982): 3–40. An essay on film music: "The Material," "The Literature," and "The Present State of Research into Film Music" plus an annotated bibliography divided into three parts: "Bibliographies," "Sources from the Silent Period (through 1929)," and "Books, Dissertations, Pamphlets and Periodicals on Film Music, from 1930 to the Present."

Mercer, John. *An Introduction to Cinematography*. 2d ed. Champaign, Ill.: Stipes, 1974. Three parts: silent cinematography, producing sound films, and film in television. Numerous drawings. Bibliography and index.

Pirie, David, ed. *Anatomy of the Movies*. New York: Macmillan, 1981. Essays organized under four headings: money and power, creators, craft, and the product. Photographs and index.

Reisz, Karel, and Gavin Millar. *The Technique of Film Editing*. Enlarged edition. New York: Hastings House, 1968. Written in 1953, then revised, the book gives a short history of editing and a discussion of editing techniques and principles. Includes excerpts divided into shots, often with accompanying frame enlargements. Glossary and index.

Roud, Richard, ed. *Cinema: A Critical Dictionary: The Major Filmmakers*. 2 vols. New York: Viking, 1980. Contains 234 critical essays by various authors. Most of the essays are about directors and their films, but also included are entries for *The Cabinet of Dr. Caligari, Gone with the Wind*, actors, comic teams, writers, periods of national cinema, etc. Some of the entries are written for the advanced student.

Sitney, P. Adams, ed. *The Avant-Garde Film: A Reader of Theory and Criticism*. New York: New York University Press, 1978. Contributors include Vertov, Eisenstein, Deren, Brakhage, Snow, and Mekas. Stills and an index. For advanced students.

Skaggs, Calvin, ed. *The American Short Story*. 2 vols. New York: Dell, 1977 and 1980. Reprints the short stories used as a basis for the films shown on the PBS series, plus critical essays, interviews, six screenplays, excerpts from screenplays, and black-and-white stills.

Thomas, Tony, ed. *Film Score: The View from the Podium*. South Brunswick, N.J.: A. S. Barnes, 1979. Mainly interviews with 20 leading composers, plus short biography and photograph of each. Discography and bibliography, but no index.

Weiner, Janet. *How to Organize and Run a Film Society*. New York: Collier Books, 1973. Organization, finances, selecting and booking films, publicity, presentation. Some illustrations. Index.

Youngblood, Gene. *Expanded Cinema*. New York: Dutton, 1970. Concentrates on advanced technologies of computer films, television experiments, laser movies, and multiple-projection environments, with analysis of different kinds of works in each field. Includes interviews, 284 photos (60 in color), bibliography, and index. For advanced students.

Film Reference

The American Film Institute Catalog of Motion Pictures Produced in the United States: Feature Films 1921–1930 and *The American Film Institute Catalog of Motion Pictures: Feature Films 1961–1970*. New York: R. R. Bowker, 1971. Alphabetical listing of feature films by title. Lists production company, date released, full credits and cast, summary of plot. Comprehensive listing.

The American Film Institute Guide to College Courses in Film and Television. 7th ed. Ed. Peter Bukalski. Princeton, N.J.: Peterson's Guides, 1980. Lists U.S. colleges and universities offering course work in film and television. Arranged by state, then alphabetically by school. Each entry includes type of school, accreditation, location, campus size, enrollment, faculty size, calendar, course offerings, majors, and degrees in film and television.

Bisplinghoff, Gretchen. "On Acting: A Selected Bibliography." *Cinema Journal* 20, no. 1 (Fall 1980): 79–85. Annotated bibliography.

Cushing, Jane. *101 Films for Character Growth*. Notre Dame, Ind.: Fides, 1969. For each of these 101 short films, the following information is supplied: a rating (good, excellent, etc.), topic heading, synopsis, age level suitability, and questions for discussion.

Ellis, Jack C., et al. *The Film Book Bibliography, 1940–1975*. Metuchen, N.J.: Scarecrow, 1979. An unannotated record of about 5,500 books on film in English published between 1940 and 1975. There are 10 major classifications in the book and detailed subdivisions. Title and name indexes.

Enser, A. G. S. *Filmed Books and Plays: A List of Books and Plays from Which Films Have Been Made, 1928–1974*. London: Andre Deutsch, 1975. Mostly British and U.S. titles. Includes film title index, author index, and change of original title index.

Feature Films on 8 mm, 16 mm, and Videotape: A Directory of Feature Films Available for Rental, Sale, and Lease in the United States and Canada. 7th ed. Ed. James L. Limbacher. New York: R. R. Bowker, 1982. Entries include title, country of origin (for U.S. films, distributor), year of release, running time, format, major cast members, director, indication of rental/lease/sale, and company. Includes list of serials for rent or sale, index of directors, index of foreign-language films, short bibliography, and list of film companies and distributors with addresses and phone numbers. Seventh ed. lists some 23,000 titles. New edition every few years.

Film Literature Index. Albany, N.Y.: Film and Television Documentation Center, 1973 + . Indexes articles in more than 300 international film and nonfilm periodicals. Entries are arranged alphabetically by author and subject (including film titles). Also includes a section on book reviews.

The Focal Encyclopedia of Film and Television Techniques. Ed. Raymond Spottis-woode. New York: Hastings House, 1969. Contains 1,600 entries on film and TV. Cross-references. Nearly 1,000 illustrations. Some entries are quite technical, some are not. Extensive index.

Glossary of Film Terms. Compiled by John Mercer. University Film Association, 1978. Comprehensive dictionary of film and television terms.

Halliwell, Leslie. *The Filmgoer's Companion.* 7th ed. New York: Scribner's, 1980. More than 10,000 entries on English-language films, performers, directors, other filmmakers, technical terms, series, remakes. Many stills, list of title changes, bibliography, more.

Index to Critical Film Reviews in British and American Periodicals, 1930–1972. 3 vols. Ed. Stephen E. Bowles. New York: Burt Franklin, 1974–1975. Detailed index to reviews of films and reviews of books about films. Alphabetical listing by title. Volume 1: A–M, volumes 2 and 3 (bound together): N–Z, plus book review index and five additional indexes.

Index to Critical Film Reviews: 1972–1976. Vol. 4. Ed. Stephen E. Bowles. New York: Burt Franklin, 1979. A continuation of *Index to Critical Film Reviews in British and American Periodicals, 1930–1972* (see above).

International Film Guide. Ed. Peter Cowie. New York: A. S. Barnes. Since 1964, these volumes have been published annually. Include articles on five featured directors of the year, information on major films produced in each country, sections on short films, festivals, film schools, archives, magazines, books, and more.

International Index to Film Periodicals: An Annotated Guide. New York: R. R. Bowker, 1972 +. Published annually with the assistance of the International Federation of Film Archives (FIAF). Each volume lists articles and essays on film that have appeared during the past year in 90 + world film magazines. Most entries are annotated. Each volume includes various indexes.

Katz, Ephraim. *The Film Encyclopedia.* New York: Thomas Y. Crowell, 1979. A comprehensive encyclopedia of world cinema with 7,000 entries in one volume. Mostly short essays on people: directors, producers, performers, cinematographers, writers, composers, art directors. Also histories of all major national cinemas and of major studios. Articles on styles, genres, schools of filmmaking, organizations, inventions, techniques, technical terms, and more. No photographs.

Leff, Leonard J. *Film Plots: Scene-by-Scene Narrative Outlines for Feature Film Study.* Vol. 1. Ann Arbor, Mich.: Pierian, 1983. Scene-by-scene descriptions of 67 films often studied or written about. Also included are locations and times, transitions between scenes, names of characters, occasional dialogue or intertitles, plus running times and selected credits.

MacCann, Richard D., and Edward S. Perry. *The New Film Index: A Bibliography of Magazine Articles in English, 1930–1970.* New York: E. P. Dutton, 1975. Lists articles covering all aspects of film, such as actors/actresses and acting, directing, writing, lighting, editing, sound, animation, theory, history, nonfiction films, and film societies. Also includes a listing of "Extended Analysis of Single Films" and an index to the volume.

Newsbank Review of the Arts. New Canaan, Conn., 1975+. A microfiche collection of newspaper reviews and background stories on films, books, plays, TV programs, art exhibits, concerts, and other cultural events throughout the U.S. Compiled from over 125 newspapers, at least one from each of the 50 states. The Review of the Arts is divided into four sections: Film and Television, Fine Arts and Architecture, Literature, and Performing Arts (theater, music, dance). Index is monthly and yearly. Indexed by film titles, people, and subjects.

The Oxford Companion to Film. Ed. Liz-Anne Bawden. New York: Oxford University Press, 1976. An encyclopedia-style reference book with information on films and filmmakers, companies, genres, national cinemas, technical aspects, etc. Illustrations are usually frame enlargements in original aspect ratios.

Rehrauer, George. *The Macmillan Film Bibliography: A Critical Guide to the Literature of the Motion Picture.* 2 vols. New York: Macmillan, 1982. A comprehensive reference source on film literature in the English language. More complete and more current than the author's earlier *Cinema Booklist* and its two supplements. Volume 1 includes more than 7,500 annotated reviews of books on film and related film subjects (such as biographies, reference books, film scripts). Nearly all the entries include description and evaluation. The entries are alphabetized and numbered, and include books published between 1900 and 1982. Volume 2 is an index of names, films, and topics in the books reviewed in volume 1.

———. *The Short Film: An Evaluative Selection of 500 Recommended Films.* New York: Macmillan, 1975. The 500 films, all 60 minutes or less, include many fictional ones. Virtually all are post-1920s sound films. For each film the following information is included: title, release year, producer or distributor, running time, animated, wordless, black-and-white or color, annotation or description, suggested audience by age, suggested areas of use (subject index), and books that recommend the film. The book also includes "Other Sources of Short Film Information," "Selected Film Periodicals Which Deal with the Short Film," and "Subject Listings" (subject headings and film titles).

Robertson, Patrick. *Movie Facts and Feats: A Guinness Record Book.* New York: Sterling, 1980. First published in Great Britain under the title *The Guinness Book of Film Facts and Feats.* From the preface: "This book is unashamedly about *quantity*—together with 'firsts,' records, oddities, remarkable achievements, historic landmarks and the wilder extravagances of the motion picture business. . . ." The information is grouped under 19 categories, including The Industry, Story and Script, Characters and Themes, Performers, Music, Censorship, Awards and Festivals, Animation, and Shorts and Documentaries. Includes numerous lists and many photographs, some in color. Name, subject, and title indexes.

Sadoul, Georges. *Dictionary of Films.* Trans., ed., and updated by Peter Morris. Berkeley: University of California Press, 1972. Brief credits, synopsis, and short essay for about 1,300 major feature films.

St. James Films and Filmmakers Series. 4 vols. Ed. Christopher Lyon. Chicago: St. James Press, 1983 and in press (vols 3 and 4). Information and signed critical essays on 500 major films, 500 directors/filmmakers, 700 actors and actresses, and 500 writers and production artists (including cinematographers, producers, editors, and designers).

Salem, James M. *A Guide to Critical Reviews, Part IV: The Screenplay from "The Jazz Singer" to "Dr. Strangelove."* 2 vols. Metuchen, N.J.: Scarecrow, 1971. Lists reviews of about 12,000 U.S. and foreign feature films. Reviews listed are in U.S. or Canadian general, nonfilm periodicals and in the *New York Times*.

———. *A Guide to Critical Reviews, Part IV: The Screenplay, Supplement One, 1963–1980.* Metuchen, N.J.: Scarecrow Press, 1982. A continuation of Salem's earlier work.

Schuster, Mel. *Motion Picture Performers: A Bibliography of Magazine and Periodical Articles, 1900–1969.* Metuchen, N.J.: Scarecrow, 1971.

———. *Motion Picture Performers: A Bibliography of Magazine and Periodical Articles, Supplement No. One, 1970–1974.* Metuchen, N.J.: Scarecrow, 1976. Updates all coverage in earlier volume through 1974; the number of performers covered has been doubled, to 5,500, and the runs of several publications not covered in the earlier volume are added. Articles are arranged alphabetically by performer's last name. Entries include author and title of article, publication title, volume, issue, and pages.

Stewart, William T., et al. *International Film Necrology.* New York: Garland, 1981. An alphabetical listing of deceased actors and actresses and (less completely) directors, writers, cinematographers, and composers working in film. Includes date and place of birth, date of death and age at death.

Subject Guide to Books in Print. Vol. 2. New York: R. R. Bowker. Under "Moving-picture" followed by some noun (such as "direction") are listed appropriate books currently in print. Many cross-references. New edition every year.

TV Feature Film Source Book. New York: Broadcast Information Bureau. Published yearly since 1949. More than 21,000 "motion picture features and other hour-long films, currently available to television, or which have been shown on television, are listed alphabetically. . . ." Kinds of information supplied include: awards, type of picture (for example, western, science fiction, romance), year of theatrical release, projection process film was shot in (such as CinemaScope or VistaVision), an "audience tune-in expectancy indicator," running time, major performers, director, original distributor, and a short description of the story.

TV Movies, 1983–84 Edition. Ed. Leonard Maltin. New York: New American Library, 1982. Brief description and evaluation of 15,000 theatrical films and 1,500 made-for-TV movies. No photographs.

Third World Cinema. Washington, D.C.: National Education Services, American Film Institute, 1977. Lists schools, organizations, and archives in Third World countries; festivals; distributors; and guides to books and periodicals in or about Third World cinema.

Truitt, Evelyn Mack. *Who Was Who on Screen.* 3d ed. New York: R. R. Bowker, 1983. Lists over 13,000 actors, actresses, nonperformers, and animal actors, who died between 1905 and 1981. Alphabetically arranged listing includes professional and real names, places and dates of birth and death, cause of death (if known), marital history (sometimes), awards, and screen credits.

Variety International Show Business Reference, 1983. Ed. Mike Kaplan. New York: Garland, 1983. In this revised version are included information on Oscars and "All-Time Film Rental Champs," plus nearly 6,000 biographies, a Necrology for 1976–1980, and additional information on plays, TV, and music. Name and title indexes of films, TV programs, plays, and award credits.

The Video Source Book. 5th ed. Syosset, N. Y.: National Video Clearinghouse, 1983. Information on 35,000 programs available on video from over 700 sources. Separate list of videodiscs. Each entry gives title, release date, type of show, brief description, awards, distributors, etc. Also included are main category index, subject category index, and video program sources with addresses and phone numbers.

Welch, Jeffrey Egan. *Literature and Film: An Annotated Bibliography, 1909–1977.* New York: Garland, 1981. Lists and annotates entries on major books and articles published in North America and Great Britain having to do with relationships between films and literature. It also lists interviews with directors, screenwriters, novelists, actors/actresses, and playwrights. Notes published screenplays adapted from literature and feature articles on how to teach film and literature courses. Index.

The Whole Film Sourcebook. Ed. Leonard Maltin. New York: New American Library, 1983. Sixteen contributors wrote material divided into three parts: Education and Careers, Access to Films, and Research and Reference (including pp. 287–388: an annotated bibliography of film books and periodicals). The book has as its goal the supplying of useful and current information.

Writers' Program, New York. *The Film Index: A Bibliography, Vol. 1: The Film as Art.* New York: Arno Press for the Museum of Modern Art Film Library, 1966. Originally published in 1941, the book contains 8,600 entries, most of them annotated, on film books, articles, and film reviews or material dealing with a particular film. Part I: History and Technique; Part II: Types of Films. In Part II, synopses are provided for numerous pre-1915 films and for some post-1915 films. Alphabetized index includes authors, books, 500+ films, and 4,200 filmmakers.

Indexes for Film Reviews in Magazines

Humanities Index, April 1974+, listed under "Moving Picture Reviews." At end of each volume: section on book reviews.

Multi Media Reviews Index, 1970+, later *Media Review Digest,* listed in film section, alphabetically by title.

New Periodicals Index, 1977+, listed under "Motion Pictures—Reviews."

Popular Periodicals Index, 1973+, listed under "Motion Pictures."

Reader's Guide to Periodical Literature, 1910–March 1977, Under "Moving Picture Plays"; March 1977+, under "Motion Picture Reviews." Since March 1976 (vol. 36), book review citations are listed at the end of each volume.

Indexes for Film Reviews in Newspapers

Los Angeles Times Index, under "Motion Picture Reviews."

New York Times Index, under "Motion Pictures: reviews." *New York Times* reviews have been collected and reprinted in separate volumes called *New York Times Film Reviews.*

The Times Index (London), under "Films."

Current Film and Video Journals

American Cinematographer. Published monthly since 1920 by the American Society of Cinematographers, an "educational, cultural, and professional organization" in Hollywood. Reports on current film and video productions, articles on production techniques and equipment, interviews, book reviews.

American Film. Published by the American Film Institute 10 times per year since 1975. Articles, interviews, book reviews. Discusses both film and video.

Cineaste has been published quarterly in New York City since 1967. Articles, interviews, book reviews, film guide (to current films). International coverage. Often Marxist perspective in its analyses.

Film and History. Published quarterly since 1972 by the Historians Film Committee in Newark, N.J. Film reviews, and articles on history as seen through films.

Film Comment. Published bimonthly since 1962 by the Film Society of Lincoln Center in New York. Film reviews, book reviews, interviews, articles on film festivals, television, the industry, and independents.

Film Criticism. Since 1972, published three times a year; partially funded by a grant from Allegheny College, Meadville, Pa. Book reviews, interviews, film analyses.

Film Quarterly. Since 1945, published quarterly by the University of California Press, Berkeley. Articles, interviews, film analyses, book reviews.

Films in Review. Published 10 times per year since 1950 by the National Board of Review of Motion Pictures, New York. Interviews, articles, reviews of current theatrical films and films for TV, music, sound, films on 8 mm and 16 mm, festivals, book reviews.

The Journal of Popular Film and Television (formerly *Journal of Popular Film*) is published four times a year and has been since 1972. Its articles concentrate on commercial cinema and TV. Interviews, book reviews, one poem in each issue.

Jump Cut. Published (usually) four times a year since 1974 from Berkeley and Chicago. Film reviews, including Third World films, interviews, articles, and critiques. Special emphasis on Marxist, feminist, and gay criticism.

Literature/Film Quarterly. Published four times a year since 1973 by Salisbury State College in Maryland. Articles on "individual movies, on different cinematic adaptations of a single literary work, on a director's style of adaptation, on theories of film adaptation, on the 'cinematic' qualities of authors or works, on the reciprocal influences between film and literature, on authors' attitudes toward film and film adaptations, on the role of the screenwriter, and on teaching of film." Also interviews and book reviews.

Monthly Film Bulletin. Published by the British Film Institute in London since 1934. Detailed credits, plot summary, and review of feature films and short films, contemporary and "retrospective." International coverage.

Post Script: Essays in Film and the Humanities. Published three times a year at Jacksonville University since 1981. Includes interviews, articles, book reviews, and a readers' forum.

Sight and Sound. An independent critical magazine published by the British Film Institute, London, since 1932. Book reviews, film reviews, articles covering films, festivals, and TV.

Variety. Newspaper published weekly since 1905. Top grossing films, film festivals, film reviews, sound, video, cable, music, talent, stage, financial and legal news, and obituaries.

Video Review. Published monthly since 1980 in New York. Information on videogames, special programs on cable, videotape and videodisc releases, and new equipment. Feature articles and special reports.

Wide Angle. Since 1976, a quarterly publication edited and published at Ohio University and distributed by Johns Hopkins University Press. Film analyses, other articles, interviews, book reviews. International coverage.

Index

Index*

---

* Page numbers in bold type refer to figures and tables.

images, cinematic, 62–73, 105–106, 134–135, 146, 147, 150, *see also* camera angles, camera distances, color, composition, grain of image, lenses, lighting, moving camera, objective camera, and subjective camera
intentions, 187
intertitle, 183
Intolerance, 59, 304
Invasion of the Body Snatchers (1956), 145–146, 287
It Happened One Night, 149–150
Ivan the Terrible, 39, 250

Jacobson, Herbert L., 215
James, Henry, 51
Jaws, 57, 94, 95, 98, 101, 138–141
judgment, *see* evaluation
jump cut, 77

Kael, Pauline, 8, 91, 231
Kane, Carol, **197**
Karas, Anton, *see The Third Man:* personnel
Kaufman, Deborah Helfman, 132–133
Keaton, Buster, 235, **236**
Keaton, Diane, 196
Keaton, Michael, 55
Kipling, Rudyard, 77
Kitchen, Jan E., 142–143
Knife in the Water, 127
Korda, Alexander, *see The Third Man:* personnel
Kramer vs. Kramer, 52
Krasker, Robert, *see The Third Man:* personnel
Kubrick, Stanley, 278, **279**
Kurosawa, Akira, 154, 155, 156, 262, **263**

Lady in the Lake, 312
lap dissolve, 77

Last Laugh, The, 129, 312
Lawrence, D. H., 187
Lawrence of Arabia, 168, 171, 176
Leigh, Janet, 123
lenses, camera, 70, 71
    normal, 71
    telephoto, 71
    wide-angle, 71
Leone, Sergio, 53
Let's Spend the Night Together, 305
Letter, The, 34
Letzte Mann, Der, see The Last Laugh
liberal arts education, 4*n*
lighting, 62–65
    back, **64**
    bottom, **64**
    catch light, 63
    hard/harsh, **63**
    low-key, 27
    main and fill, **65**
    main frontal, **65**
    side, **65**
    soft/diffused, **63**
    top, **64**
Little Caesar, 132–133
long shot, **67, 68,** 70
low (camera) angle, **73,** 219
low-key lighting, *see* lighting: low-key
Luce, Henry R., 230

M, 34, 177*n*
made-for-TV movies, *see* television, movies made for
Magnificent Seven, The (U.S., 1960), 261, **261**
Maltese Falcon, The
    1941 film, 34, 56, 89, 151–153, 307
    novel, 151–153
Mankiewicz, Herman J., 219, **220**
"March of Time, The" (newsreels), 230
Margolin, Janet, **197**
Marxist film criticism, 10, 98–99

masking, 171, **255**
match cut, 77, **282**
meanings, 93–99, 107, 145–146, 147,
    148, 149–150, 155–156
medium close-up, **68**
medium shot, **67**, 68
Meisel, Edmund, 251
Mercury Theatre Company, 222
Middleman, Louis I., 124
Mifune, Toshiro, 262
Miles, Vera, 122, 186
Minelli, Liza, 52
Minot, Stephen, 57
mise en scène, see composition
Mr. Hulot's Holiday, 127
mixing console, *see* mixing sound:
    mixing console
mixing sound, **79**, 82–84
    final mix, 82
    mixing console, **24, 83**
    premix, 82
    recording and mixing sound, **82**
    (sound) transitions between scenes,
        83, 84
Moby Dick (novel), 57
Moews, Daniel, 245
Morris, George, 53
Mother, 128
moving camera, 72
Murch, Walter, 78
Murnau, F. W., 129
music, *see* sound: music
My Dinner with André, 56, 89

Nanook of the North, 304
Naremore, James, 231
narrator, 183
Nelson, Thomas Allen, 285
neorealism, 210–211
Newman, Paul, 53, **54**
Night Shift, 55
nitrate film stock, 168
Nosferatu (1922), 179

notes (foot- and end-), *see* writing
    about films: notes
note-taking, *see* writing about films:
    note-taking

objective camera, 72
Occurrence at Owl Creek Bridge, An,
    52, 56
Odd Man Out, 33, 39
Oliver!, 45
Olson, Gene, 3, 117
Olson, Leslie Ellen, 134–135
Once Upon a Time in the West, 53–54
Open City, 119, 210
outlining essays, *see* writing about
    films: outlining
outlining films, 112, 191
out-takes, *see* editing: out-takes

pace, 86–87, 107, 146
parallel editing, *see* editing: cross-
    cutting
Pather Panchali, 291, **292**
Patton, 122, 183
performers, *see* characterization:
    people, characters, performers
Perkins, Anthony, 186
photography, *see* images, cinematic
Picasso, Pablo, 184
Pittenger, William, 235, 236, 246
plot, 57–60, 105
    arrangement of scenes, 59–60
        chronologically, 59
        flashback, 59
        flashforward, 59
    experience and plot, 57–58
    selection of scenes, 58–59
poetry and film, 185
point-of-view shot, *see* subjective
    camera
Popeye, 101
Potemkin, 4, 75, 75, 101–102, 128,
    248–260, 308, 309

About the Author

WILLIAM **H. P**HILLIPS was born in Indianapolis, Indiana. He received his B.A. from Purdue University, where he majored in philosophy and minored in mathematics, his M.A. in English literature from Rutgers University, and his Ph.D. in English (narrative film and British drama) from Indiana University. He has taught at Toledo University, Indiana University, and the University of Illinois. His publications include a book, *St. John Hankin: Edwardian Mephistopheles* (1979), which analyzes the works of a British playwright. He and his wife, Eva Santos Phillips, and their son, Rey, live in Turlock, California, located 100 miles east of San Francisco. Currently, Dr. Phillips is a professor of English at California State College, Stanislaus, where he teaches courses in expository writing, script writing, and film analysis.

To the Reader

Your comments, corrections, and suggestions about any aspect of this book are welcomed and will be considered in future revisions. Please tear out this sheet, fill it in, and mail it to Film Editor, College Department, Holt, Rinehart and Winston, 383 Madison Avenue, New York, NY 10017.

Comments, Corrections, Suggestions:

School:
Course Title:
Instructor:
Other Books Assigned in Course: